# net mode

## WEB FASHION NOW

LAIRD BORRELLI

# net mode

## WEB FASHION NOW

Thames & Hudson

First published in paperback in the United States of America in 2002 by Thames & Hudson Inc., 500 Fifth Avenue, New York, New York 10110

thamesandhudsonusa.com

Library of Congress Catalog Card Number 2002101766
ISBN 0-500-28380-X

Printed and bound in Hong Kong

Half-title page: The inside angle – Ruth Spivey wears Bruce. Photograph by Andreas Rhuen. Courtesy of ZooZoom.

Title page: Hot to trot – Eva models selections from Net-a-Porter. Photograph by Barbara Metz and Eve Racine. Creative direction by Megan Quinn-Newall. Courtesy of Net-a-Porter.

# contents

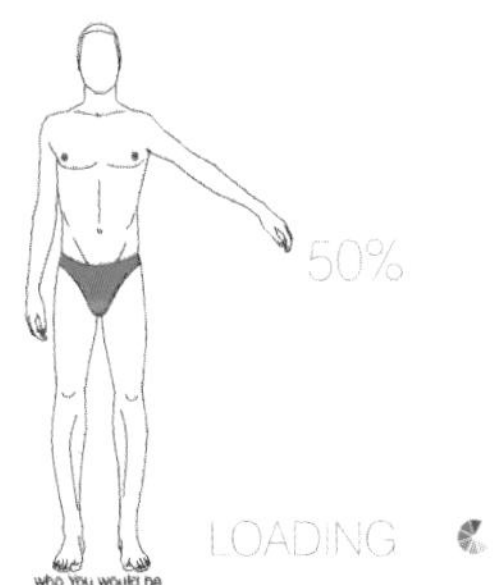
50%
LOADING

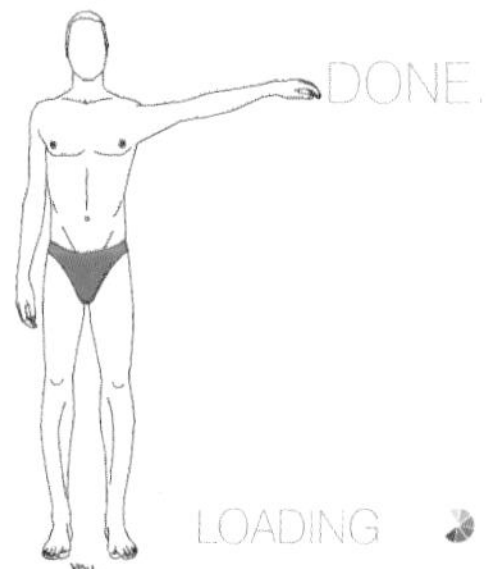
DONE.
LOADING

# introduction

Seven years into the new media revolution, no formal analysis of fashion on the Internet has been undertaken, nor has the time been right – until now. *Net Mode* records, explains and celebrates a vital area of Web design, concentrating specifically on fashion and focusing on designer, shopping and editorial sites.

In talking to me about his company's intuitive and ethereal Website, Dior Homme's Hedi Slimane did so in part by saying that it is different from what (traditional) fashion sites look like. That someone can speak of 'traditional' fashion Websites suggests that the standards that have been established are at last ripe for analysis. We are in urgent need of some bearings before the next phase begins, either through upgrading (in the first instance via speedy Broadband access) or, more fundamentally, through a rethink based on solid experience.

The design of fashion sites (and I've looked at hundreds of them) is either very, very good, or – more commonly – completely without merit. 'When the Internet first burst onto the scene in a big way a few years ago', wrote Melanie Kletter in *Women's Wear Daily* in 2001, 'the visual presentation of Internet sites often took a back seat to getting something – anything – up and running.' It was little wonder that the early sites – with no base in experience to guide them – were mostly unconvincing.

Fashion was first propelled onto the Internet by what María Contreras in *Vogue España* refers to as that old refrain, the 'adapt or die' (*adaptarse o morir*) mentality. The culture of fashion did not help. 'Whatever its claims to forward-thinking-ness and however self-amplified its worship of the modern', Ginia Bellafante, of the *New York Times*, observes, 'the fashion world is essentially a technophobic place.' Unfamiliar with the Web, its functionality and its lingo, early (fashion) sites often fell into one of two traps. They either tried to mimic print layouts, or to recreate brick-and-mortar shopping experiences. Worse, some site development was outsourced to designers who indulged in explorations of the 'Flash-y' pyrotechnics of which the new technology was capable, but which few users had the technological means to access. However, by the time DigitalForm designed the award-winning Versace site, which was launched in December 2000, they were savvy enough to offer users two practical options: a Flash-enhanced or an html experience.

Showy technology would seem to go hand-in-hand with high fashion, but through lessons learned the hard way designers have found that functionality and interactivity cannot be ignored. Patience runs at a premium on-line. At the same time, the Internet does offer a fruitful and exciting multi-layered tool for fashion, via 'the choreography of content, sound image, animation' – to quote DigitalForm's enthusiastic Farhad Farman-Farmaian, who sees it as 'a whole new language' with many more possibilities than print.

*Net Mode's* tripartite organization into Fashion Identity, Fashion Sale and Fashion Talk reflects the different ways that fashion exists on the Web. Each category of site has distinct functions, restrictions and goals but what I looked for in all cases was organic design that marries content and purpose in a manner that is delightful to the eyes, 'fluid, in a visual and auditory sense', as Farman-Farmaian says. When the design and functionality of a site merge successfully, interactivity is encouraged and a singular user experience is created. The sites that are most instructive (and appealing) are generally those that amuse, that inform, that are easy to use and that express personality.

## FASHION IDENTITY

Designer, or vanity sites (as they are referred to in industry parlance), exist as brand-building vehicles. Almost never self-standing, they are now a necessary part of many-tentacled marketing plans. The Web, moreover, is an ideal medium of expression for an era summed up by Teri Agins in her 1999 book *The End of Fashion*, since today 'a designer's creativity expresses itself more than ever in marketing rather than in the actual clothes .... In a sense, fashion has returned to its roots: selling image. Image is the form and marketing is the function.'

What are the specific strengths of the medium? Unlike a print ad, billboard, catalogue or television commercial, Websites offer 'bidirectional communications' (according to Web Analyst Deborah Kania); they invite dialogue and interaction between the brand and the consumer. Almost all sites have a 'Contact Us' feature, where users can submit comments and ask questions. As simple as this seems, the Web has created a new vehicle for customer service and sometimes creates highly personal brand experiences. On BCBG, for example, designer Max Azria answers customer's queries personally in *Style Tips.* There is a *Guest Book* on www.emiliopucci.com, in which users are invited to share their own Pucci stories, while users are encouraged to 'whisper sweet words to John Galliano or confide in Miss Galliano' in the *Love Letters* section of www.galliano.com.

The content of most designer sites is visual, built around imagery, both from designers' collections and advertising campaigns. Theoretically, high fashion seems particularly well suited to new media, since both are eminently image-centric (intangible/virtual) and, notes celebrated fashion photographer and showstudio.com founder Nick Knight, about 'speed of change'.

In other ways, however, fashion and the Internet make strange bedfellows. The Internet is inherently democratic – total access, all the time, by anyone – whereas high fashion is built upon exclusivity. It was in the 1960s that *Vogue's* Diana Vreeland celebrated 'youthquake', ostensibly the end of fashion dictatorship, but the Internet has gone much further. Websites not only provide a kind of insider's ingress to the catwalk – usually the bailiwick of international press and celebrity – but offer varying runway and backstage experiences through technologies such as streaming video, slideshows and reviews.

While the focus of *Net Mode* is high fashion – which produces the most far-flung and fantastic fashion images, and provides the opportunity for cross-media analysis – it is not a compendium of luxury goods sites. In keeping with the democratic nature of the Web, I have mixed corporate and indie sites and placed young designers such as Alexandre Herchcovitch and Dorothée Perret side-by-side with heavy-hitters such as Christian Lacroix, Helmut Lang and Dior Homme to show the breadth and variety of the best and most 'sticky' designs: the ones that encourage loyalty, affection – and repeat visits. These are the sites where, to borrow Deborah Kania's words: 'The brand *is* the experience on the Website. The experience is the brand.'

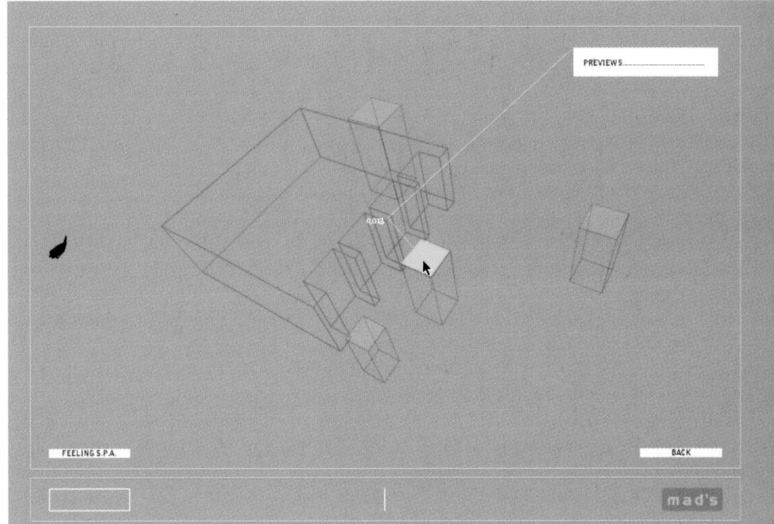

Above: A page from the mads.it Spring 2002 game-style site.



## FASHION SALE

Among the most extraordinary characteristics of Web culture is the way that the Internet first captured the imagination, igniting Utopian dreams. The Web, it seemed, could fashion a new world, streamlined and uncluttered – in which shopping lines would be eliminated, traditional media would be repackaged and the workplace would be a dressed-down Eden where in-chair massages would be quotidian fare.

The same media would not let failed dot-coms die with a whimper, but rather wrote miles of copy casting e-commerce in the role of the mouse (as it were) that roared. Though millions of dollars of revenue are generated on-line, it is understandable that many have bought into the dot-bomb/dot-bust theories. The essential points are that the Web is better suited to some sectors than others and that the learning curve is still on the ascendant.

And among those helping to define luxury sales on the Internet are the e-commerce and teaser sites (store sites that show merchandise but that do not fulfil orders on-line) included in the second chapter of *Net Mode*.

The demographics of the Web audience (above-average income and education) seem ideally suited to moving luxury goods. Early sites have been criticized for trying to replicate in-store experiences in cyberspace. The considerable success of Net-a-Porter is based on the editor's common-sense observation that not only do women use *magazines* as shopping guides, they also often carry tear sheets with them when they shop. Accordingly, Net-a-Porter is designed to let women shop as if from magazine pages. Similarly, A.P.C.'s site design correlates with its catalogue design.

E-commerce is actually very close to catalogue shopping, which set a precedent for shopping without being able to try things on or feel a fabric, although the merchandise on the Web is often more contextualized. Instead of focusing on the physical comfort of the consumer, sites are consciously built to aid the thinking shopper's search for product. Most sites are organized in categories that reflect the way that people approach shopping: usually by designer, category, price and trend.

Convenience is, of course, a prime motivation for buying on-line, but – especially in the luxury goods sector – not the only one. When www.colette.fr reports that one of its first customers lives five minutes from the actual store, it is clear that ease of access is not the only factor at play. All the sites in this chapter confer 'cool' by associating themselves with certain products and brands. In effect, they validate the product.

The shopping sites in *Net Mode* possess what Marilyn Bender called the 'boutique mystique' in the 1960s – the special quality that attracts and defines 'the swingers'. Now shopping on-line guarantees modern-day 'swinger' status. Add convenience and access to merchandise for which there is necessarily a limited market and availability (think $600 T-shirts, $1,000 stilettos), take away the intimidation of store clerks, and much of the appeal of on-line shopping is explained.

## FASHION TALK

Editorial fashion sites exist somewhere between fanzine and cinema. This genre of fashion site most obviously exhibits the all-access, democratic bent of the Web. Vanity and shopping sites are necessarily related to business concerns, a line of clothing, a shop, but anyone with an opinion who desires to analyse *la mode* can launch a Website. This chapter includes editorial sites that have print sisters, such as www.vogue.co.jp and www.nylonmag.com, but also those that exist exclusively in cyberspace. Significantly, however, in this realm truly independent publications can co-exist with corporate/established brand names.

Like the team at itfashion.com, the founders of these editorial sites believe 'that the existence of paper magazines is necessary'. And, in fact, 2fanzine, Nylon and Vogue Nippon exist in print, while many of the other sites receive requests for print versions. None of the editors to whom I spoke doubted the usefulness or necessity of the glossies. The Web doesn't challenge the existence of magazines, so much as extend their reach and/or encourage further exploration of various media and definitions of what fashion is. For example, only two of the sites in this chapter have advertisers, hintmag.com and vogue.co.jp, and most editorial fashion sites have the 'media filter' removed. This is, to an extent, pure editorial, which often relies on random collaborations that are encouraged by the Internet. It is in this space that Net-a-Porter's Natalie Massenet sounds most convincing when she says: 'Everything that everybody said about the Internet is true: it is wonderful, it is a creative Disneyland for adults.'

In order for an editorial Website to be effective, it needs a Web identity. Content directly transferred from print to the Internet has been found to be less effective than content that takes advantage of the Web's strengths, such as real-time capacity and interactivity. Editorial on the Internet can be a multi-dimensional as well as a multi-sensory experience.

Independent sites include It Fashion (operating on a budget of '0 pesetas') and Dresslab in Barcelona, and ZooZoom in New

York. Nick Knight's site, showstudio.com, is less a zine than an on-line gallery, a place where fashion artists are encouraged to use the Web page as a blank canvas and to explore Web-specific technologies. The results lead us to expand our definition of fashion – and to have fun doing so.

Kania reports that the Web's main usage 'center[s] on information, utility, entertainment, shopping and community'. Play is most encouraged on editorial sites where interactivity is showcased. On Dresslab, for example, there is an entire section called *Play*, while 2fanzine allows users to customize its editorials with the virtual equivalent of the geometric stickers that come with the print version to encourage customization. In the 21st century, the Web is still confirming the assertion made by Barthes in 1967, that 'Fashion time is essentially festive time.' The party continues, especially on editorial fashion sites where image, information and play unite. The Web allows editorial freedom that is unthinkable in print and gives greater financial freedom by reducing costs: a potentially bewitching combination.

*Net Mode* became an historical document long before it was sent to the printer. Fashion sites update apace, so don't be surprised if you log on to find a site looking very different than it does on one of these pages. As with other forms of populist art (flyers, posters, graffiti), there are no agreed rules for archiving or recording Web design, despite its importance and ubiquitousness. *Net Mode* sets out to make a record by identifying and explaining good fashion Web design, but it also has a simpler objective: to celebrate the imagination and creativity of Web pioneers.

The twenty-nine sites showcased in *Net Mode* are not only survivors, but those setting the standards against which future design will be judged. *WWD's* Peter Braunstein might be correct in stating that the Web is 'a utopia that didn't happen', in the sense that it has become a tool for living rather than an all-pervasive way of life. Yet it has also become an important destination, where fashion's reality, defined by Barthes as 'a reality experienced fantastically', is given free and elegant expression.

lairdy718@aol.com

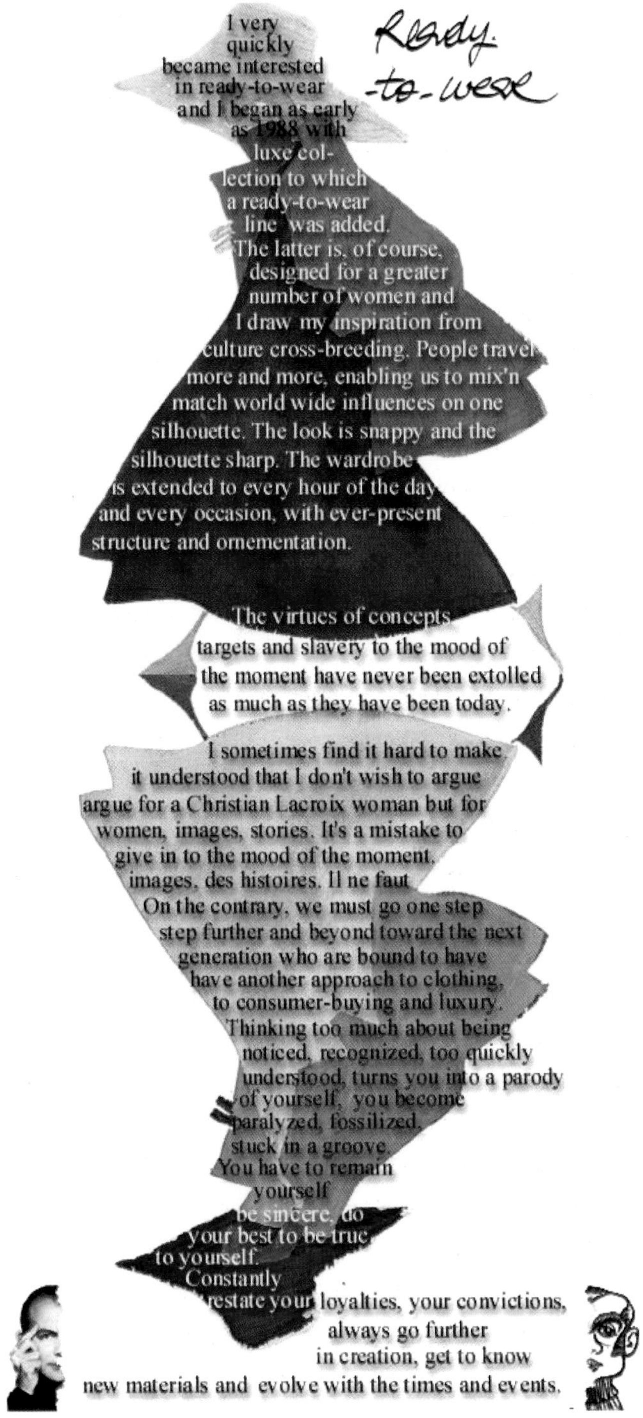

Above: An illustration from christian-lacroix.fr, with a two-faced navigation featuring the designer's portrait, half-drawn and half-photographed.

# fashion identity

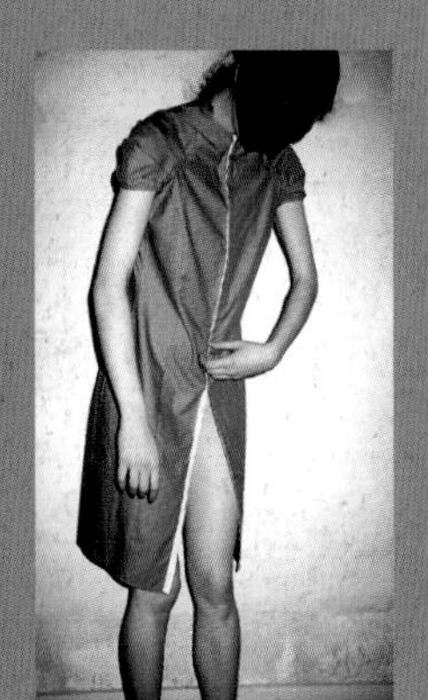

# 1

www.uol.com.br/herchcovitch

www.amayaarzuaga.com

www.bcbg.com

www.christian-lacroix.fr

www.costumenational.com

www.dior.com

www.dorotheeperret.com

www.emiliopucci.com

www.helmutlang.com

www.mads.it

www.pleatsplease.com

www.xuly-bet.com

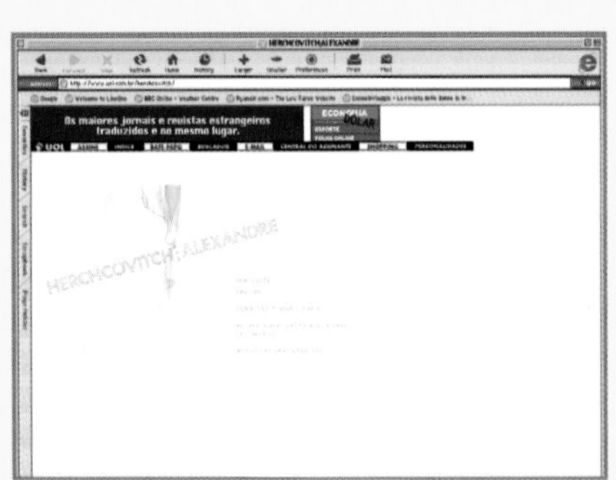

# www.uol.com.br/herchcovitch



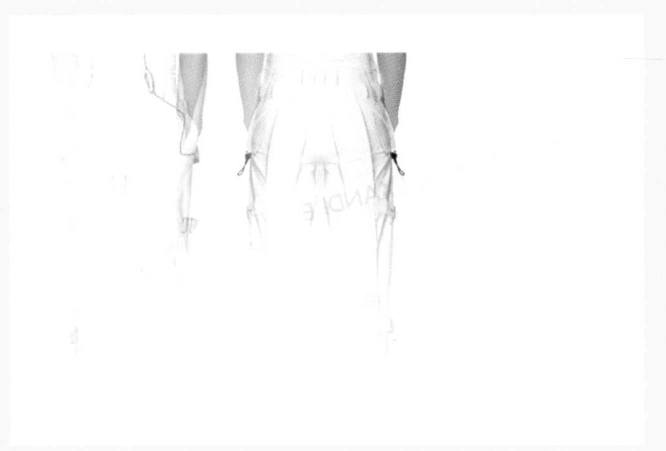

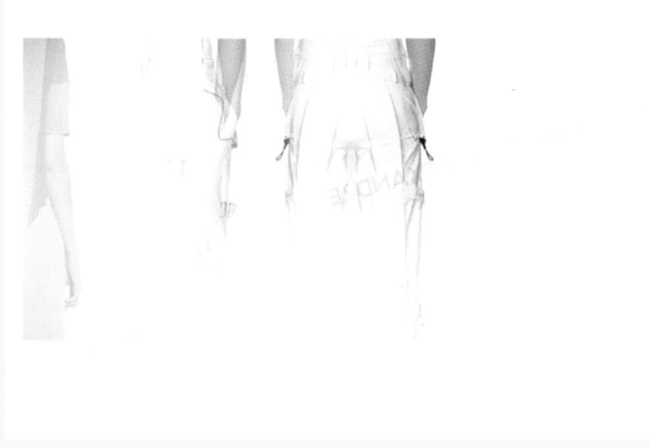

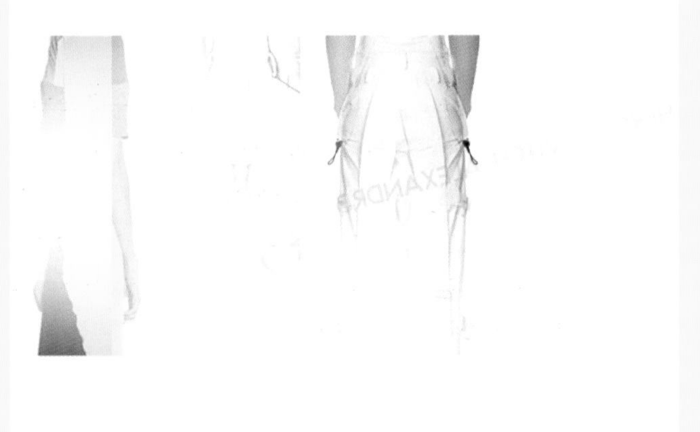

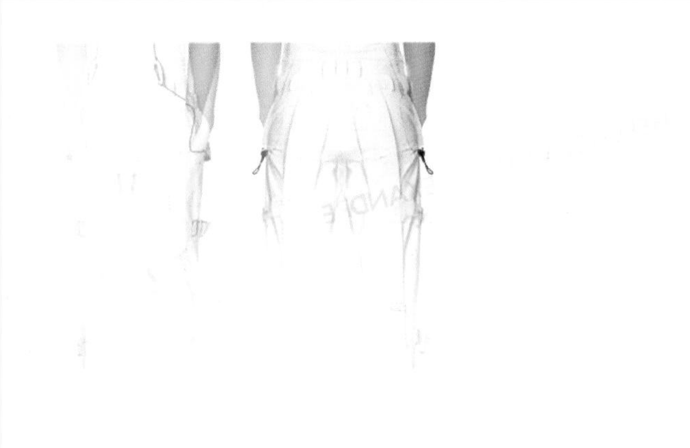

Top left: The Home page, framed and in detail, with its diagonal title. Below left: Screen shots of section Top pages from the Spring 2002 version of the site. These photos show front and back views of various looks and are deliberately washed out, as if blanched by a terrific paparazzi-style burst of flashbulb. The accompanying electronic audio for this season lends a circus-like mood to the site, since it incorporates ambient street ruckus and whistle-blows in a continuous loop.

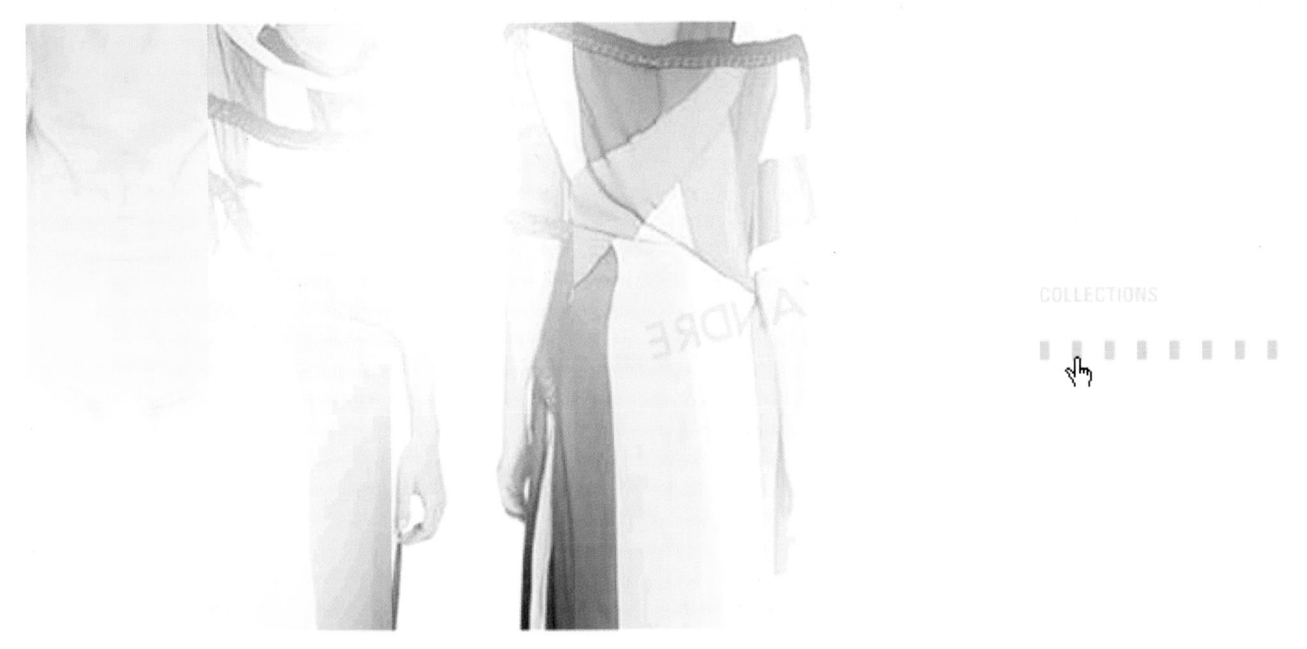


'What sets me apart…it's the freedom I give myself to mix fabrics, cuts, colours, culture', says star Brazilian designer Alexandre Herchcovitch, who often shows in Paris. The Web is, of course, a perfect vehicle for cultural bricolage, since it is without boundaries. Each season the Web designers at Grafikonstruct play with Flash animations and audio to showcase and set the mood for Herchcovitch's 'emotional' garments. For the Spring 2002 version of the site, Grafikonstruct visually deconstructed the designer's brilliantly coloured collection by over-exposing images of it. The blinding flashes of white that temper the fevered yellows and pinks of the collection refer to the brilliance – figural and literal (via crystal appliqués) – of Herchcovitch's designs.

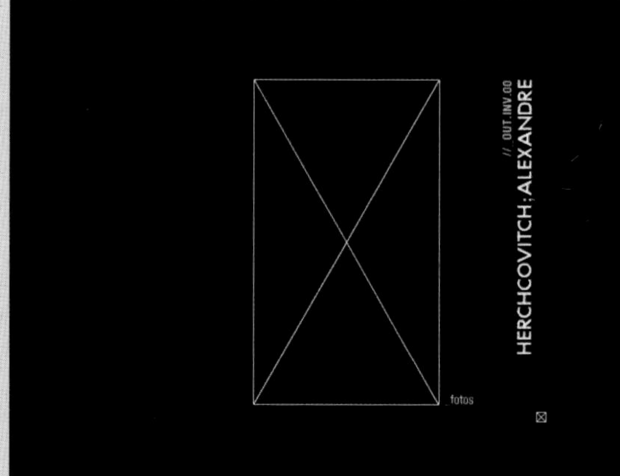


The path into Herchcovitch's Fall 2000 women's collection is shown on this page.
Top left: A Top page from the Fall 2001 season. Shown fully resolved here, it is built in tiny knife-like cuts, like those patterning the image above. The slideshows of the most current seasons' collections populate from a black layout page marked for visuals (top right), which fills with runway images, such as the one shown, near right, from Fall 2000. The navigation allows for forward and back movement.
Herchcovitch is involved in all aspects of branding his collection.
Opposite: Invitations from past shows, specifically Fall 1998 (chair), men's and women's Spring 2002 (apples) and women's Fall 2001 (hand). The site is made more personal, user-friendly and comprehensive with the addition of archives such as these. In addition to the invitation and press clippings archives, there is a photo album in the Bio section containing images of the designer, as well as his friends and beloved dogs.

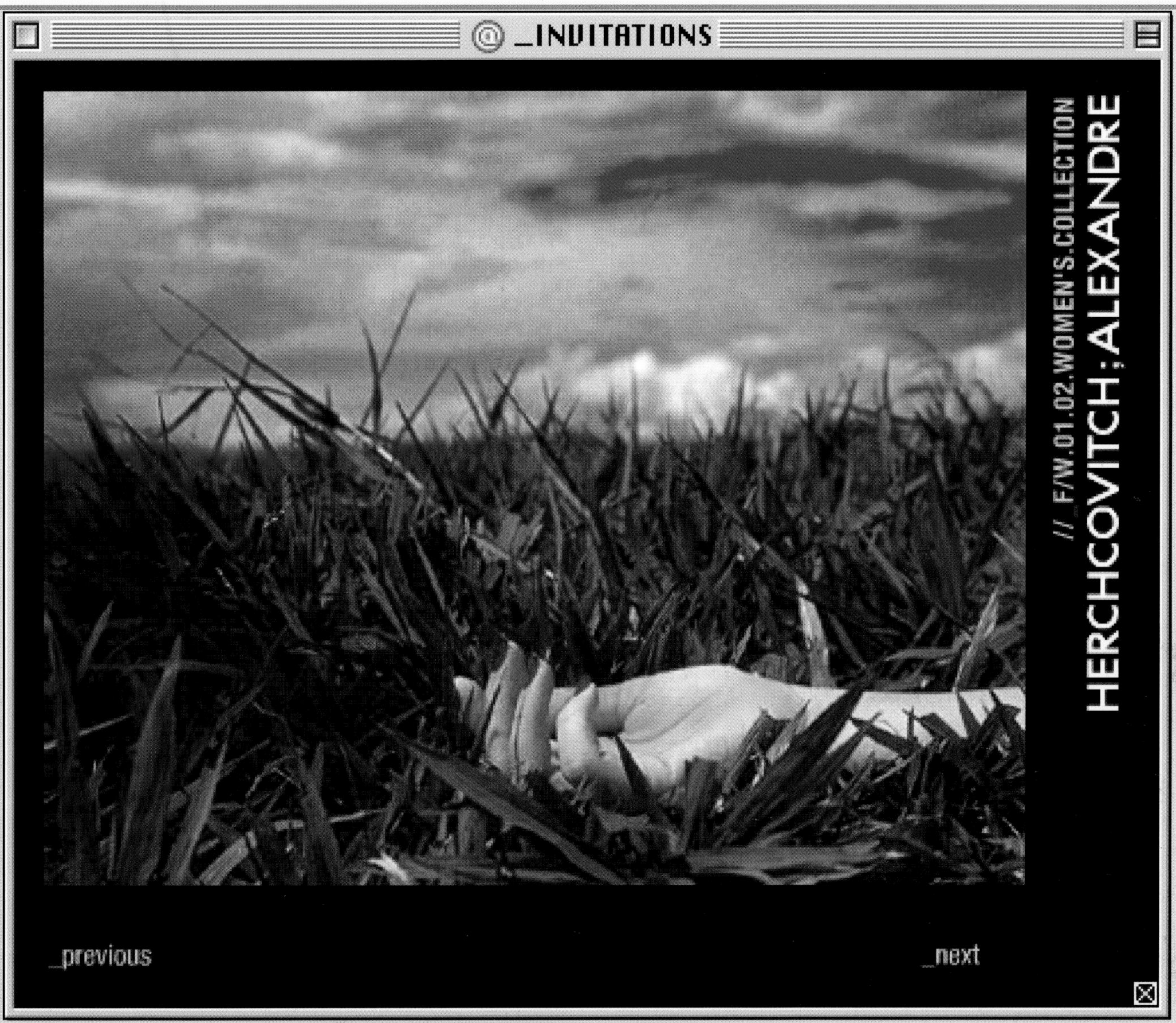

@ _INVITATIONS
// _F/W.01.02.WOMEN'S.COLLECTION
HERCHCOVITCH;ALEXANDRE
_previous
_next

// CONVITE.OUT/INV.98
HERCHCOVITCH;ALEXANDRE
D 018
_anterior
_próxima

// CONVITE.PRI/VER.01/02.FEM/MASC
HERCHCOVITCH;ALEXANDRE
_anterior
_inicio

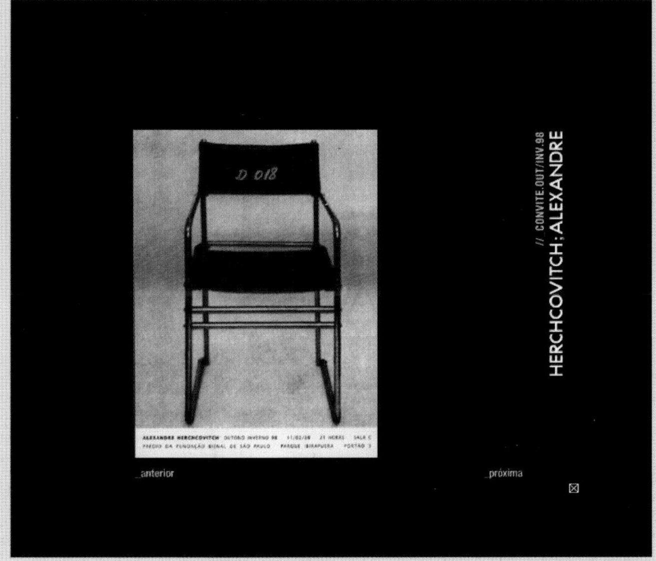

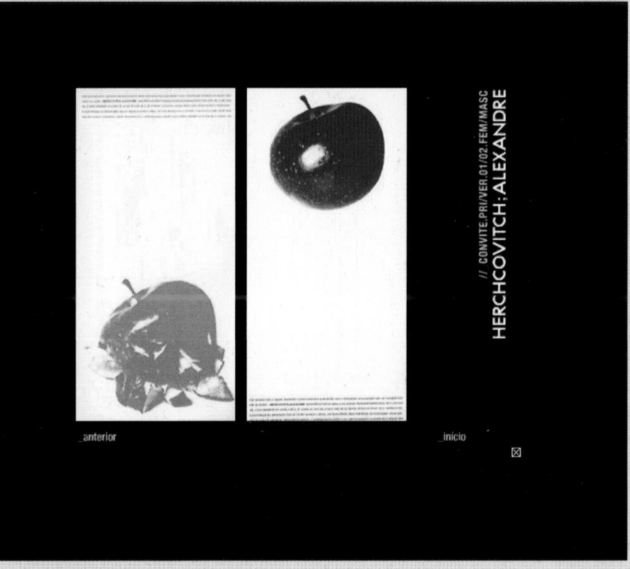

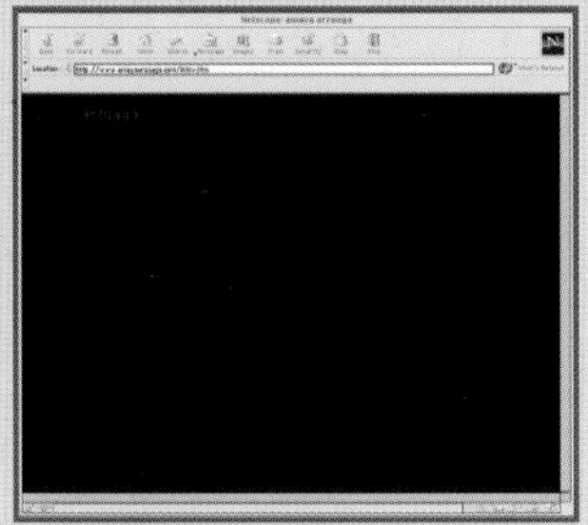
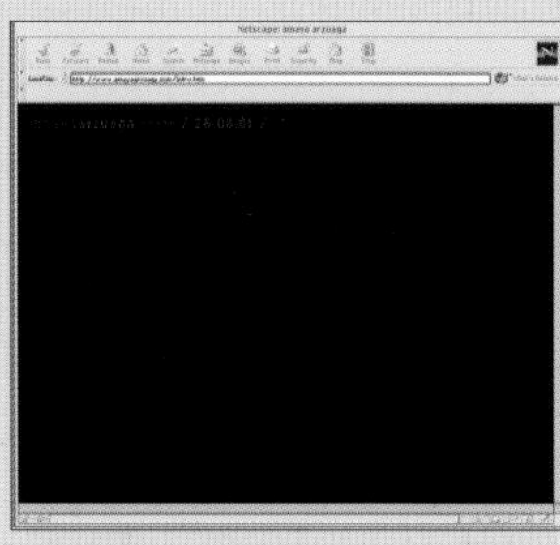

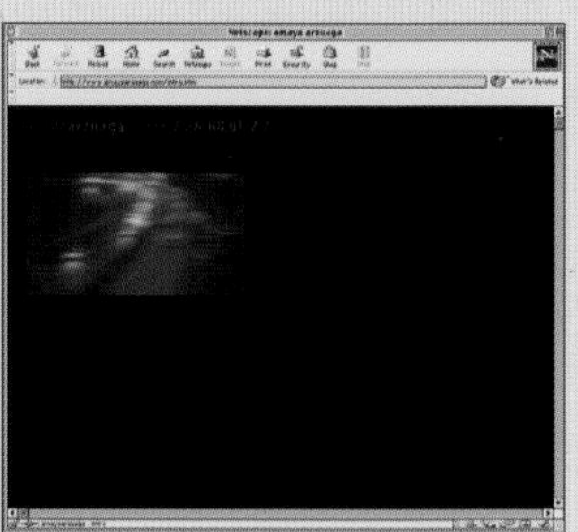

# www.amayaarzuaga.com



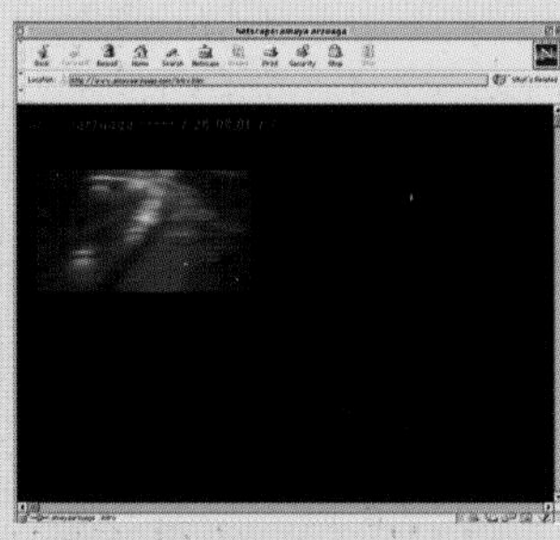

The echoing, empty sound of typing greets viewers to Amaya Arzuaga's Website: a line of text builds rapidly, letter by letter, on a black ground, each keystroke heralding the next. Then, with a roaring swoosh, a blurred reportage-style photograph of fluid strands of jewel-coloured traffic flowing through a dusky Barcelona night appears in one, two and then three layers on the chaste black ground, creating a charged and mysterious atmosphere. The mood having being set, it's time for fashion, and two entwined modish young people appear, again in layers. The staggered transformation of the images, which move from left to right, becomes a clever pathway into the site. The accompanying sweeping swoosh-zoom audio suggests that Arzuaga makes fashion for the fast lane, baby.

The development of the Home page is shown here, top and bottom, left to right.

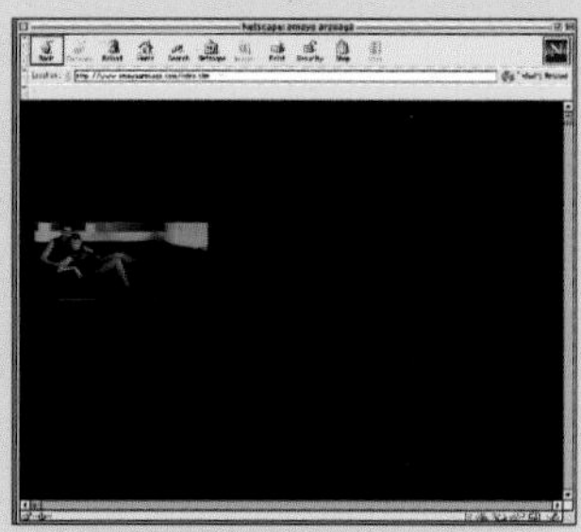

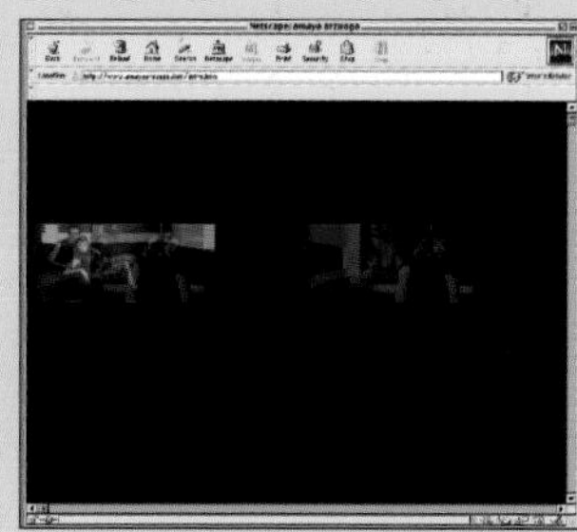

Amaya Arzuaga, a Spaniard who shows in London, is a young designer who enjoys great commercial success. She is known for her use of asymmetry and colour. Quim Nolla, the award-winning graphic designer who created the Fall 2001 version of the site, describes it as 'active and dynamic'. The site was programmed by Toni Sánchez of Alteraciones and is archived at http://idd02g7q.eresmas.net/amaya/index.html.

amayaarzuaga / / / autumn-winter 2000/2001
accesories +
2
< / >
< / >
4
< / >

Introduced in negative form, photographs of Arzuaga's accessories (left) 'develop' (via Shockwave and html or Flash) before the user's eyes to glow against a black ground. The simple graphic brackets and mathematical-style forward/back navigational symbols give context to the images, indicating that they have been specially chosen for display.

'About my work' (sobre mi trabajo) is the title Arzuaga has given to the Press section of her site. It is designed with the same restraint as the rest of the site, allowing the images to speak for themselves (right and below).

Launched in 1997, bcbg.com is an extremely comprehensive site, built, says founder and designer Max Azria, 'to provide the consumer an inside view of BCBG Max Azria'. The company's sophisticated advertising images are transformed into moving, layered Top pages and section markers using Flash technology, effectively building the brand and providing the user with a unique, Web-specific experience of the campaign.

# www.bcbg.com

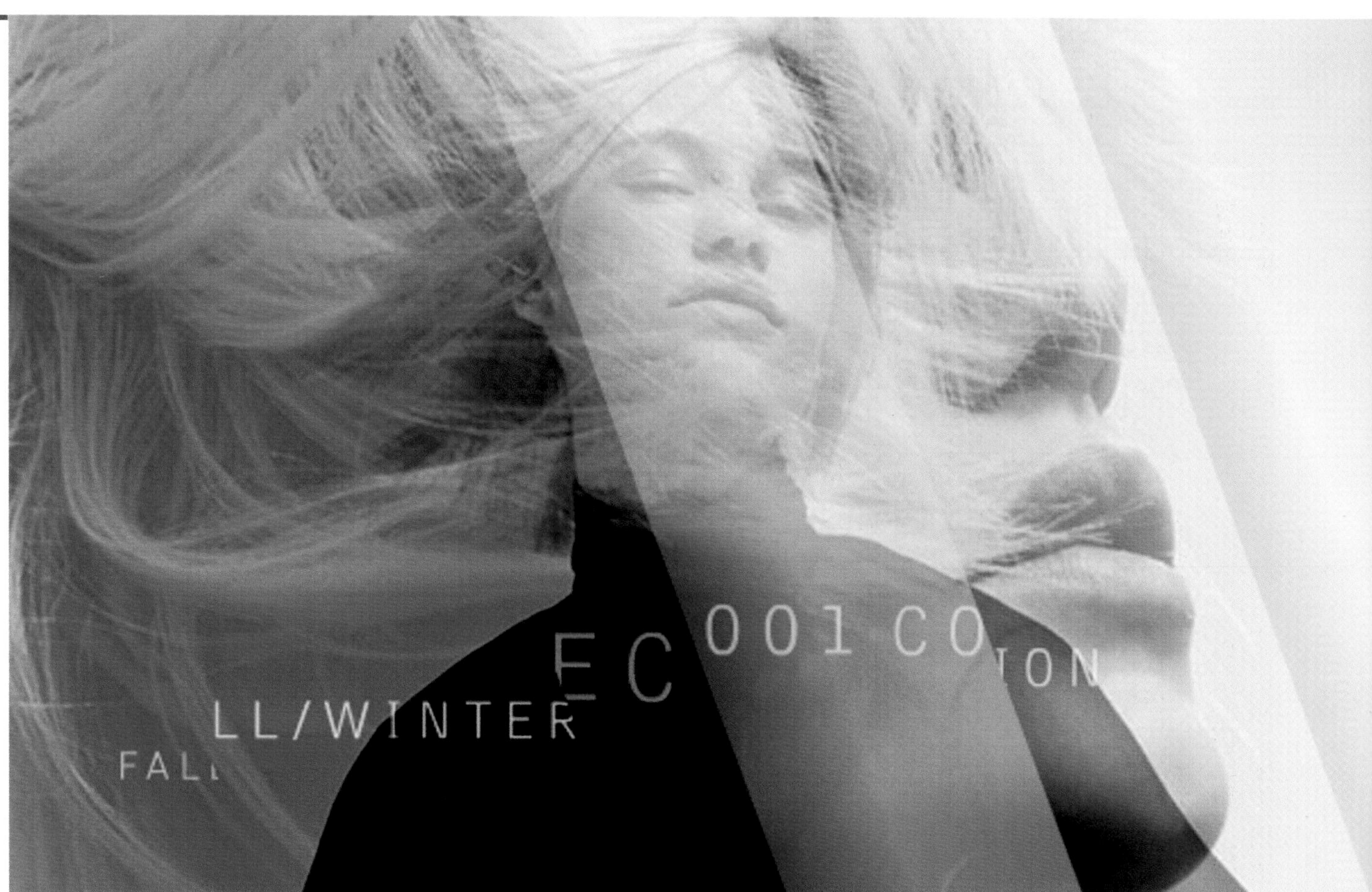


Tow-headed model Delfine Bafort is the star of BCBG's Fall 2001 print campaign – and the season's edition of the site. The images above and to the right, variously transfigured with Flash, are taken from the introductory sequence to the site.

ALL/WINTE 001 COL
FAL
FALL/WINR 2001

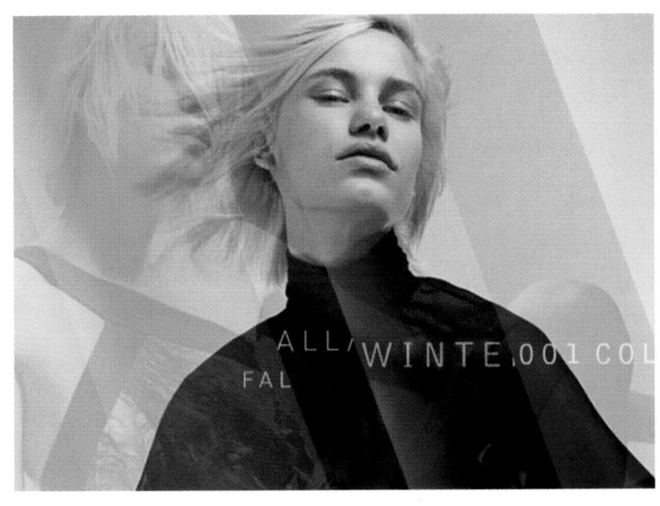

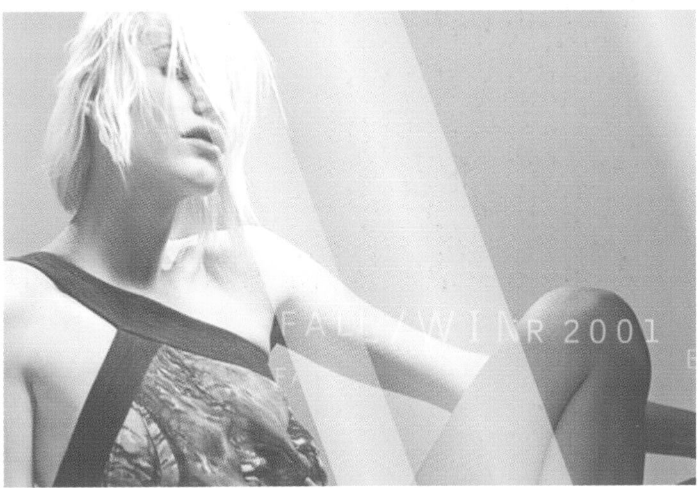

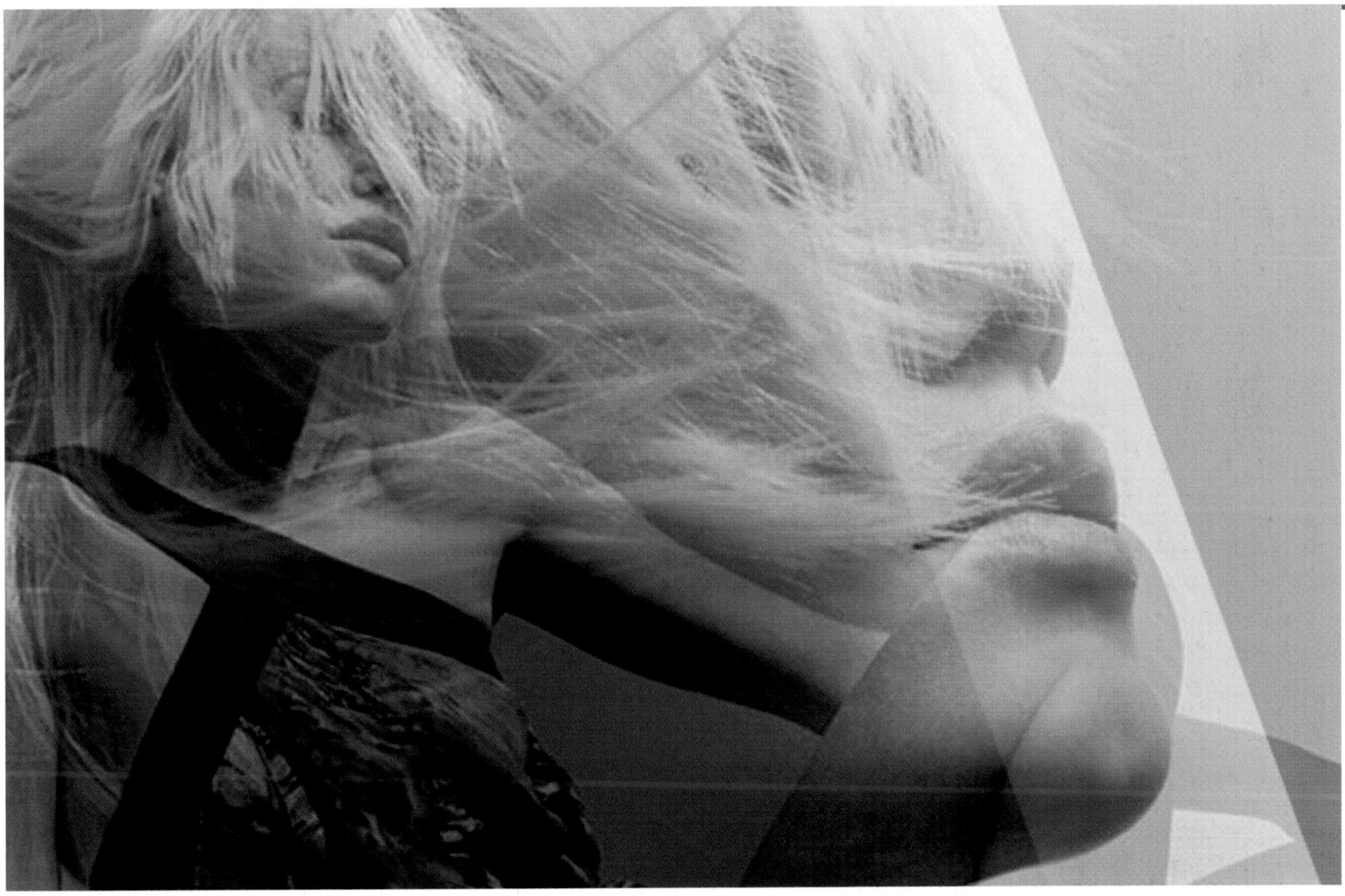

Runway shows are exclusive, by-invitation-only affairs attended by buyers, press and celebrities. The Web, in contrast, is about accessibility and interactivity. BCBG makes its collections available to its users in a variety of formats. In addition to runway and backstage photographs, there are still shots of accessories, as well as a streaming video of the show. 'Not only do we reach the fashion forward via our Website but also consumers that may not have had the privilege of becoming familiar with our merchandise', says Azria.

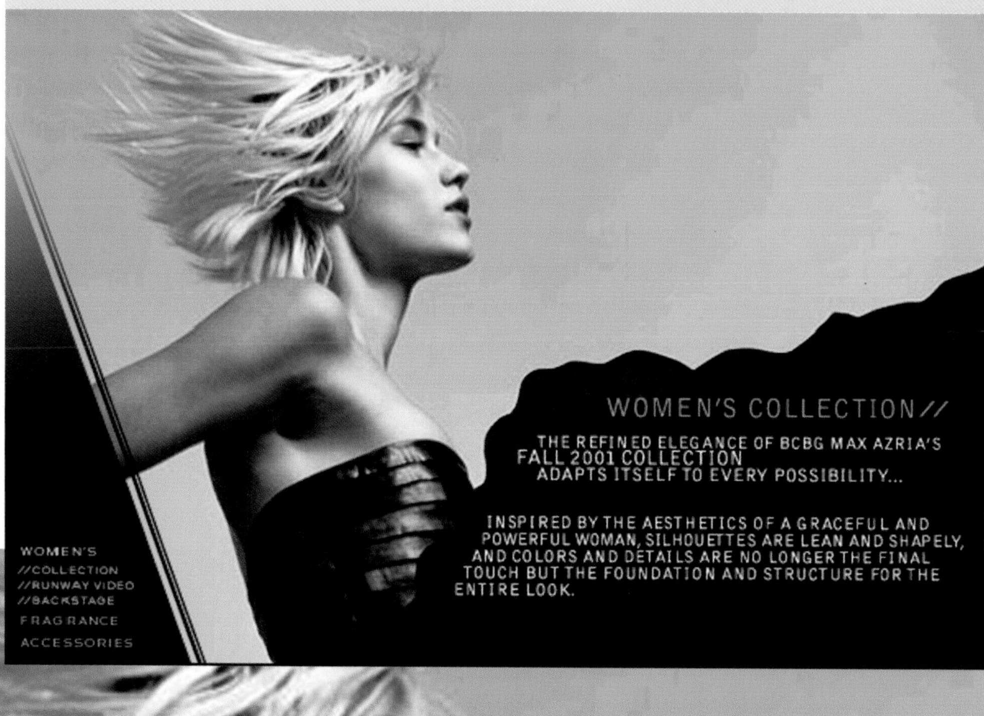

Clockwise from bottom left: The final state of the Collection Top page. One layer in: Collection/Women's selected. Text describing the inspiration of the collection appears over the Top page image. Two layers in: Collection/ Women's/Collection showing a series of images from the catwalk. When Collection (a subcategory of Women's) is selected, the Top page image shifts to the left to become a horizontal page marker. Each section of the site is thus 'branded' with a specific image. As the inset demonstrates (right), users can click to enlarge any runway image and can elect to send the resulting large-size pop-up to friends as a 'fashion e-card', which is an interactive element of the site.

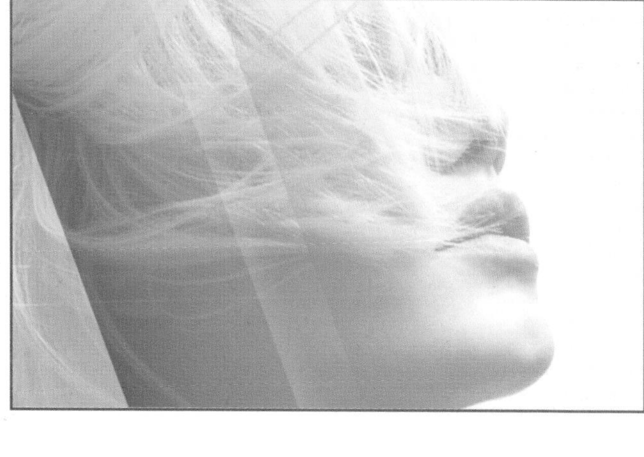

BCBG's site is redesigned each season using images from the campaign. The image at top left was grabbed from the Fall 2001 site. The other images on these pages, featuring model Liisa Winkler, are Top pages from the 2001 edition, which employed horizontal Flash enhancements. In contrast, those for Fall moved in sweeping vertical motions.

The main categories of the BCBG site are: Collection; What's New; Company; Stores; Catalog; and Contact Us. Each has subdivisions. The site provides another means by which the company is able to provide customer service and to interact in other ways with customers through, for example, advice columns (answered by Azria himself) or a contest to win tickets to a BCBG fashion show.

This page: Christian Lacroix invites users to explore his world (in French or in English) on the Home page, from which the latest collection is available in video and slideshow formats. The coeur of the Summary page (top right) is a flaming heart accompanied by audio of a fire being lit. The writing is Lacroix's own, as is the collage. A chameleon-like chirping cricket directs users through the What's New page (middle right).

# www.christian-lacroix.fr

The most personal of designer sites, christian-lacroix.fr is also one of the most joyous. 'Fashion is one of the favoured domains of the Web', says Anne Lardeur, who designed the site in close collaboration with Christian Lacroix with the aim of 'permitting the user to discover the whole of the designer's work without an intermediary'. To that end, Lacroix's illustrations, as well as his wonderfully expressive calligraphy, are used throughout the site, giving it a warm, 'signature' feel.

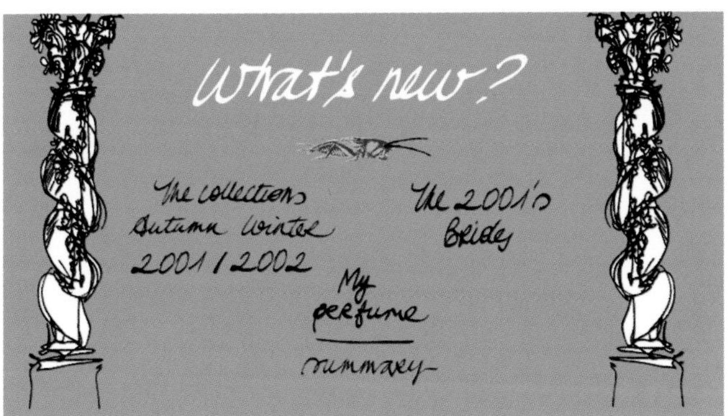


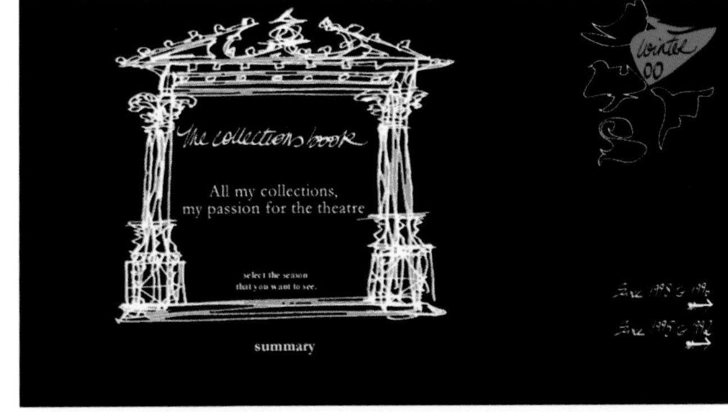

If Collections are selected, the user will be led to the Autumn/Winter 2001 page (above).

The Collections Book is a complete archive of the designer's work from 1987, when his fashion house was founded (middle right).

Above: The Shops page is accessible from the Summary page with the burning heart.

Opposite: Stills from the Flash pop-up slideshow of the Spring/Summer 2002 collection. Model Vivien Solari becomes visible through a Swiss cheese peep show.

Streaming video provides the user with a multi-sensory experience of the show, including audio. The stills are beautiful documents in themselves. The Web allows many technologies to be used, creating different types of experiences of a single event.

prêt-à-porter printemps été 2002
-wear spring summer 2002
prêt-à-porter printemps été 2002
ready-to-wear spring summer 2002
prêt-à-porter printemps été 2002
ready-to-wear spring summ
prêt-à-porter printemps été 2002

The training years
Arles
London
Paris

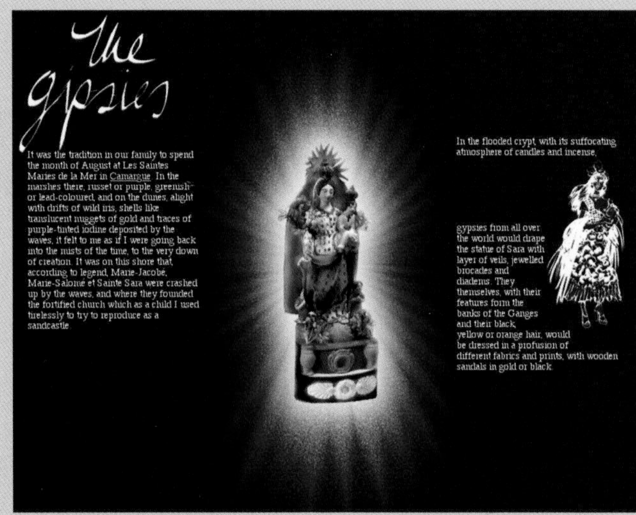
The gipsies
It was the tradition in our family to spend the month of August at Les Saintes Maries de la Mer in Camargue. In the marshes there, russet or purple, greenish or lead-coloured, and on the dunes, alight with drifts of wild iris, shells like translucent nuggets of gold and traces of purple-tinted iodine deposited by the waves, it felt to me as if I were going back into the mists of the time, to the very down of creation. It was on this shore that, according to legend, Marie-Jacobé, Marie-Salomé et Sainte Sara were crashed up by the waves, and where they founded the fortified church which as a child I used tirelessly to try to reproduce as a sandcastle.
In the flooded crypt, with its suffocating atmosphere of candles and incense,
gypsies from all over the world would drape the statue of Sara with layer of veils, jewelled brocades and diadems. They themselves, with their features form the banks of the Ganges and their black, yellow or orange hair, would be dressed in a profusion of different fabrics and prints, with wooden sandals in gold or black.

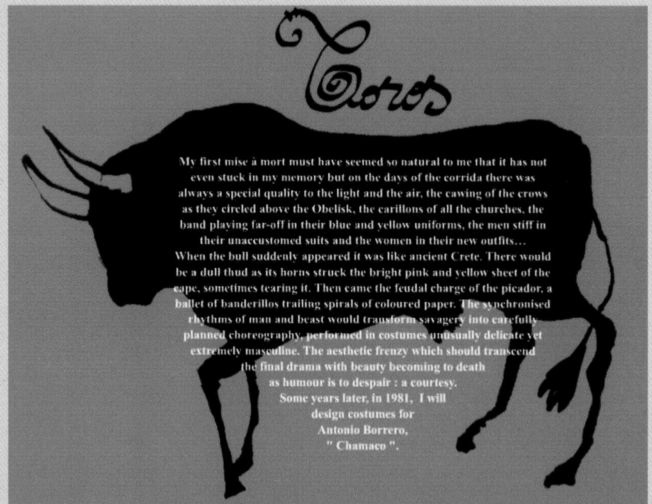
Toros
My first mise à mort must have seemed so natural to me that it has not even stuck in my memory but on the days of the corrida there was always a special quality to the light and the air, the cawing of the crows as they circled above the Obelisk, the carillons of all the churches, the band playing far-off in their blue and yellow uniforms, the men stiff in their unaccustomed suits and the women in their new outfits...
When the bull suddenly appeared it was like ancient Crete. There would be a dull thud as its horns struck the bright pink and yellow sheet of the cape, sometimes tearing it. Then came the feudal charge of the picador, a ballet of banderillos trailing spirals of coloured paper. The synchronised rhythms of man and beast would transform savagery into carefully planned choreography, performed in costumes unusually delicate yet extremely masculine. The aesthetic frenzy which should transcend the final drama with beauty becoming to death as humour is to despair : a courtesy.
Some years later, in 1981, I will design costumes for Antonio Borrero, " Chamaco ".

## Sublime arlésiennes

**The Arlésiennes, the napes of their necks shown off by the five ritual pleats of their chantilly lace fichus,, their Greek profiles harmoniously balanced bythe traditional velvet ribbon, their shoulders thrust back and their trains caught up with a silver clasp, would elbow their way through the crowd to the front seats.**

**In one hand they held lace parasols and in the other beaded or tapestry -work purses, or some- times the painted and sequinned fans behind which they laughed and gossiped.**

My Itinerary is Lacroix's first-person narration of his life in design, from Arles, through London to Paris. Top left: The Training Years Top page. The Gipsies; Toros; and Sublime Arlésiennes pages (some of the designer's main inspirations), seen at bottom left and above, are all reached by links through the following path: My Itinerary/The Training Years/Arles/Walking on Thursday. The Flash-enhanced bull paws the ground and raises his head up and down, reacting as if the user were a torero.

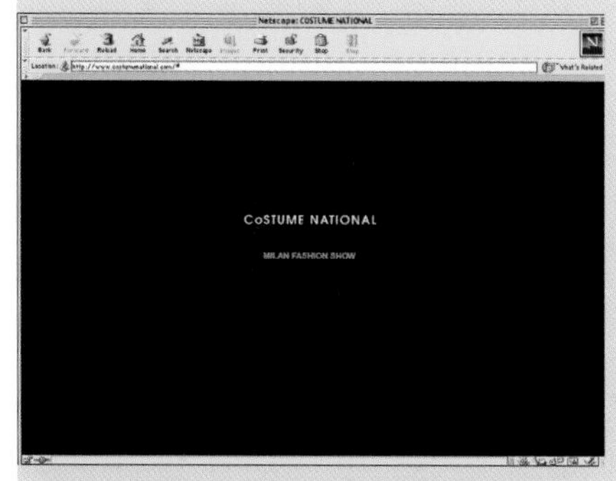

Top row: The spare black and white Home page gives way to a kinetic index-in-motion by way of the 'o' in costume, which is used throughout as the window into the world of Costume National.
Middle row: A raven heralds Winter 2001/2; the Men's Collection page.
Bottom row: The Women's Collection, highlighted, and (top right) selected, enlarged and colourized.
Bottom right: Living large – Erika Wall on the runway.

# www.costumenational.com



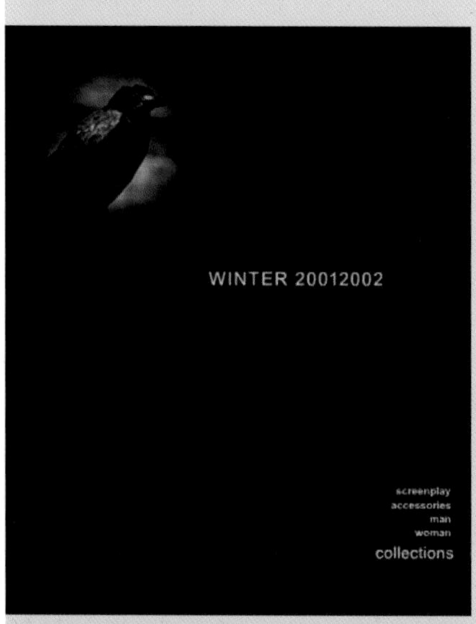

'It feels like we are behind the computer screen', says designer Ennio Capasa when asked what the distinguishing characteristic of his company's site is. Capasa's precise, streamlined aesthetic is at work both on the catwalk and on the Web. Family-owned, Costume National is an Italian company with a French name taken from an antique book on Gallic uniforms. Unique to the Costume National site is the Screenplay section, where Flash and Shockwave technology are artfully used to create a Web-exclusive experience that combines elements of film and fashion. 'Fashion and the Web', states Capasa, 'are both about updating. They are modern and fast and have a long way to go.'

John Akehurst's Winter 2000/1 image campaign for Costume National is suffused with a glowing golden light that creates a hothouse atmosphere within which three women and a man enact a languid and slightly ominous scenario. Manipulated using Web technology, the images are layered and dissolved one over the other, allowing for the story to evolve seamlessly. The fluid and easy glamour of the Screenplay mirrors Capasa's achievement in his clothing designs.

This page: Stills from the Winter 2000/1 Screenplay show the visual evolution of one image into another. The face of a pensive woman surfaces from behind an image of a lounging man, who then fades away, leaving her alone, centre stage.

John Akehurst shot the Winter 2001/2 Screenplay entirely in black and white. A feeling of stillness pervades this season's Screenplay which is less plot-orientated – and contains more still-lifes – than others. Images dissolve through black grounds and/or are surrounded by black circular frames, which mimic the 'o' navigation through which the site is accessed.

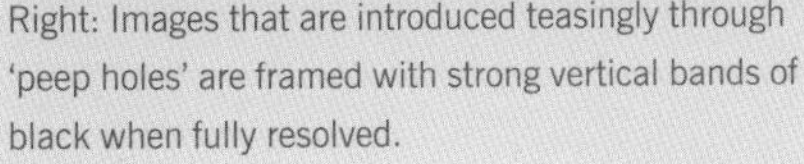

Right: Images that are introduced teasingly through 'peep holes' are framed with strong vertical bands of black when fully resolved.

SUMMER 2001
woman
man
accessories
screenplay

Models Amanda Moore and Griet Toch star in the sexually charged Summer 2001 Screenplay, suffused with blue light. Shot in a masculine wood-panelled manor-house, the Screenplay uses vertical open and close layering to add an erotic rhythm to the whole.

Shimmering and textured fabrics, as well as brightly coloured clothes, stand out against the empty industrial building in which Akehurst shot the Summer 2000 Screenplay. A mysterious tension is created between the seeming déshabillé (cracked paint, worn floors) of the setting and the carefully dressed and posed models.

**SUMMER2000**

woman man accessories underwear

*screenplay*

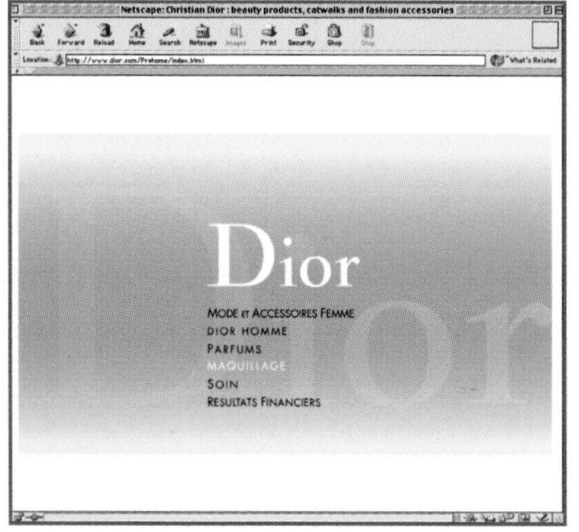


Left: The Dior Homme site is accessed through the Dior Home page.
Below: Users are greeted by an advertising image from the Spring 2001 Dior Homme collection by Hedi Slimane. The designers used Shockwave to moult, subtley, the hues of black, white and grey, which brighten and fade in 'windswept' waves.

Right, clockwise from top left: The splintered Dior logo, moving towards resolution. The logo dissolves in a six-pronged sparkle (second and third images). Each sector of the 'star' is a room. 'The experience', explains the team, 'is to enter an ethereal space and to gain access to the rooms, following the animations and sounds as they inspire you.' The fourth image is one of the navigations in use on the site.

# www.dior.com

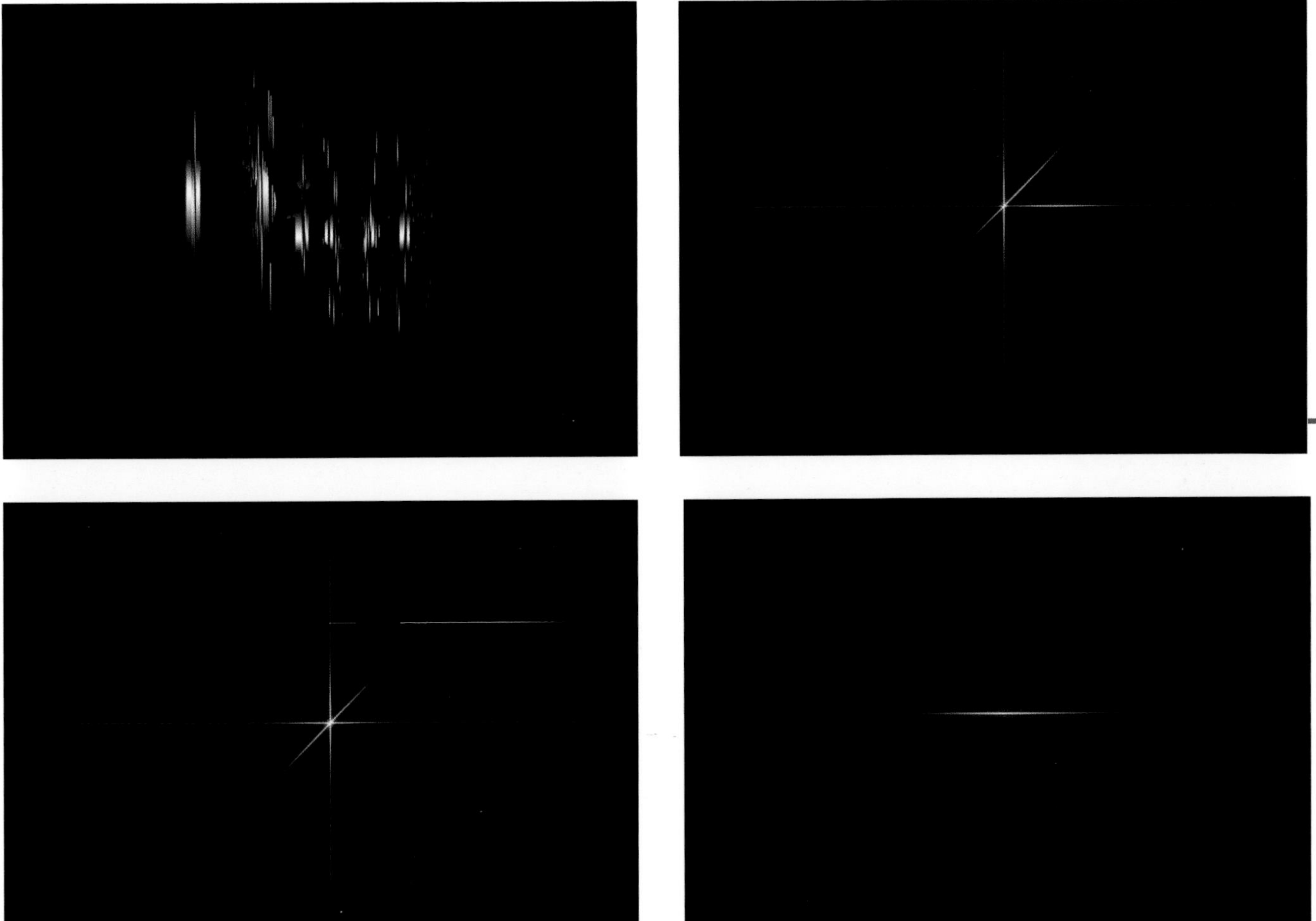

The Dior Homme site 'is intuitive', says menswear designer Hedi Slimane. 'We do not want it to look like a fashion site.' Rather, it is the internet extension of the universe Hedi Slimane set out to create at Dior, specifically the studio he designed at 40, rue François 1er in Paris. Working against conventions, the Dior Homme Web team built a site that leads people through 'a journey "at random" in this space, where visuals and sounds are key media, showing or suggesting information or events linked with Dior Homme, but in an allusive and intuitive way.'

Left: Vertical navigation bars burning red from within a black background. Below: A runway image from the Spring 2001 Solitaire collection by Hedi Slimane for Dior Homme.

Opposite, top left: White-hot horizontal navigation bars. Opposite, top right: Text in an in-between state of resolution. Opposite, below: Moving vectors of light. Users who click on these 'sweepers' are led to screen savers, which can be downloaded.

40 FRANÇOIS 1ER

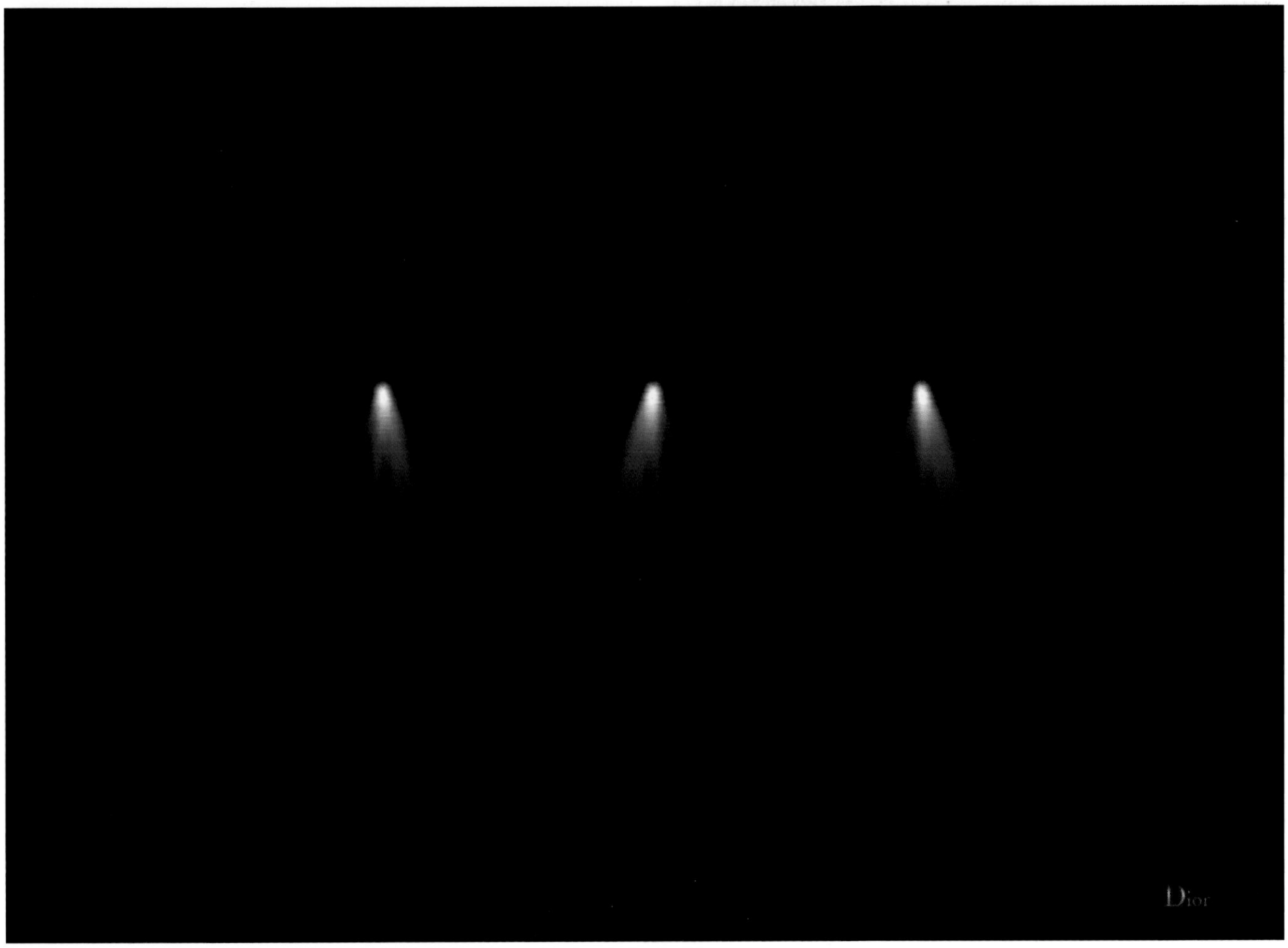

Left and below: The pixilation of the red house that welcomes users to Dorothée Perret's site indicates that the image has been mechanically reproduced. This deliberate choice introduces the idea of alteration, which is taken further in the manipulation of the typeface on the rest of the page.

# www.dorotheeperret.com

Dorothée
Perret was
born in
October
1972 in

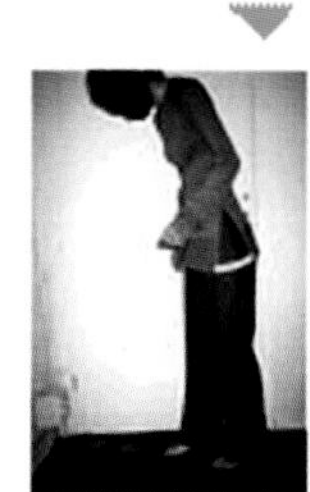

Dorothée Perret
Spring / Summer 00

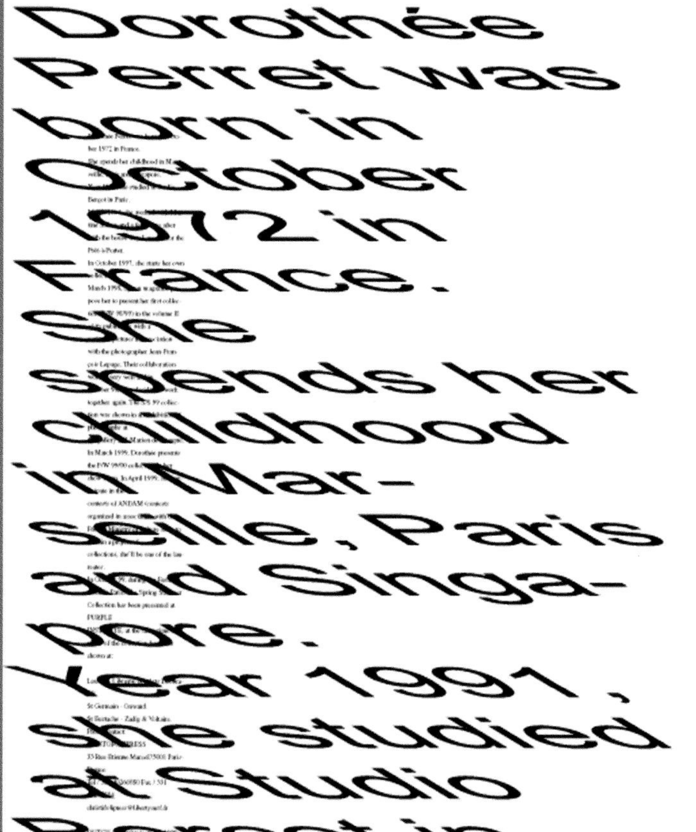

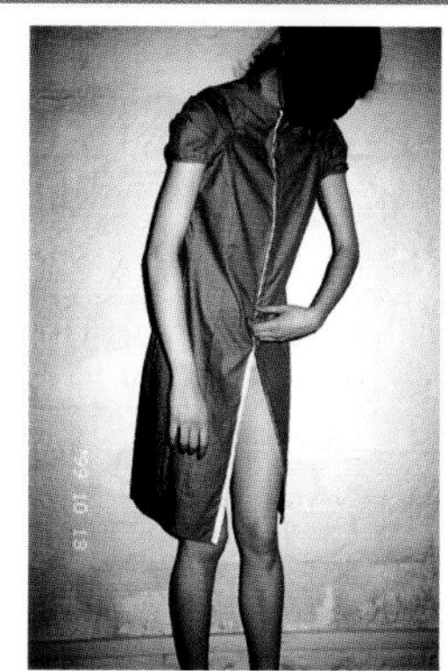

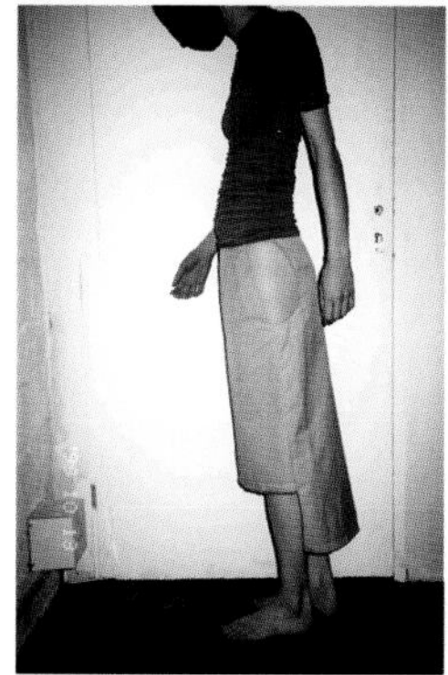



An intuitive designer, Dorothée Perret drapes all of her collections on her own body, cutting the pieces flat. Her Website, a single page with pop-ups and a video, is similarly flat (rather than deep). Perret's clothes have been variously described as 'abstract', 'psychologically fragile' and as having 'a wounded look'. Almost as interesting as her work is Perret's concern as to how it is presented. Rather than traditional runway shows, she has displayed her collections as gallery exhibitions. Designed by The Lonely Line, Perret's site is distinct in its creative use of typography. 'The Web', she says, 'is an excellent tool to exchange ideas and meet people and propose things, and by extension it works quite well with my way of seeing fashion.'

Above left: Pop-up slideshows of past collections border the biographical text. Above right: Two images from the Spring/Summer 2000 collection slideshow. These photographs are at once lo-fi and highly composed.

Dorothée
She childhood
Year studied
March Sitbon
In
March her to present
series the photograph
October together again.
In March F/W 99/00
contests in association
In October week in Paris
INSTITUTE time

Dorothée us and mo
Paris's Sitbon,
I'm really And beca
intuition re's no glo
and elas holds sleev
clothes ok and

Dorothée born
She childhood
Year studied
March 199 Sitbon and
In she
March 199 to present
series of the photographer
October 98, together again.
In March 1999 F/W 99/00
contests of ANDAM in association
In October 99 week in Paris,
INSTITUTE, at time

Dorothée Perret More reserved, less glamorous and more

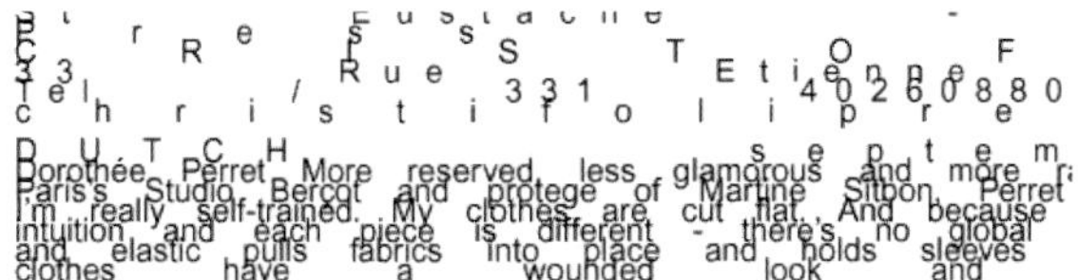

# SHO°P

DOROTHEE PERRET'S COLLECTIONS ARE SALES AT:

ONWARD / PARIS
147 BOULEVARD ST GERMAIN
75006 PARIS, FRANCE
TEL 331 55 42 77 55
FAX 331 55 42 77 51

PENELOPE / BRESCIA
VIA GRAMSCI 16
25122 BRESCIA, ITALIA
TEL 030 29 04 73
FAX 030 29 04 85

INDIVI LIFE / TOKYO
AOYAMA TEN
MINATO KU
5.11.8 MINAMI AOYAMA
107/0062 TOKYO JAPAN

Opposite: While it is not yet possible to conduct e-commerce on Perret's site, one can shop for her collection elsewhere. A comprehensive contact list of vendors is provided in the Shop section. The text that appears higher up on the page is also used in the shopping section as a cut-out graphic pattern, adding texture and depth to the design.

Left: Specific shop contact information. Below: A pop-up photograph by Marcus Bayer, with whom Perret collaborated on the documentation and presentation of her Spring/Summer 2000 collection at Purple Institute in Paris.

[1] [2] [3] [4] [5] [6] [7]

1

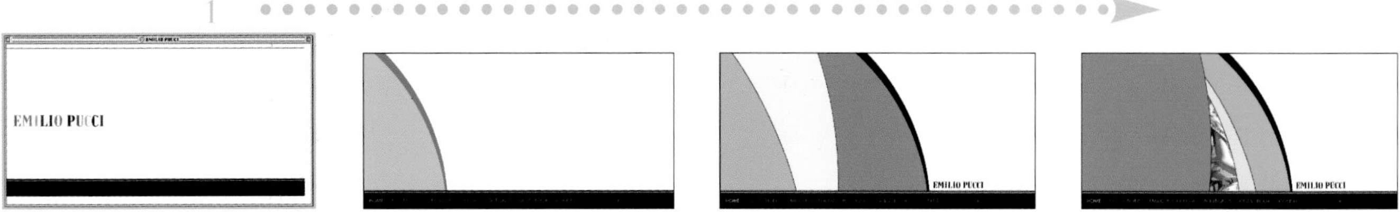


www.emiliopucci.com



2

BALANCE

'Balance', 'glamour', 'new', 'forward fantasy', 'exuberant', 'optimistic', 'joyful' – these words are all used to describe the Pucci brand championed in the site's introduction. The juxtaposition of vintage and contemporary photographs links the company's past and present, surrounded by colourful moving 'frames' designed after Pucci prints, using the house's vivid palette.

The original 'lounge-y' music composed for the site evokes, says Laudomia Pucci, 'the memory of something you've known, but which is not exactly that'.

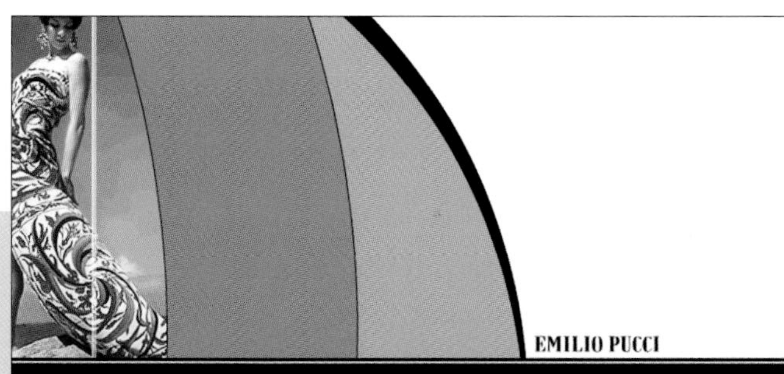


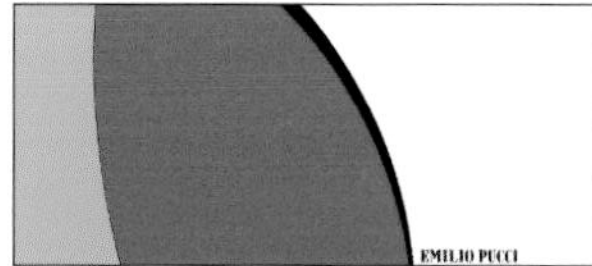

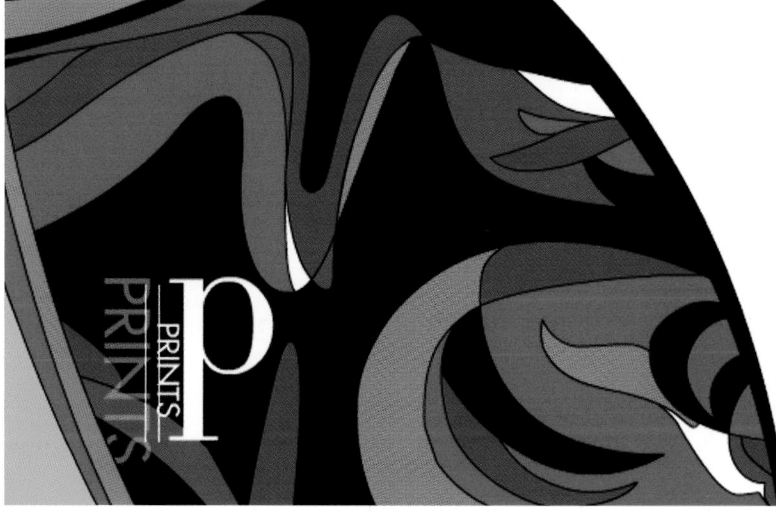

'Nouveau retro' is the phrase Laudomia Pucci uses to describe the Emilio Pucci site designed by DigitalForm. While focusing on 'forward fantasy', the rich history of the company, established in 1947 by Emilio Pucci, is not abandoned. Rather, the psychedelic prints for which the company is famous – inspired by the abstract forms and movement Pucci observed while flying – become the foundation of the form and functionality of the site, reinforcing Emilio Pucci's legacy as 'The Prince of Prints'.

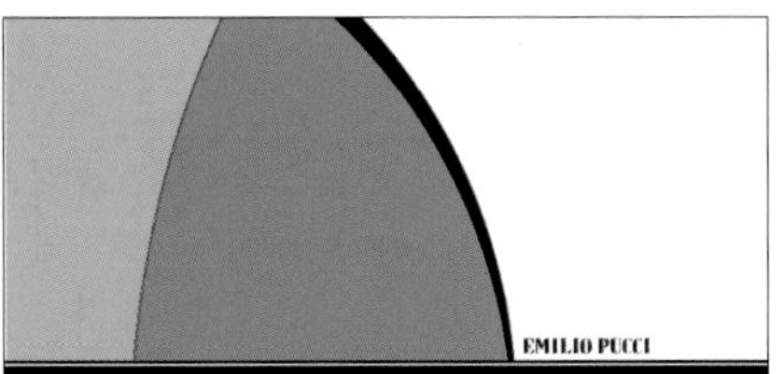

Pucci's exuberant and optimistic designs inspire not only emotional loyalty but also material lust. For Pucci addicts there are vintage dealers who specialize in the brand and a place on the site for users to share their Pucci moments via interactive e-mail. Even LVMH caught the bug, acquiring a majority stake in the company in 2000. Pucci product lust can be sated in America through the boutique section, linked to eluxury.com, which sells a selection of Pucci items on-line. What is it about Pucci that makes it ever new? 'Pucci for me', says Laudomia Pucci, 'is one of the most important historical brands in Italy.... A woman in Pucci is attractive in a modern way.'

The site must not only appeal to already-avid fans, but also inspire them to 'forward fantasies' involving the brand, if it is to fulfil the 'emotional loyalty' part of its mission. In addition, it must speak to new users about the current status of the brand in a way that incorporates the powerful allure of the company's past. This is accomplished by DigitalForm's 'image-oriented design', which combines contemporary and vintage imagery and original audio in an interactive 'print-scape'.

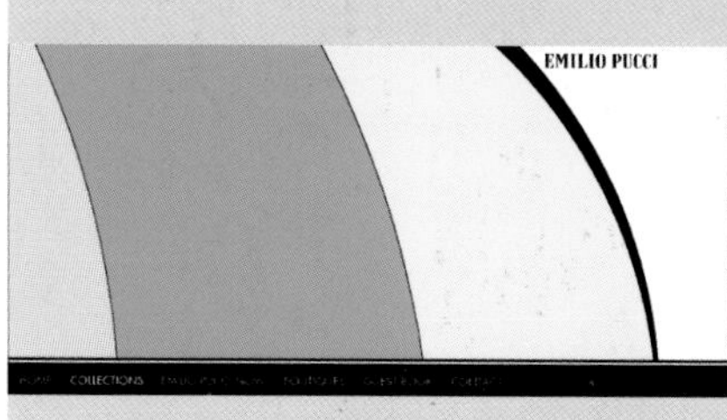


LANCE
PIANETI
NEW WAVE
BUBBLES
PESCI & RIO
VIEW BY PRINT ALL PRINTS

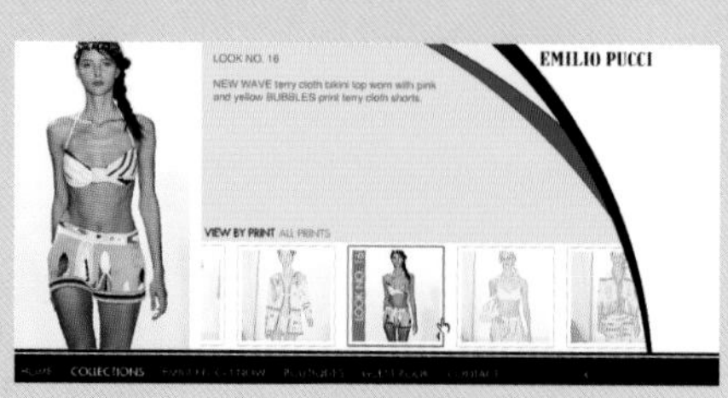


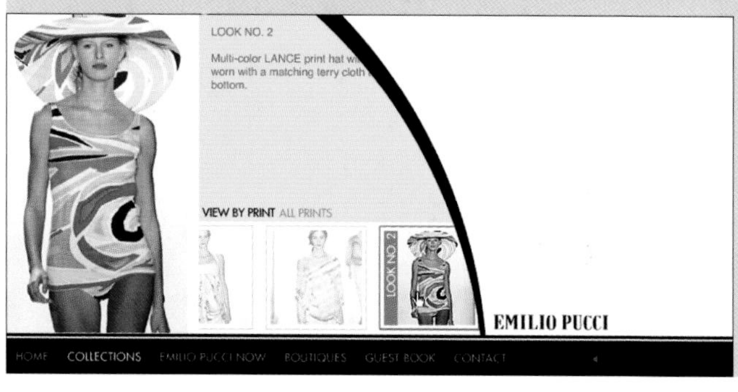


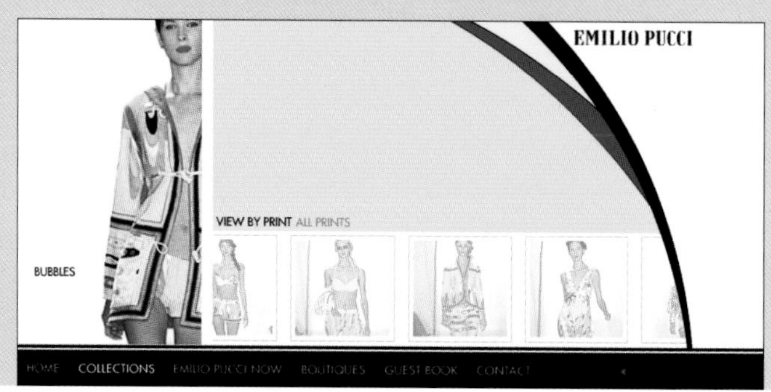

LOOK NO. 44

Mauve PESCI print long-sleeve shirt with draping, worn with matching pants.

**EMILIO PUCCI**

VIEW BY PRINT ALL PRINTS

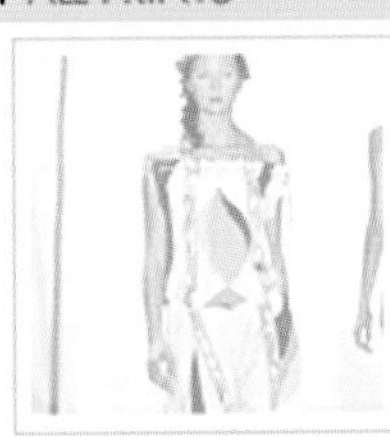

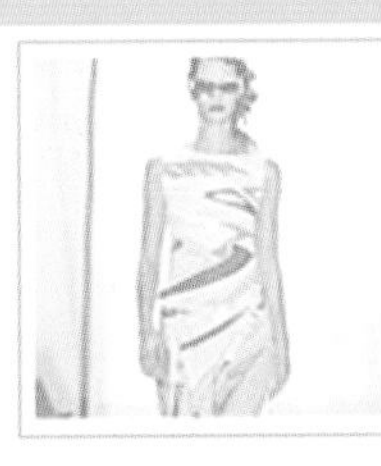

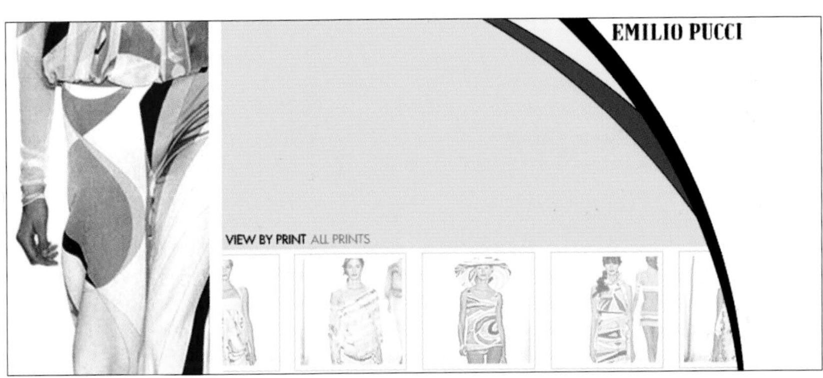


These pages: Different views of looks from the Spring 2002 collection.Users can view the season's collection look by look, or can sort by print. Sort functions are becoming increasingly popular on fashion sites. The sort-by-print function on the Pucci site does more than just enhance its functionality: it reinforces the core asset of the brand (i.e. prints) and adds an interactive element to the design of the site.

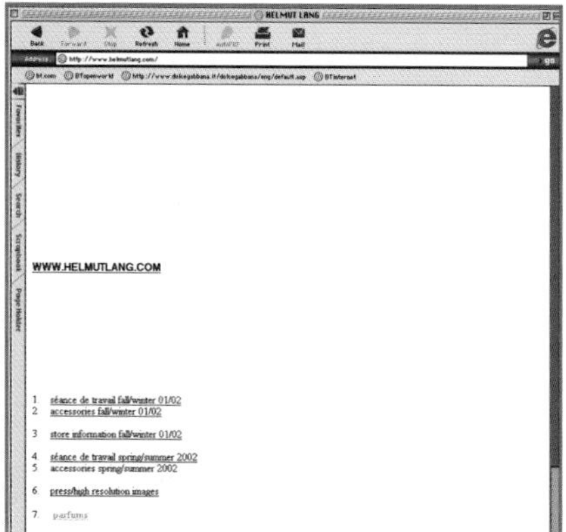

Lang chooses to showcase the images on his site against bright white, just as he does his runway shows. The Home page, seen here in full (left) and in detail (below left), gives no hint of the treasure trove of images available to the user at the click of a mouse (including Jenny Holzer's 'I smell you on my skin' piece for the recently launched parfums line).

Taken as a whole (below right), the straightforward show images, photographed by Anthony Ward, might be broadly related to the photographic experiments of Eadweard Muybridge. Opposite, above: A selection of images from the Spring 2001 show. Opposite, below: The user can click on any image to get to a larger pop-up, such as the one of Danielle Ziniach seen here.

# www.helmutlang.com

rapbook | Page Holder

WWW.HELMUTLANG.COM

1. séance de travail fall/winter 01/02
2. accessories fall/winter 01/02

3. store information fall/winter 01/02

4. séance de travail spring/summer 2002
5. accessories spring/summer 2002

6. press/high resolution images

7. parfums

Helmutlang.com has a lo-fi appeal that complements the designer's clean, utilitarian aesthetic. Unlike Lang's clothes, however, the site is often described as being 'un-designed', though the look is deliberate and created by Corsis. A classicist and non-conformist, Lang has long embraced technology and bucked traditional means of fashion presentation. Forgoing a runway show in 1998, he sent editors instead CD-ROMS and videos of his collection. The Internet became Lang's primary show platform in Spring 2001. Rather than show in Paris after terrorist attacks in New York, Lang posted the collection on his site, effectively staying in New York (his adopted city) and supporting business there, while making his show internationally accessible.

Anthony Ward shot Lang's Fall 2001 accessories collection as stills. These photographs are more stylized than the runway images, which are shot in real time. The functionality of the *séance de travail* and the Accessories pages is the same: users can access larger images as pop-ups from the thumbnail images.

These pages show the Women's Fall 2001 accessories collection. The inset (right) is of a marabou-trimmed leather scarf and shows the simple back/forward navigation.

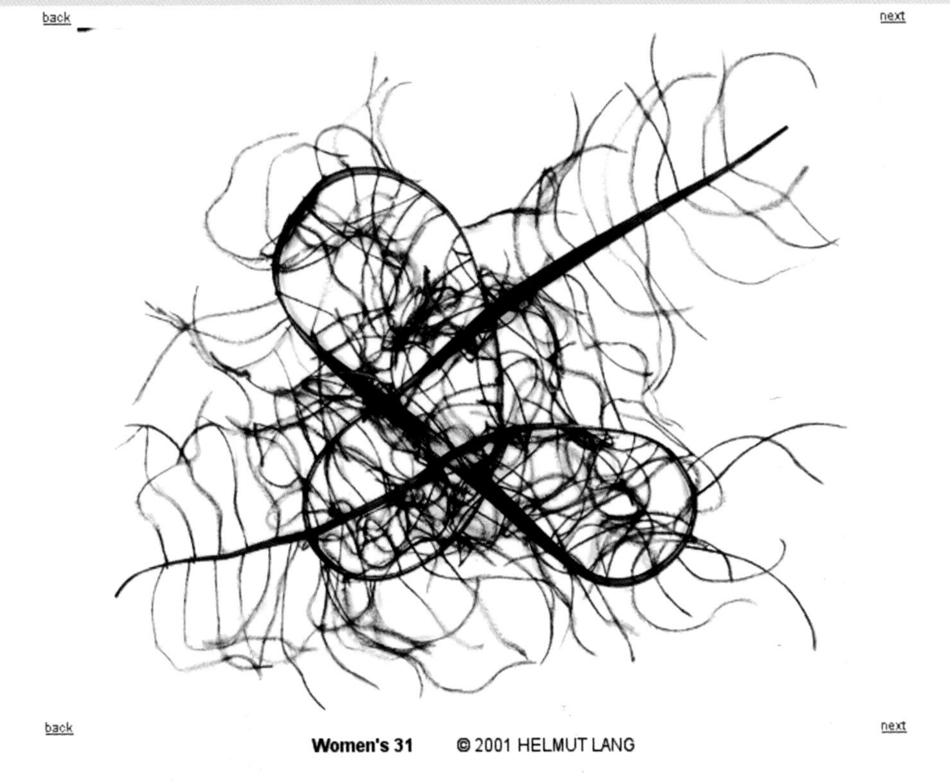

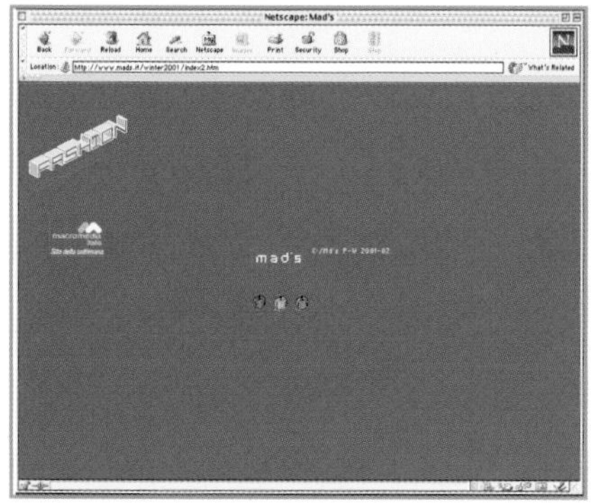

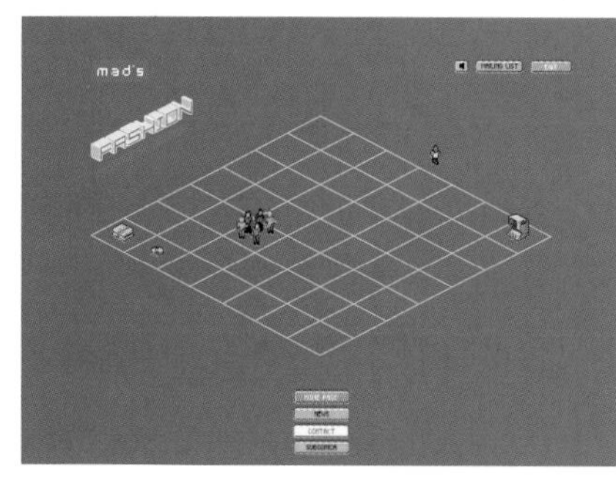

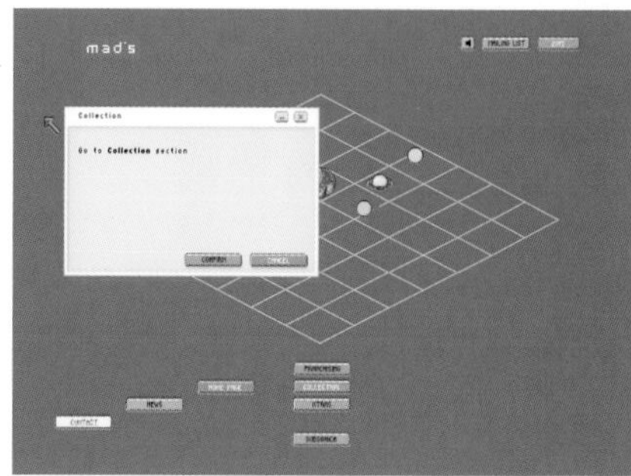

# www.mads.it



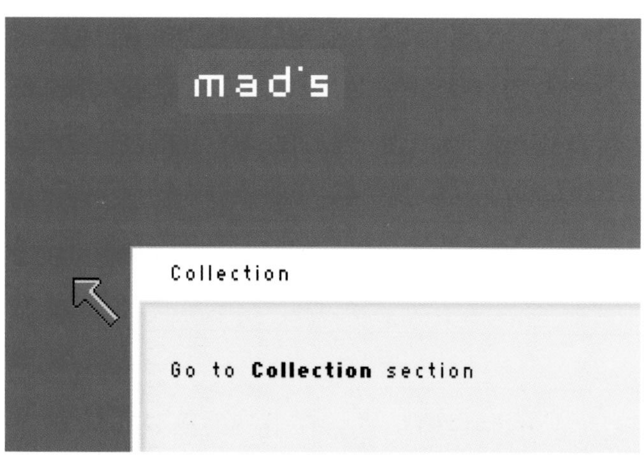


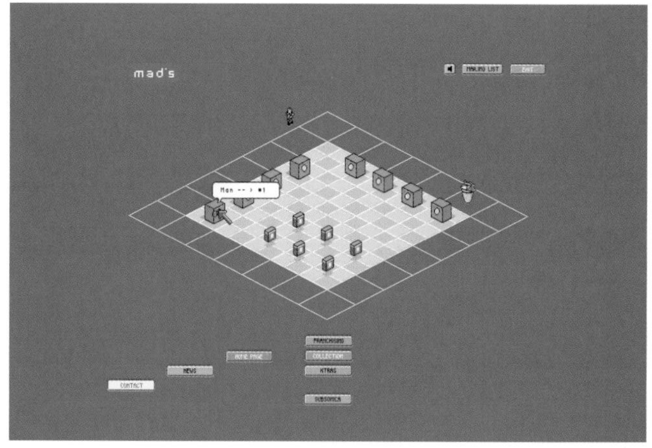

Mad's designs and sells trendy, moderately priced leisurewear through its franchises in Italy. Mads.it is redesigned every six months by the creative team at Happycentro+Sintetik, who have (via Shockwave animation) exploded the idea of the Web being a new form of entertainment by designing mads.it as if it were a game. In the Fall 2001 version of the site, video game aesthetics (think Atari, Pac Man) are transformed into the virtual world, including a beepy arcade-worthy audio track.

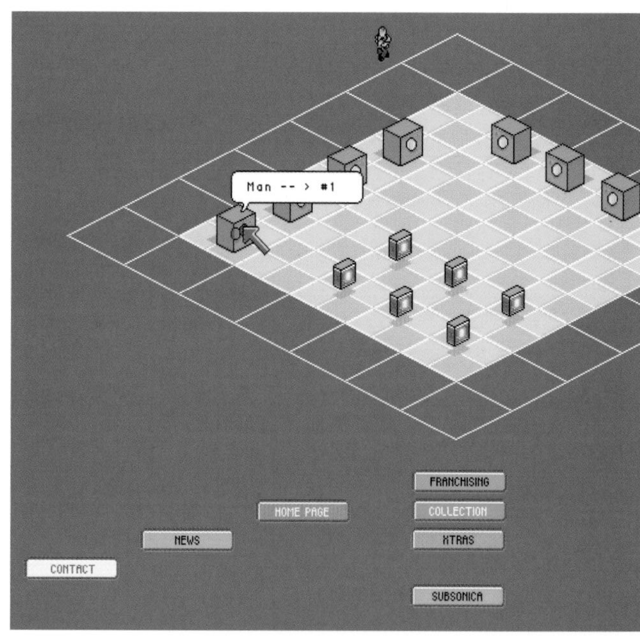

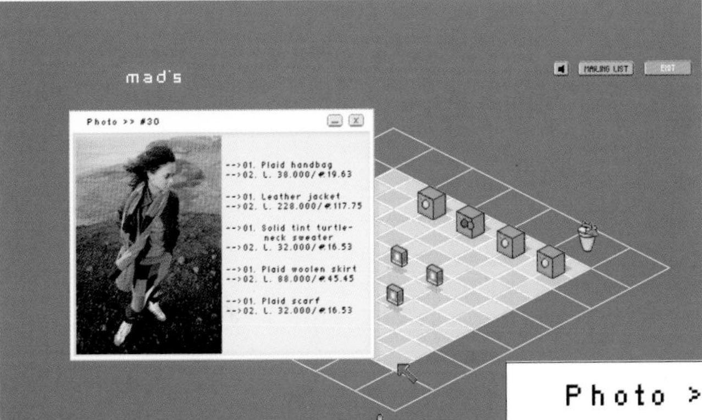


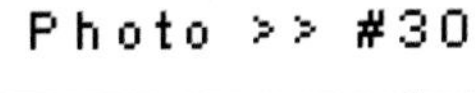

The Home page and the development of the Collections page are seen on the left. The basis of each Top page for Fall 2001 is a square grid, which is filled in and furnished with humorous icons. For example, light and dark floor tiles fill the grid before mini-washing machines and clothes baskets ricochet and bounce into position on the page. When the user clicks on a washing machine, small clickable boxes emerge. They contain photographs of looks from the collection, with product and pricing information, as seen in full and in detail on this page.

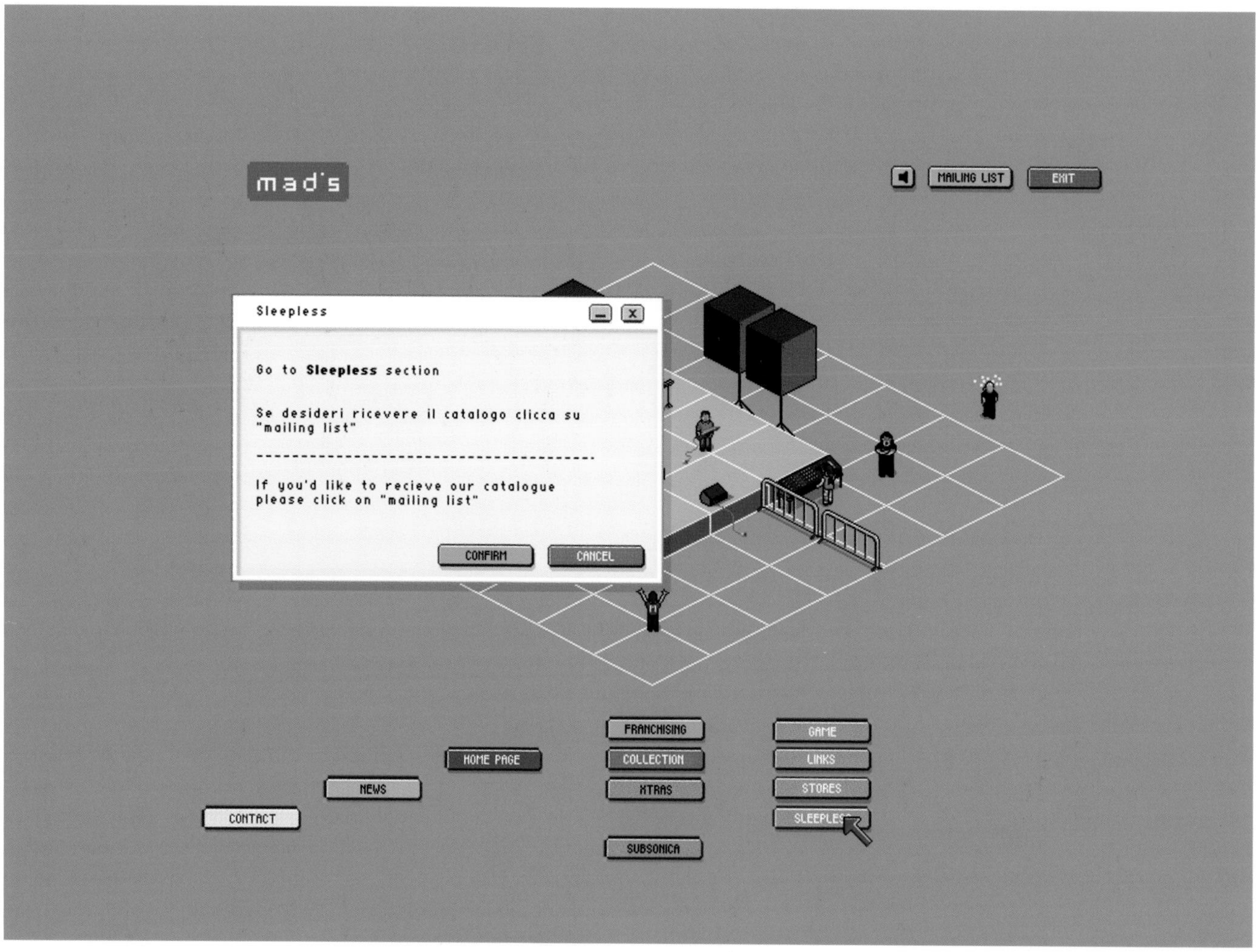

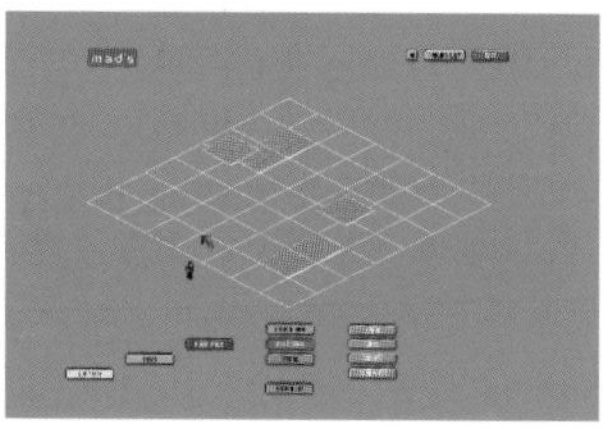

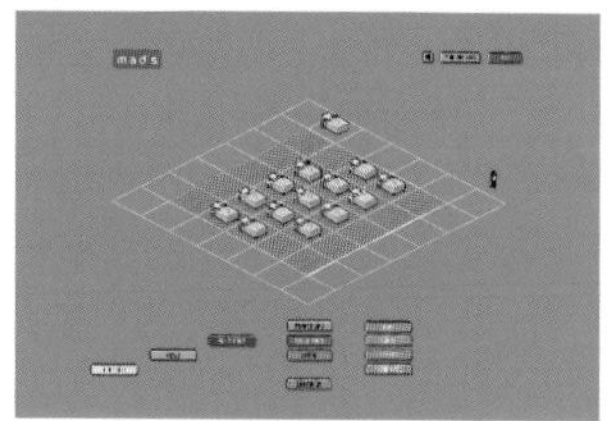

Above: The Sleepless page is seen building from the Subsonica page. (Subsonica is a Turin-based rock group sponsored by Mad's.) The Sleepless theme was inspired by the creative team's discovery of a 70-year-old Icelandic runner named Jon, who runs back and forth tirelessly between two homes. Photos from the Sleepless campaign by Emilio Casi (right) are accessed by clicking on the little cot icons, around which an icon of the 'real' Jon (pictured middle row, right) runs ceaselessly.

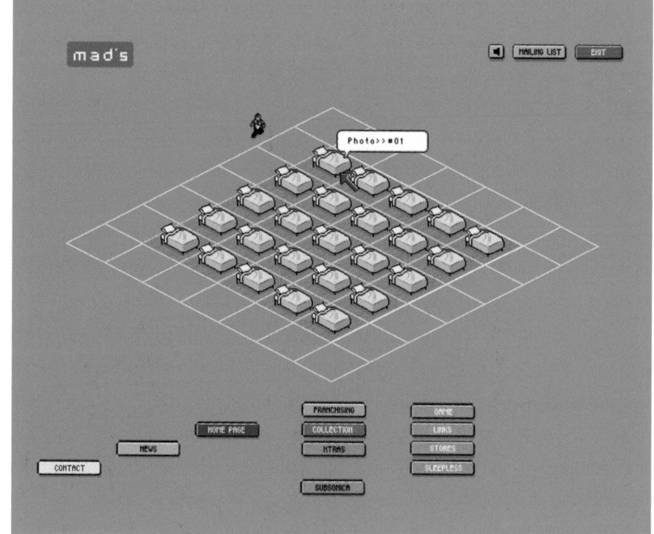

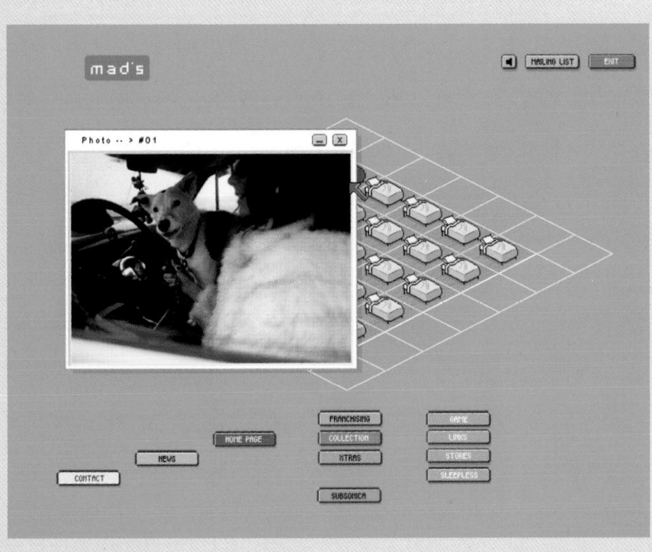
mad's
MAILING LIST
EXIT
Photo -- > #01
FRANCHISING
COLLECTION
XTRAS
SUBSONICA
GAME
LINKS
STORES
SLEEPLESS
HOME PAGE
NEWS
CONTACT

Photo -- > #03
X

Photo -- > #05
X

Photo -- > #06
X

Photo -- > #10
X

Photo -- > #20
X

# www.pleatsplease.com

'The romantic inspiration of nomads [and] wanderers' inspires Issey Miyake's Pleats Please line of easy, washable and eminently packable pleated garments designed for adventurers. An award-winning site, pleatsplease.com uses html and Flash animation to express the joy of motion. At the user's command, colourful dancing figures radiate and frolic against a simple white ground, courtesy of the sophisticated design and programming company Sayuri Studio.

Clockwise from top left: The 'E' in the logo, which is found on the upper left-hand corner of most pages, has the appearance of being pleated.

The navigation on the Home page is visual: users can click on the 'shadow dancers' to see different looks. Flash enables F. Giacobetti's photographs to move and radiate on the page.

Dancers wearing the 'multicolour knit' pattern – which is printed and pleated – from the Autumn/Winter 2001 collection. When translated into moving images in the virtual world, the effect is one of trompe l'oeil trebled: the pattern is a trompe l'oeil print, pleated – and in virtual space.

THE GARMENT IS FIRST CUT THEN SEWN TOGETHER.

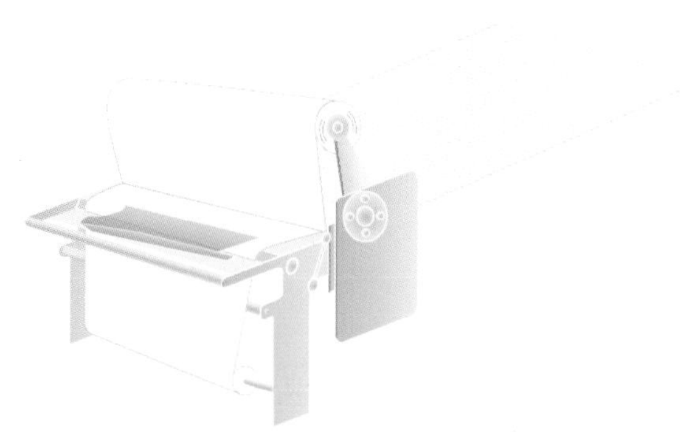

IT'S HAND FED INTO A PLEATING MACHINE.
THE PLEATED GARMENT COMES OUT IN BETWEEN RICE PAPER.

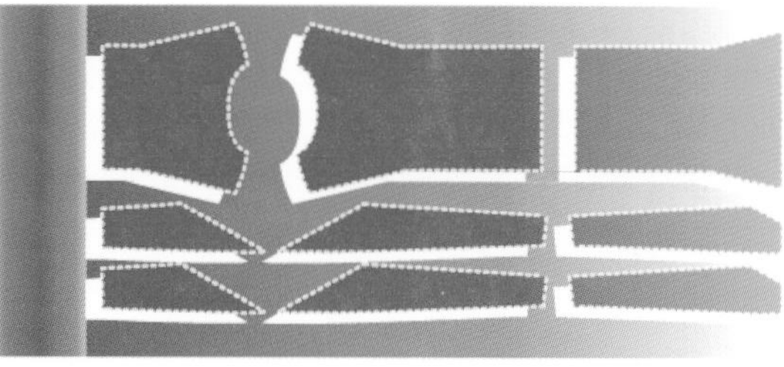

THE GARMENT IS FIRST CUT THEN SEWN TOGETHER.

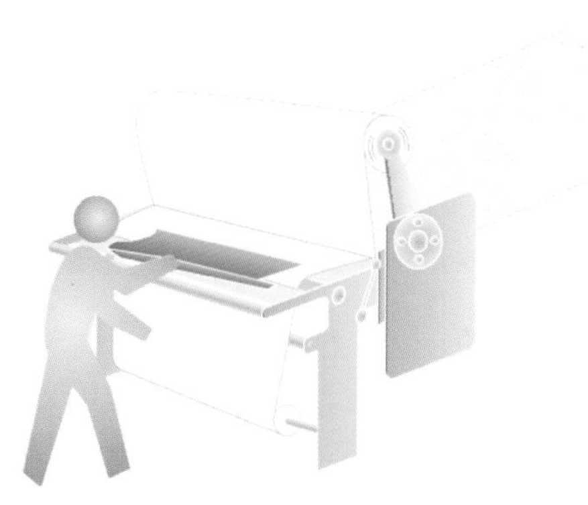

IT'S HAND FED INTO A PLEATING MACHINE.
THE PLEATED GARMENT COMES OUT IN BETWEEN RICE PAPER.

THE GARMENT IS FIRST CUT THEN SEWN TOGETHER.

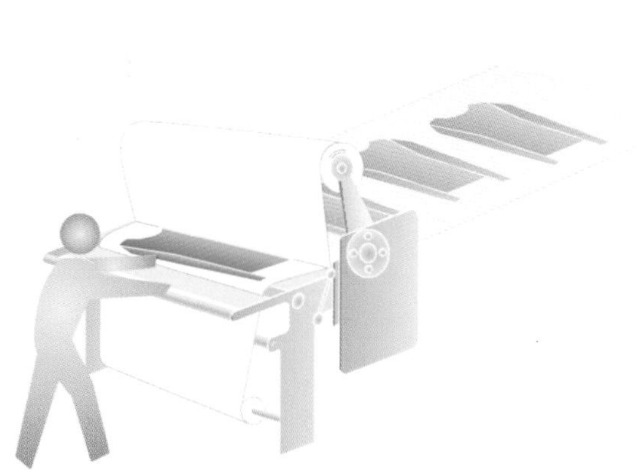

IT'S HAND FED INTO A PLEATING MACHINE.
THE PLEATED GARMENT COMES OUT IN BETWEEN RICE PAPER.

PLEATS
PLEASE

PLEATED GARMENTS COME OUT ONE AFTER ANOTHER.
THEN EACH PLEATED GARMENT IS CUT SEPARATELY.

PLEATS
PLEASE

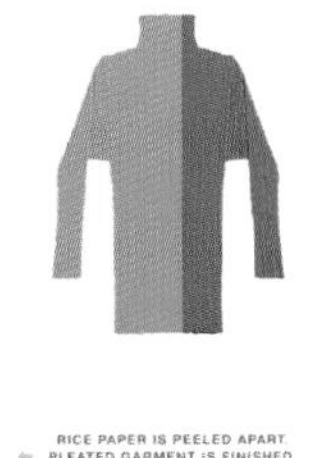

RICE PAPER IS PEELED APART.
PLEATED GARMENT IS FINISHED.

PLEATS
PLEASE

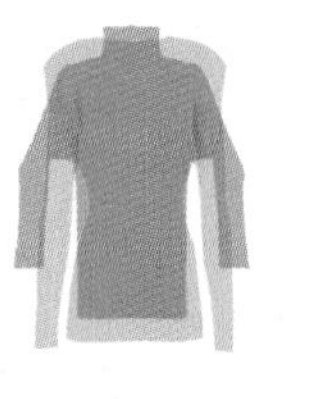

RICE PAPER IS PEELED APART.
PLEATED GARMENT IS FINISHED.

The Web is often hailed as an educational tool and an aid in the important task of brand-building. Miyake takes advantage of its didactic dimension in two sections of the Pleats Please site: via QuickTime video in 004 How to Madame-T?, a subsection of E.T.C., and in How Pleats Please are made, shown on these pages. In this section the user is walked through the making of a top – from the first cut to 'Voila!', the final product – using a series of animated illustrations that explains the magic behind these Fortuny-meets-technology-style garments.

PLEATS
PLEASE

VOILA!

The label's manifesto is put forth as an illustrated story in the E.T.C. section. Both the figures and the type morph with the scrolling movement of the mouse.

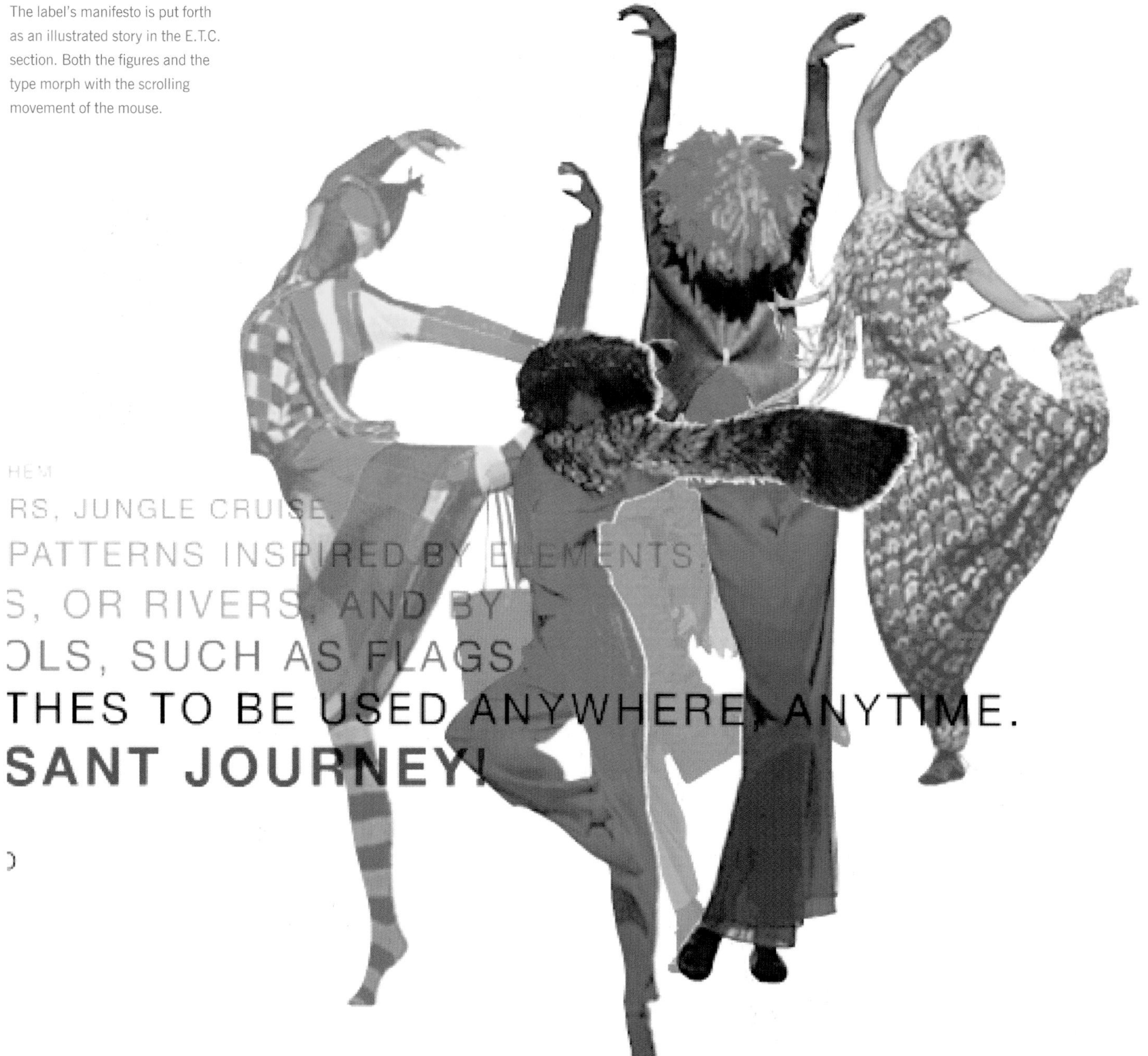

HEM
RS, JUNGLE CRUISE.
PATTERNS INSPIRED BY ELEMENTS
S, OR RIVERS, AND BY
OLS, SUCH AS FLAGS.
THES TO BE USED ANYWHERE, ANYTIME.
**SANT JOURNEY!**

PLEATS
PLEASE

PRODUCTS

E.T.C.
STORES
CATALOG REQUEST
HOME
CLOSE MENU

Flexible...

What's Pleats Please introduces the label's primary attributes in five simple terms: Pleats; Wrinkle Free; Low Maintenance; Colorful & Playful; Flexible. The last is exuberantly illustrated by dancers, who pivot around a centre point, as seen on this page.

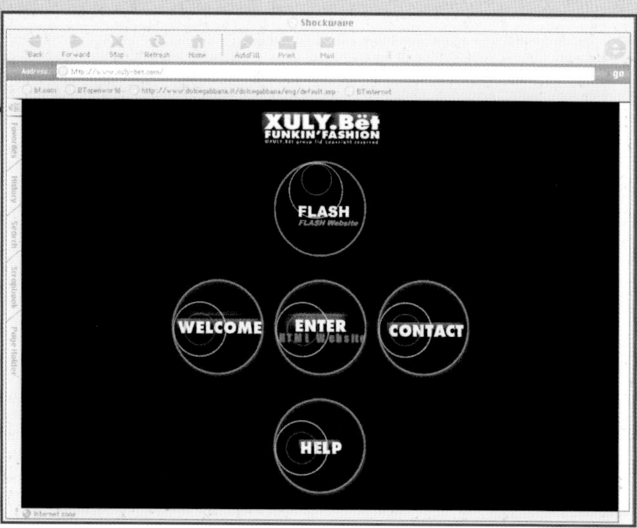


1

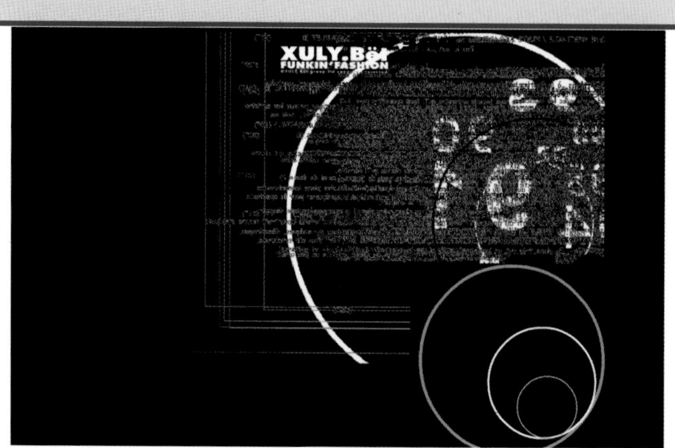


# www.xuly-bet.com

Inspired by street style, Malian Lamine Badian Kouyaté, a.k.a. Xuly-Bët, began his career in fashion 'recuperating' thrift-shop finds through recycling and re-assembly. The Website provides a global vision of his 'Funkin' Fashion' universe, and incorporates stories about music, literature, art and Africa. Designed by Human Technology and programmed by students at the Institute Telecom, it is a pastiche of images, text and wordplay ('des filles, des filles et des défilés').



2

'The Web', says Kouyaté, 'is an interesting tool for the fashion world. Fashion is often a closed universe, and the Web may open it to everybody! That's exactly the spirit which motivates Xuly-Bët – open and accessible fashion.' The development of the Home page, based on a circular motif, is shown on these pages. The site is divided into six sections: Fashion; Presse; Factory; News; Boutik; Afrique.

3

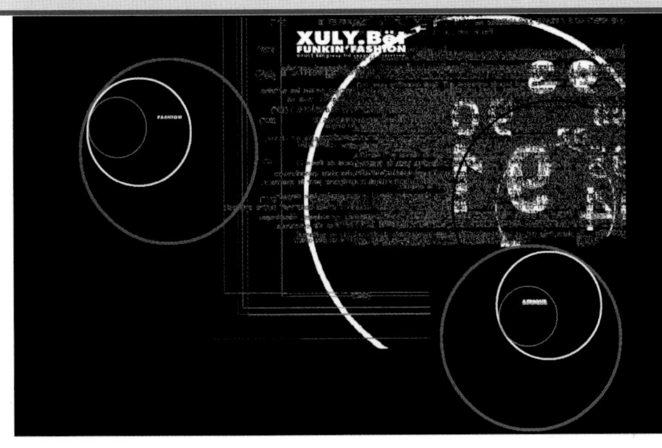
XULY.Bët
FUNKIN' FASHION

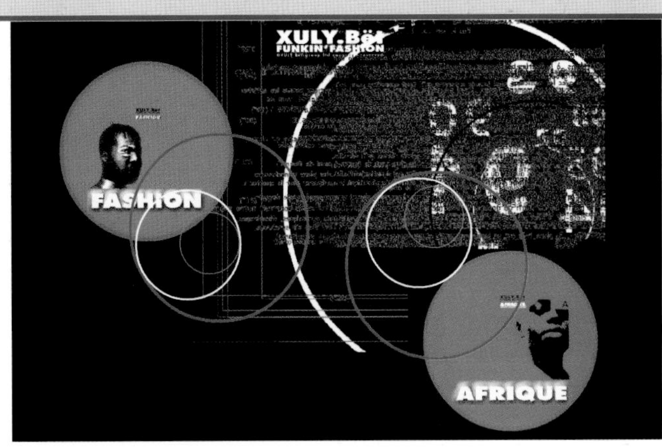
XULY.Bët
FUNKIN' FASHION
FASHION
AFRIQUE

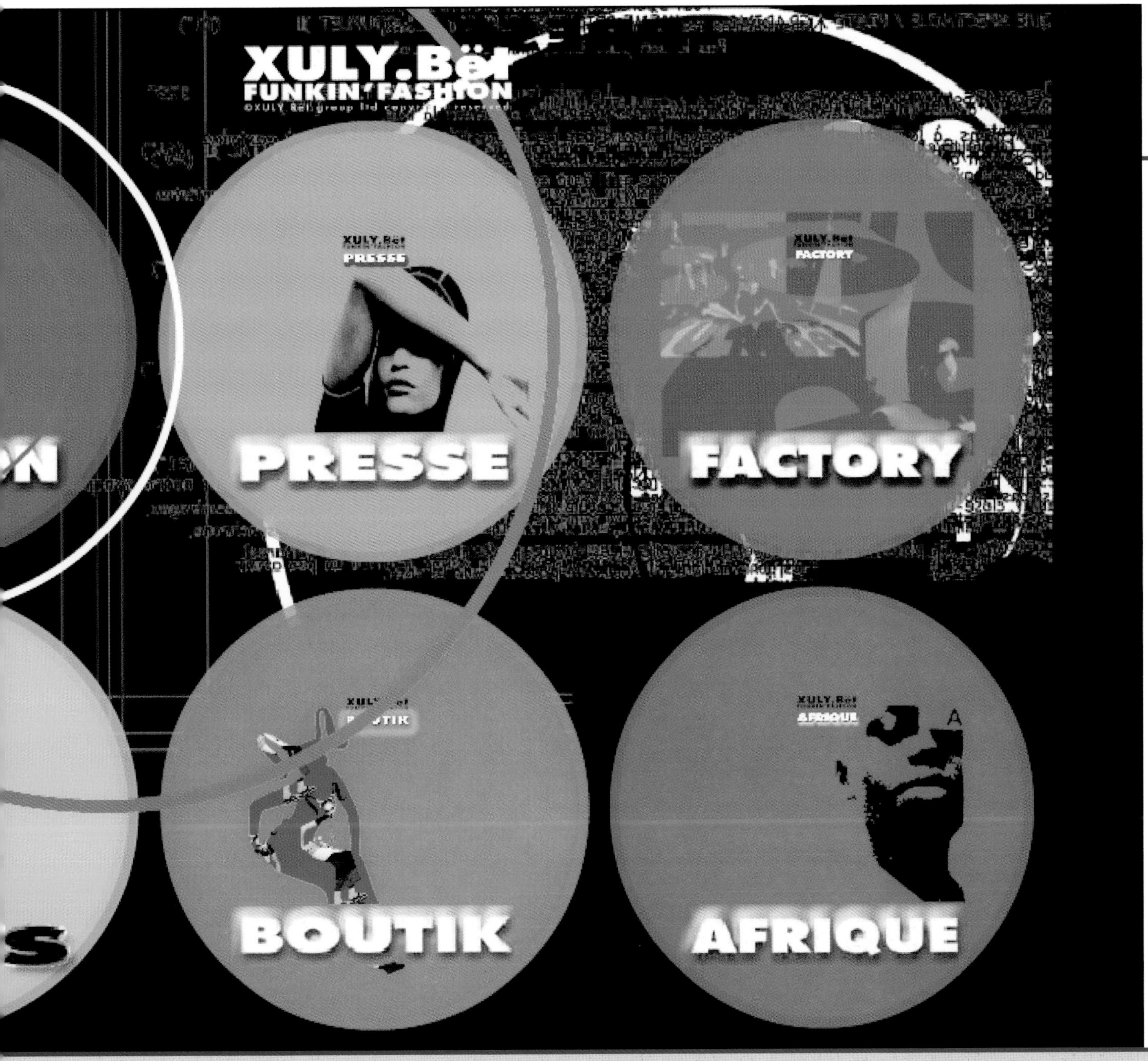

XULY.Bët
FUNKIN' FASHION
PRESSE
FACTORY
BOUTIK
AFRIQUE

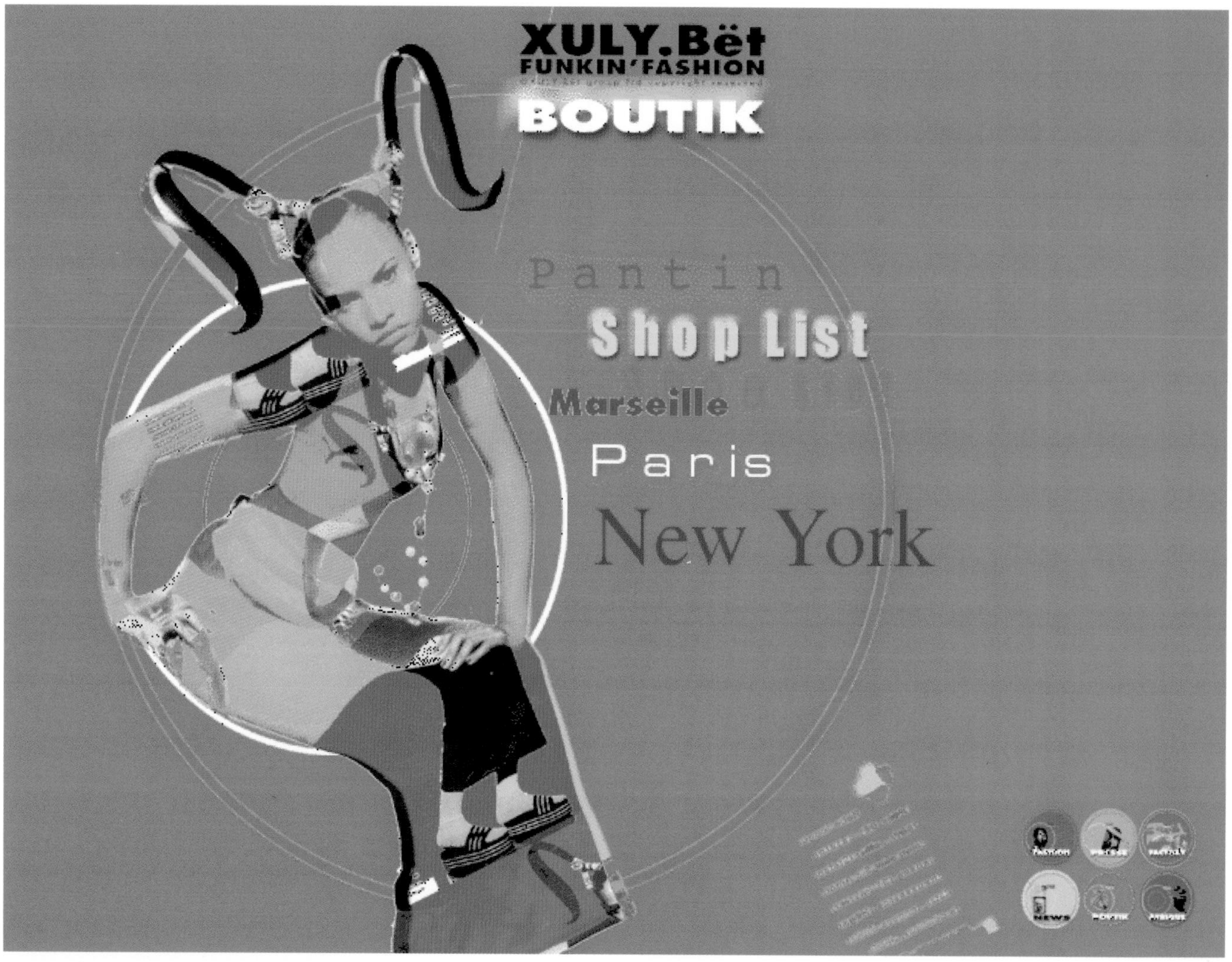

XULY.Bët
FUNKIN'FASHION
BOUTIK
Pantin
Shop List
Marseille
Paris
New York

XULY.Bët
FUNKIN'FASHION
BOUTIK
Pantin
REGARDEZ
CHANGER
Fiche Technique
ESSAYER
TOUCHER

XULY.Bët
FUNKIN'FASHION
BOUTIK
Pantin
BLANC

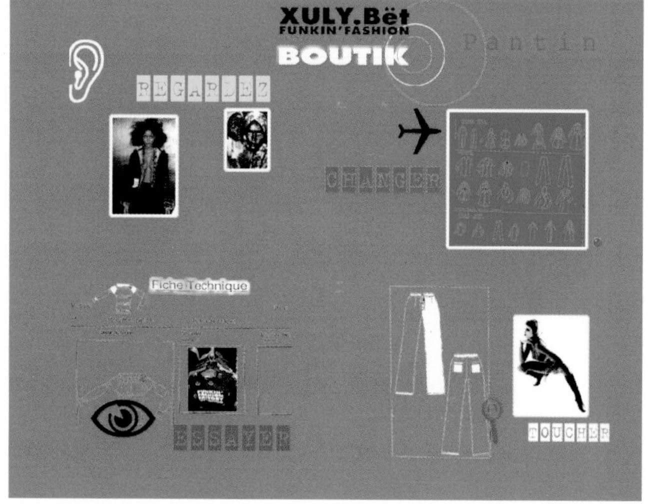

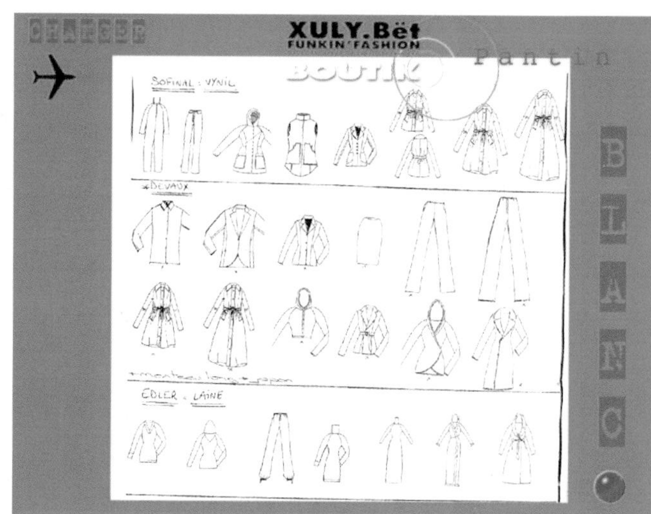

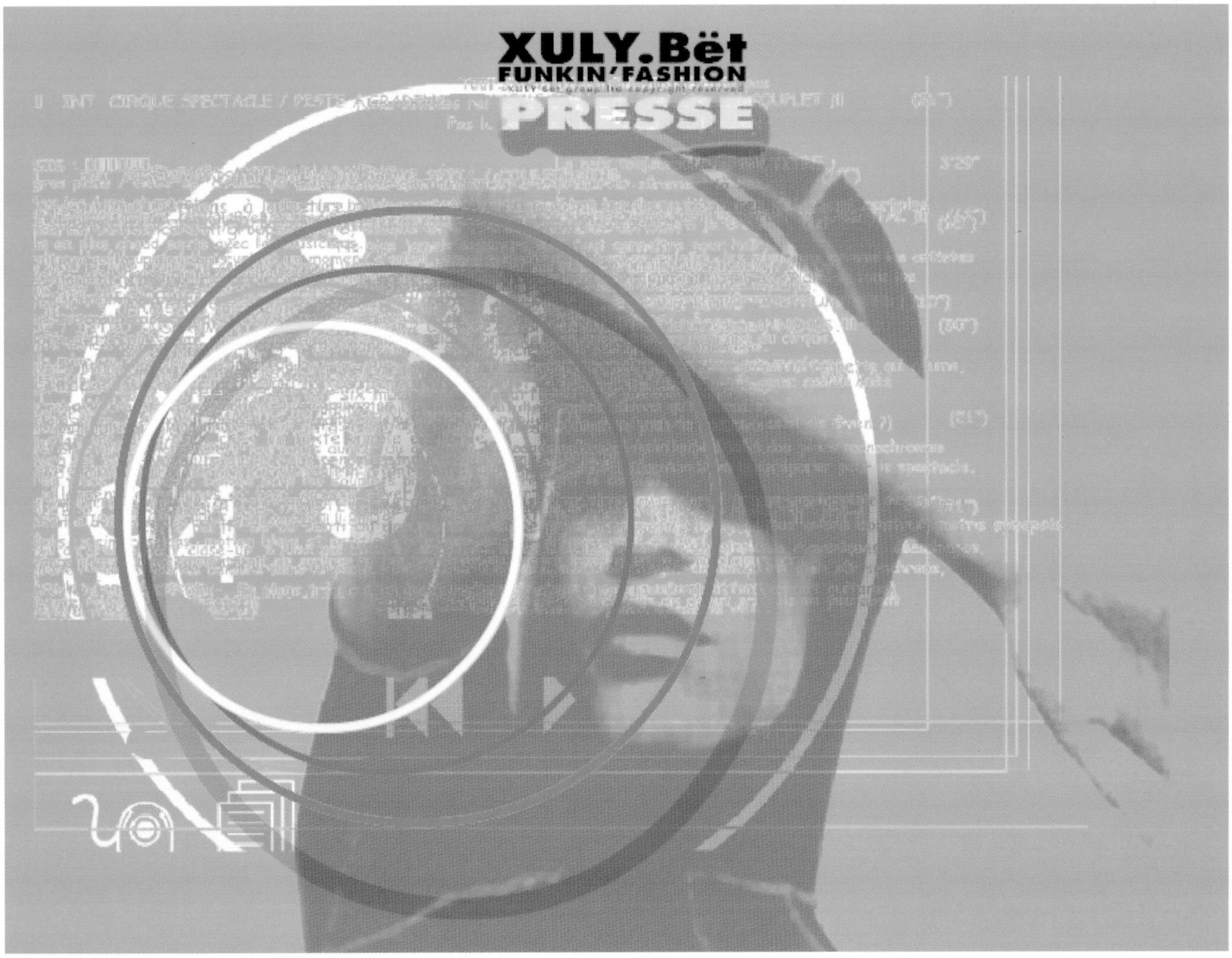

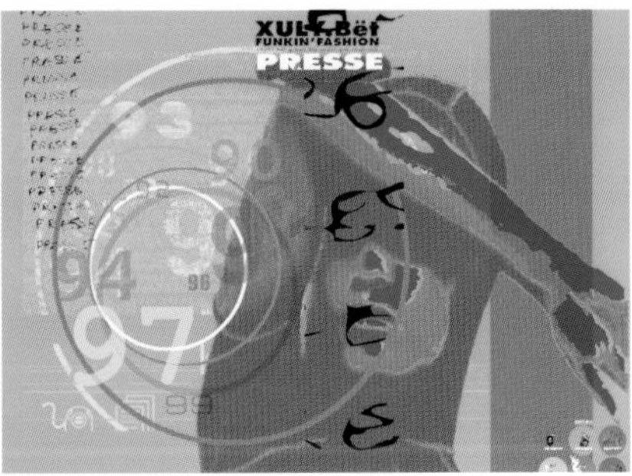

Left: The Boutik Top page and two internal pages. The text on the page at bottom left encourages customers to: Regarder (look), Essayer (try), Changer (change) and Toucher (touch). There is no e-commerce on the site, but store contact information is available.

Above: The Presse Top page undergoes multiple Warholian (Flash) transformations before reaching its final state. Users clicking on the year (94, 97) go to a page of press clippings from that year.

XULY.Bët
FUNKIN'FASHION

XULY.Bët
FUNKIN'FASHION
AFRIQUE
A
Abé tiogo di
AFRICA LIVE
xawaré

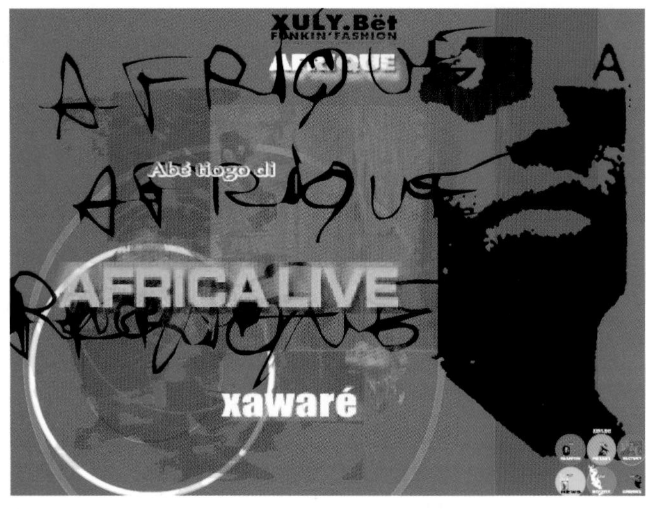
XULY.Bët
FUNKIN'FASHION
AFRIQUE
A
Abé tiogo di
AFRICA LIVE
xawaré

XULY.Bët
FUNKIN'FASHION
AFRIQUE
AFRICA LIVE
ENTENDRE
HEAR
VIVRE
BE
SEE
Pam Dakeyo
LIRE
VOIR
LISTEN
STUDIO MALICK BAGADADJI
ECOUTER

SÉNÉGAL
BE
XULY.Bët
FUNKIN'FASHION
AFRIQUE
AFRICA LIVE
VIVRE
FESTIVAL DE JAZZ DE SAINT LOUIS
"N'DAR" LA SAINT LOUISIENNE AVAIT MUSIQUE EN TÊTE
LA VILLE SE PRÉPARAIT À LA FÊTE...
SÉNÉGAL
MACEO PARKER
LIZ MC COMB
ELVIN JONES
DIDIER LOCKWOOD
FEMI KUTI
YANDÉ CODOU SENE
LE RYTHME DU SABAR CARRESSAIT DÉSORMAIS LES SONS D'HIVER
LA SAISON GLISSAIT DOUCEMENT VERS LES DOUCEURS DE L'ÉTÉ...
FESTIVAL DE SAINT LOUIS LE 14/15 ET 16 MAI 99

In the Wolof dialect, Xuly-Bët means: 'he who keeps his eyes open, when he looks he tries to see through appearances'. In the Africa Live section, Kouyaté tries to open the eyes of others to the colours, sounds and words of his country with these visual celebrations. Africa Live can have many meanings, including the use of 'live' to mean 'on line'. As he plays with words, so Kouyaté plays with the Web to create new understandings and experiences. Users can click on various elements of the Africa Live pages to access pop-up slideshows, as they can throughout this multilayered site.

XULY.Bët
FUNKIN'FASHION
AFRIQUE

xawaré

XULY.Bët
FUNKIN'FASHION
100%PURE
AFRO
FEAST OF FRIENDS
FESTIVAL
DAKAR 94

COLOR OF AFRICA

L'OUTIL EST MODESTE, MAIS LA TECHNIQUE SAVANTE. LA COULEUR ÉTANT SCIENCE, LA FEMME AFRICAINE PLEINE D'UMILITÉ EST UNE DE CES SCIENTIFIQUES QUI DONNE CES RÉPONSES DANS L'ÉCLAT DES PAGNES QU'ELLE PORTE A SES HANCHES. DANS LA TEINTURE IL Y A LA COULEUR MAIS IL Y A AUSSI LA FORME, OU AUTREMENT DIT LA COMBINAISON PARFAITE COULEUR-FORME. POUR RÉALISER CETTE DIVINE COMMUNION, IL Y A L'EAU, LE SOLEIL ET LA BASSINE. AJOUTONS QUELQUESTOUCHES DE POUDRE COLORÉE ET LE TOUR EST JOUÉ. A CECI PRÈS QU'IL FAUT MAÎTRISER L'ART, LA CHIMIE ET LE MÉLANGE DE CES TERRES AFRICAINES.

COLOR OF AFRICA COLOR OF AFRICA

# fashion sale

www.apc.fr

www.colette.fr

www.eluxury.com

www.ilovecolette.com

www.kirnazabete.com

www.net-a-porter.com

www.something.org.uk

www.sowear.com

www.style.com

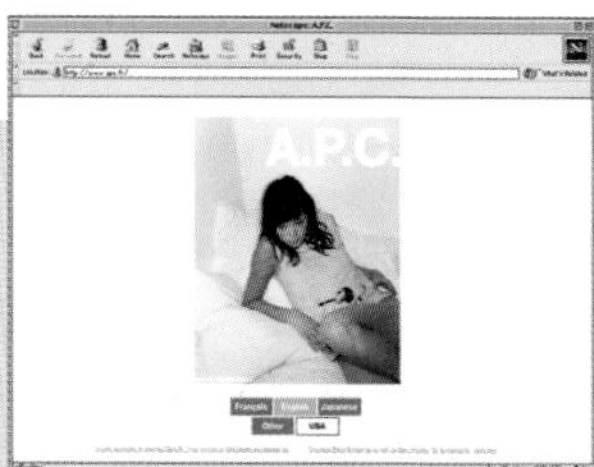


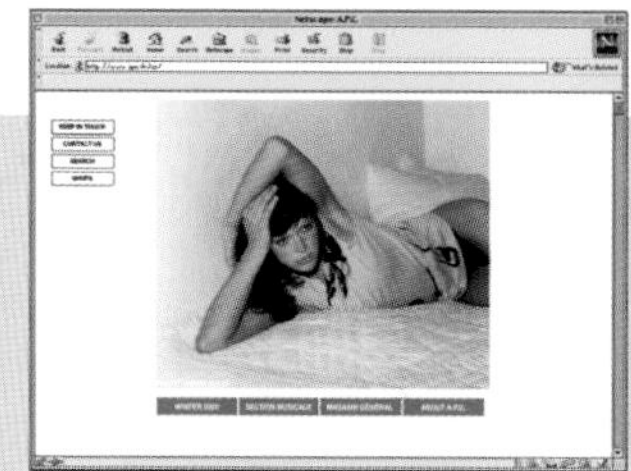

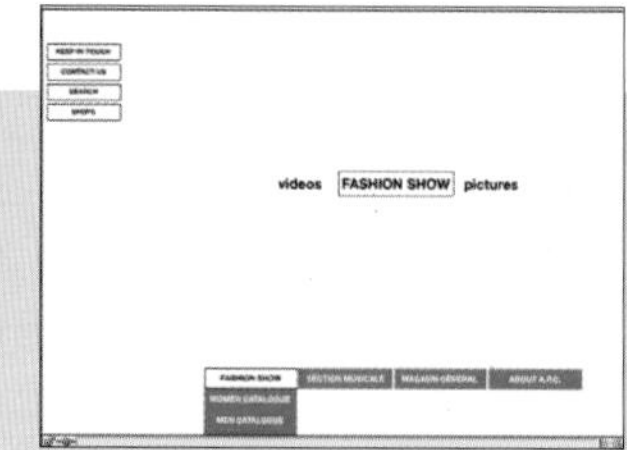


# www.apc.fr

The Home page, featuring a photograph of model Griet Toch by Pierre Bailly. The navigation is divided into four main sections, with subsections such as 'Men's Catalogue'. The advantage of the site, says A.P.C., is that 'you can see our shows and buy the clothes you see'.

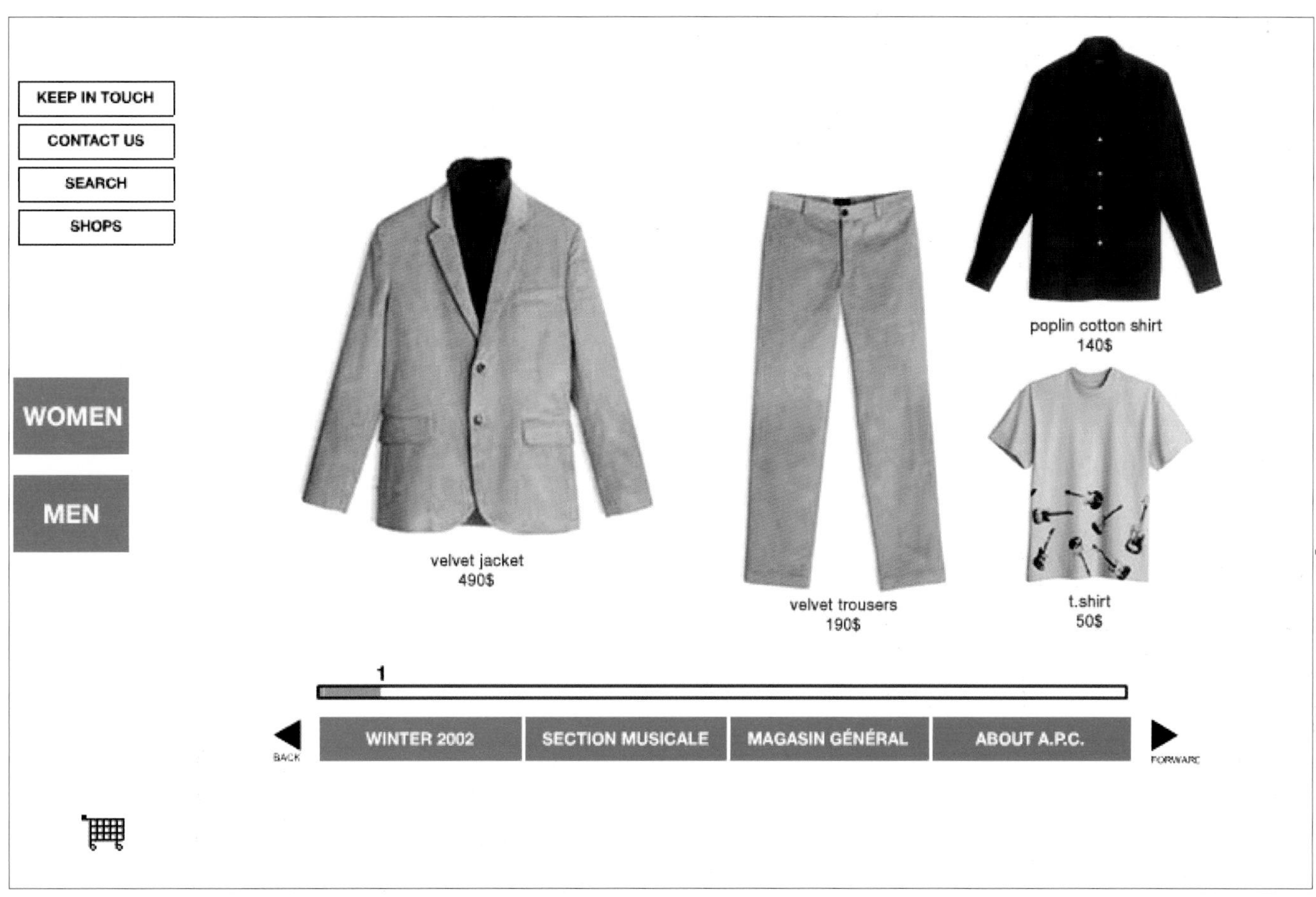


'Our site is another shop', say the team at A.P.C. 'The windows change, there's a sale period, one can listen to music, just like in any A.P.C. store. But this one is open seven days a week, 24 hours a day.' Known for their chic urban staples, A.P.C. (Atelier de production et de création) embraced simple chic long before it was co-opted by fashion and lifestyle magazines. The site was designed by Rik Bas Backer, whose aim was 'to reproduce the same whiteness and non-design' as in the printed catalogue.

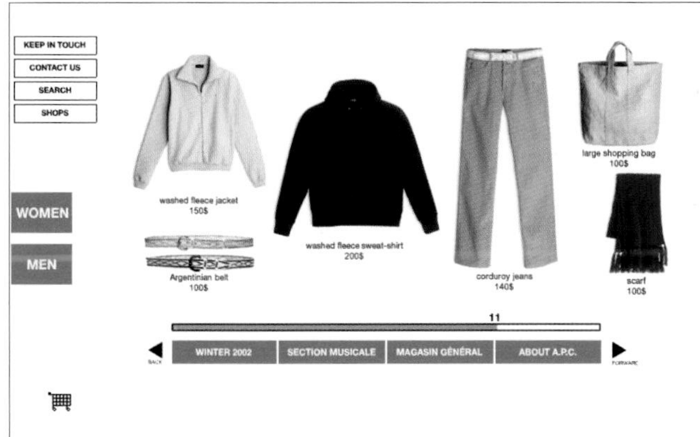

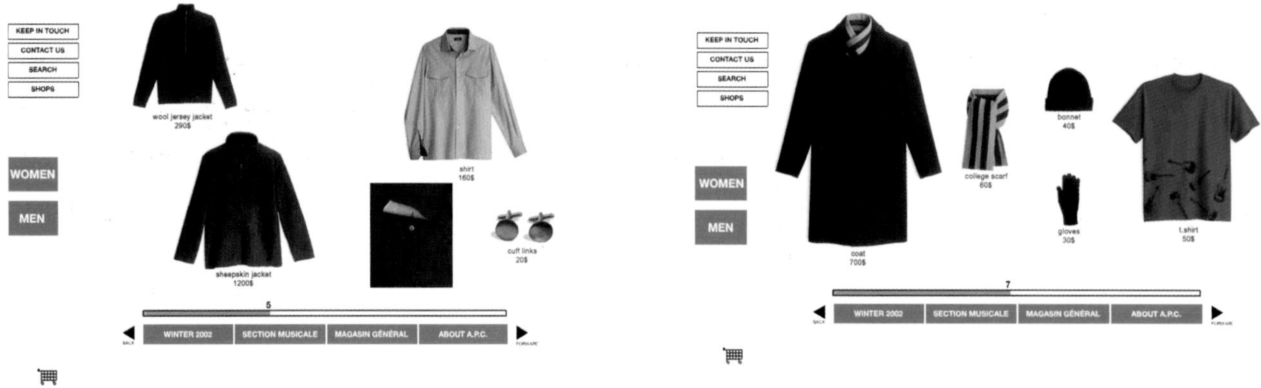
KEEP IN TOUCH
CONTACT US
SEARCH
SHOPS
WOMEN
MEN
wool jersey jacket
290$
shirt
160$
sheepskin jacket
1200$
cuff links
20$
5
WINTER 2002
SECTION MUSICALE
MAGASIN GÉNÉRAL
ABOUT A.P.C.
KEEP IN TOUCH
CONTACT US
SEARCH
SHOPS
WOMEN
MEN
bonnet
40$
college scarf
60$
gloves
30$
t.shirt
50$
coat
700$
7
WINTER 2002
SECTION MUSICALE
MAGASIN GÉNÉRAL
ABOUT A.P.C.



www.apc.fr

KEEP IN TOUCH
CONTACT US
SEARCH
SHOPS
WOMEN
MEN
poplin cotton shirt
150$
handbag
120$
raincoat
360$
13
BACK
WINTER 2002
SECTION MUSICALE
MAGASIN GÉNÉRAL
ABOUT A.P.C.
FORWARD

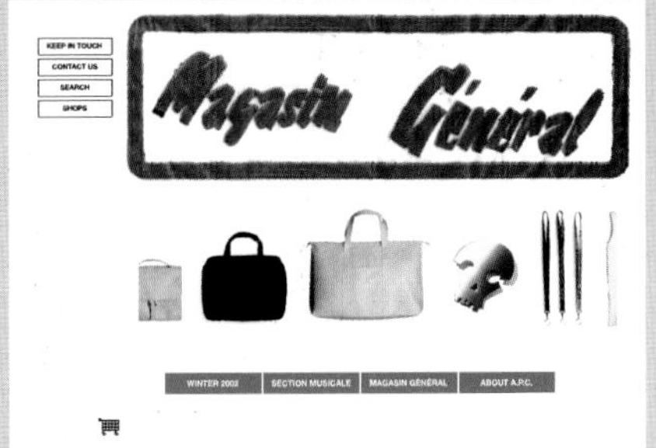


Left: Selections from the Winter 2002 men's catalogue. The cut-out images are arranged in 'vignettes' on a white ground. The navigation allows forward and backward movement. Pop-ups provide additional product information, as well as the opportunity to buy.

Backer designed the site to be simple and bold. His goal was to reach as many people as possible and not to make them feel left out. New technologies have been introduced only as it has become clear that most people have access to them. The Magasin Général (general store), seen above and below, operates like an assembly line. Users can stop the continuous (and tempting) horizontal flow of basics, such as T-shirts and jeans, with the click of a mouse. Below: Music, an integral part of the A.P.C. culture, is also an important part of the user's virtual experience of the store and the brand.

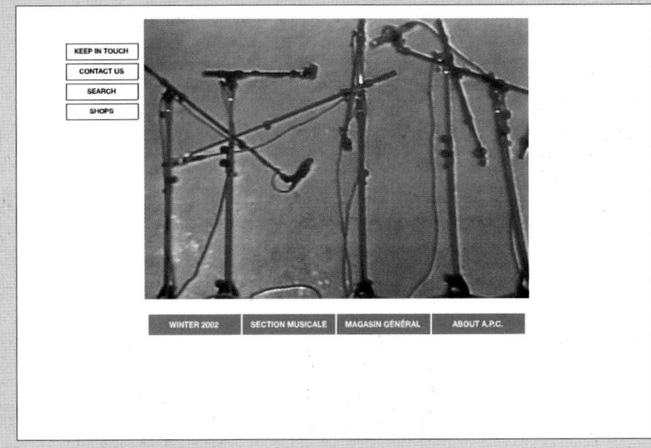


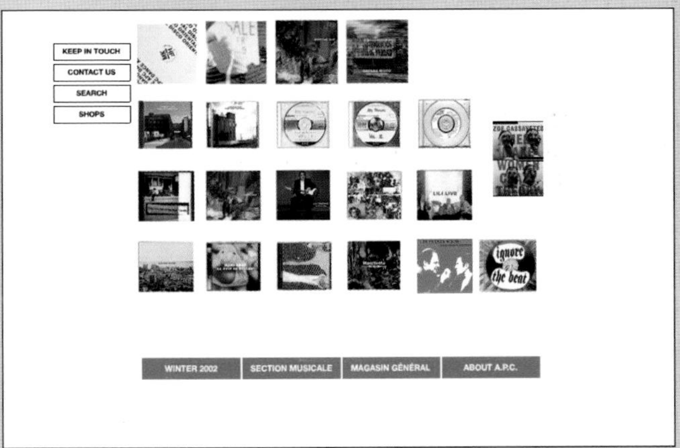

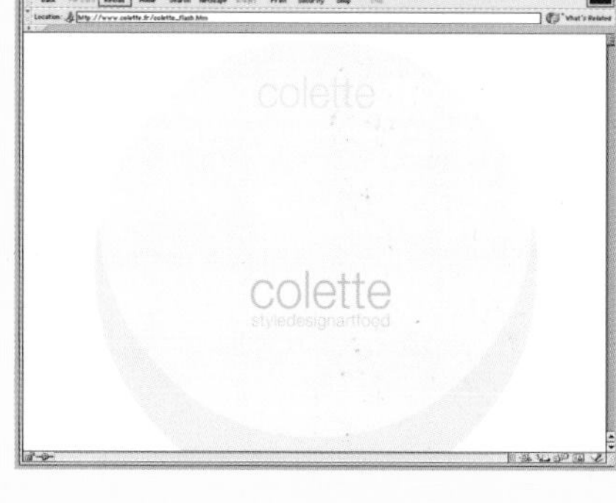

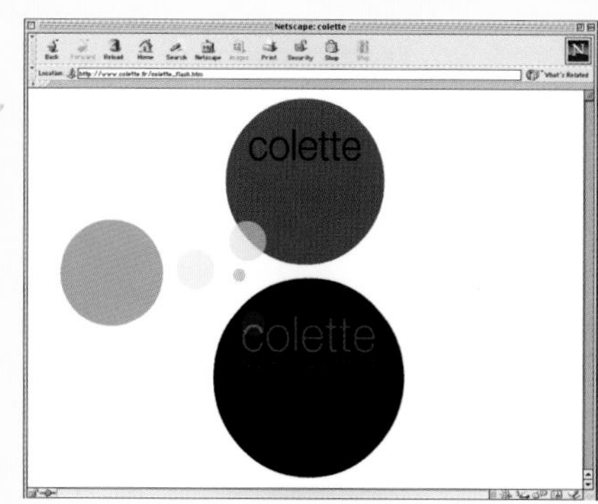

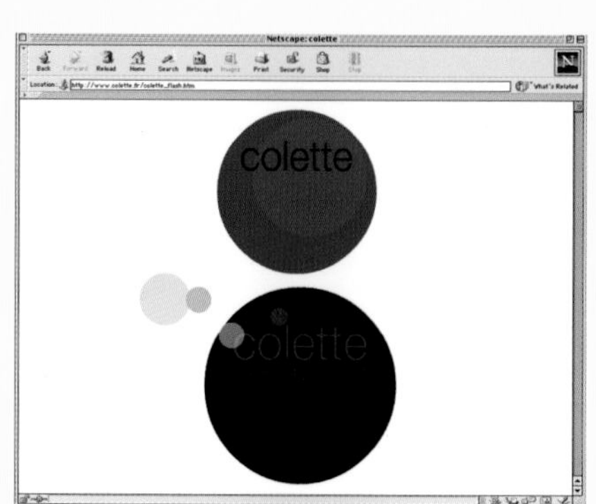


# www.colette.fr

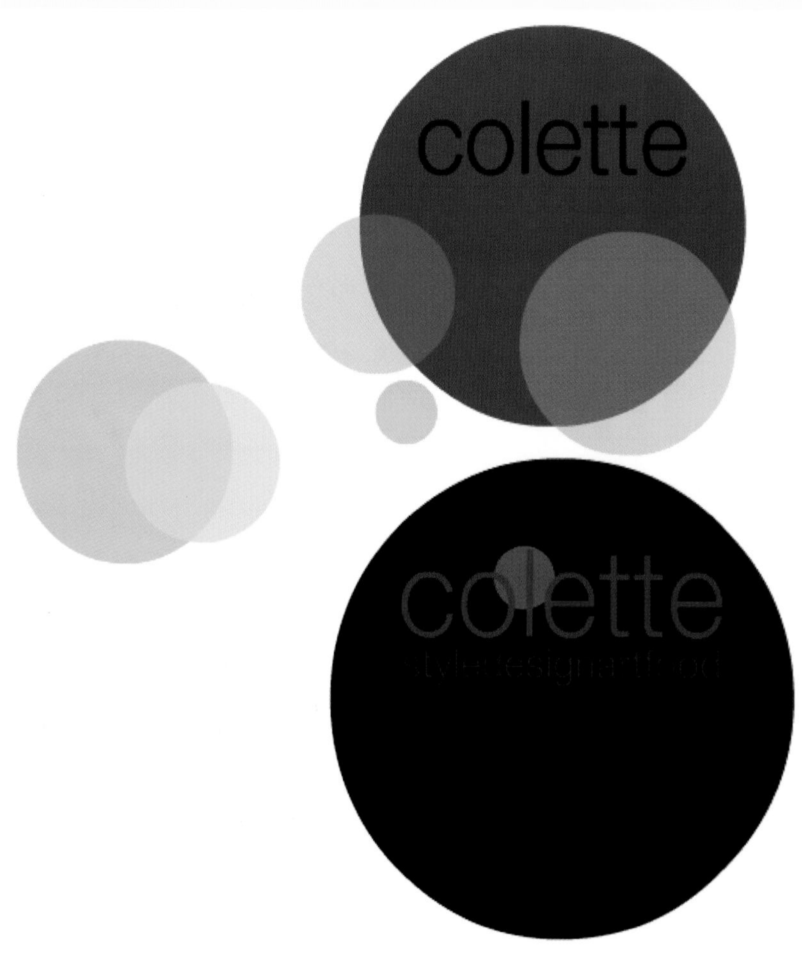

Colette is the supermodel of boutiques. An arbiter of taste in Paris, its focus is on style, design, art and food. Here shoppers can find 'all that our curiosity requires in one place'. The mission of the site, says Colette's Sarah, 'is to inform, to entertain and to sell'. These goals are met via Spill's seductive, witty and chic designs for the site, which, in keeping with the philosophy, 'favour simplicity over gadgetry'. The e-shop does not try to be like the 'real' shop, but instead a small selection of favourite items is available – essential accoutrements for the 'eclectic international lifestyle' to which Colette caters.

Above and left: Colourful circles (a play on the static double-circle logo) float through the Home page with the effervescence of champagne bubbles.

Right: The New Product page is regularly updated with news and product information.

For Fall 2001 Spill combined elements from the Fall catalogue designed by Work in Progress with a straightforward layout, great typography and Flash enhancements. Illustrations of Fall looks by designers carried by Colette are on rotation within frames along the left side of the page.

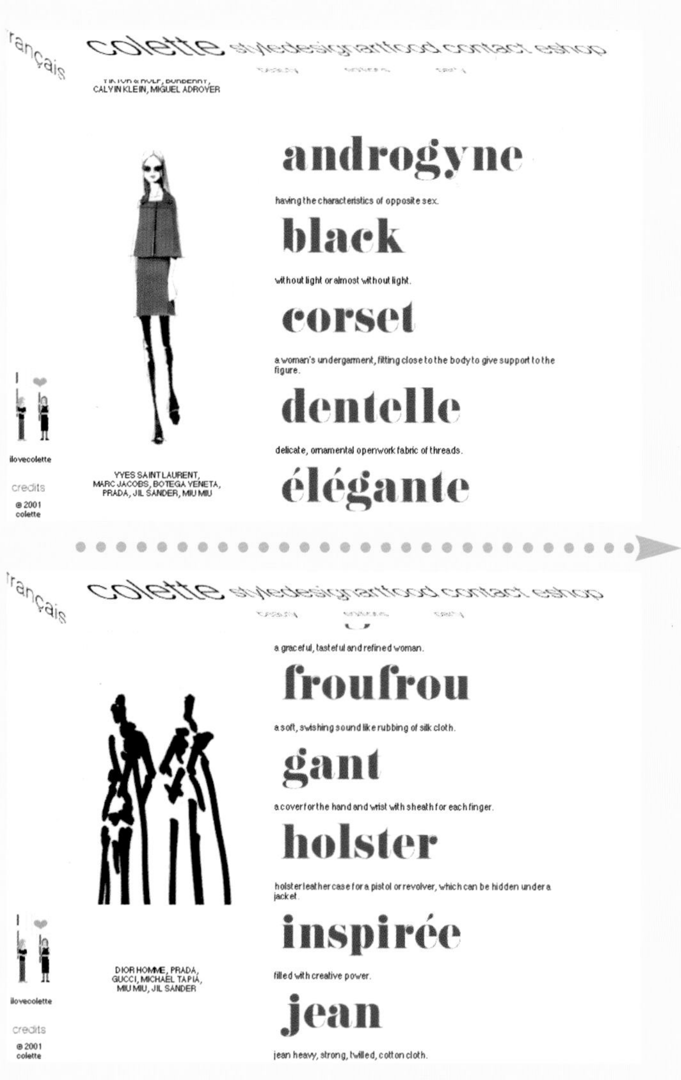

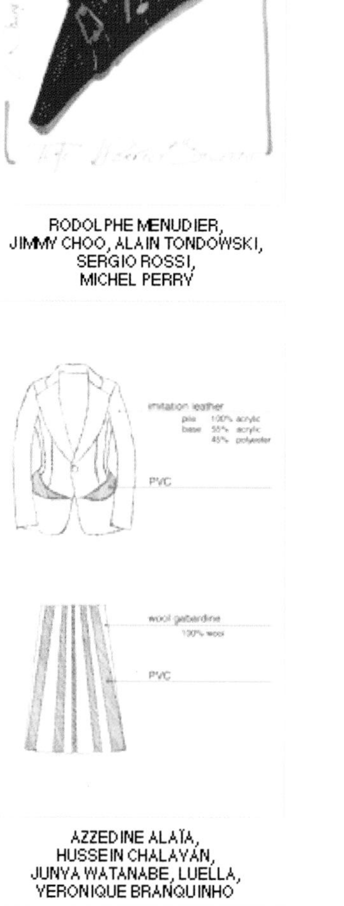

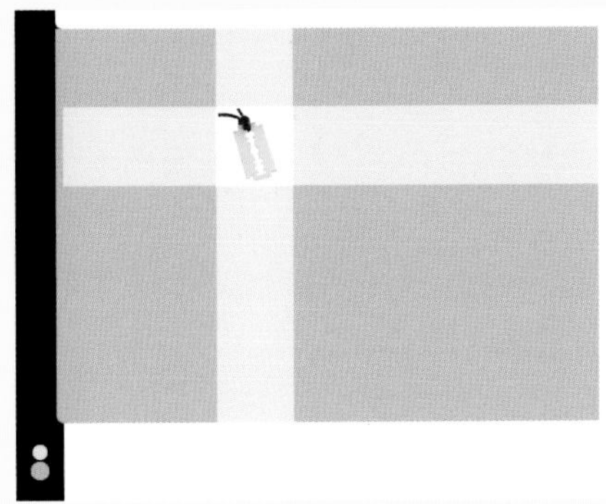

Opposite, clockwise from bottom left: Dior Homme; Prada; Viktor & Rolf; Miguel Adrover; Rodolphe Menudier (detail); Junya Wantanabe.

Above and right: The e-shop carries a select group of items from the different categories of merchandise sold at the store. Favouring 'spaces that breathe', Spill designed a blank grey page, which, when rolled over, reveals hidden treasures embedded in a simple grid. The product window is large and easy to read. The Dinh Van necklace shown here is a Colette exclusive, produced for the store in a numbered edition of 75.

Below: The dhtml navigation is enhanced visually and with audio. In addition to the mouse trailer, a different sound is associated with each section.

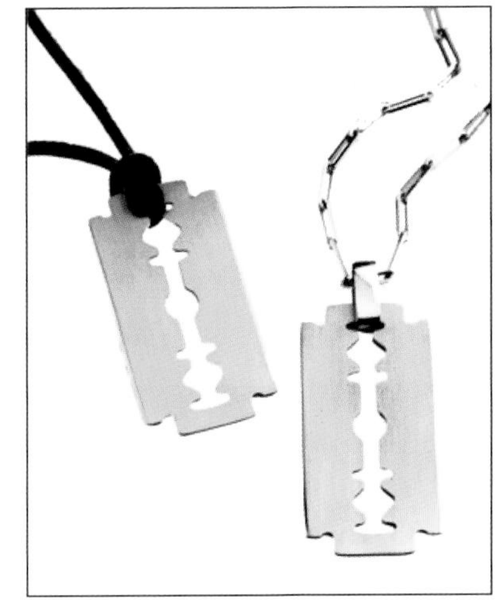


loading

loading

Left: Next model Amanda Moore on the site's 2001 Holiday Home page. Under the creative direction of Alex Gonzalez of AR Media, eLUXURY uses top models and even has a 'model of the month' feature. Opposite, above: John Galliano is profiled within the exclusive section which sells his clothes. Opposite, below: The John Galliano storefront is covered in neon signs, which flash on and off in different colours in rotation.

# www.eluxury.com

Right and below: The Shop by Category/Denim and the Gift Finder Top pages. The user can search for gifts by recipient, occasion, price range, department and brand. Fashion (for men and women) can be sorted by category and brand. Users can also choose to shop in the on-site brand shops.

eLUXURY
WOMEN_ MEN_ HOME_ GOURMET_ BEAUTY_ BRAND SHOPS_
MAGAZINE_ TRAVEL_ SIGN IN MY LUXURY GIFT FINDER HELP SHOPPING BAG SEARCH GO

SHOP BY CATEGORY_
READY TO WEAR COLLECTIONS
SWEATERS
KNIT TOPS
DENIM & CORDUROY
DENIM & CORDUROY
LINGERIE & HOSIERY
HANDBAGS
SMALL LEATHER GOODS
SHOES
JEWELRY
WATCHES
ACCESSORIES

DENIM & CORDUROY_
Hot denim in the new, slimmer silhouette. Sexy, wear-everywhere stretch jeans. A girl's gotta have perfect pants.

FEATURED_
Stretch Corduroy Original Low Rise $124.00
44 Extra Low Rise Stretch Denim Jean $107.00

Pages 1 | 2 | 3

Marc by Marc Jacobs
SF Blackwash Jean with Pocket Detail
$148.00

Marc by Marc Jacobs
SF Wash Cuffed Jeans with Patches
$148.00

Marc by Marc Jacobs
San Francisco Wash Denim Skirt
$128.00

DKNY
Jean with Angled Pocket and Cuff
$107.00

Pages 1 | 2 | 3

eLUXURY
WOMEN_ MEN_ HOME_ GOURMET_ BEAUTY_ BRAND SHOPS_
MAGAZINE_ TRAVEL_ SIGN IN MY LUXURY GIFT FINDER HELP SHOPPING BAG SEARCH GO

GIFT FINDER_
ENTER A KEYWORD GO
Choose a Recipient
Choose by Occasion
Choose by Price Range
Choose by Department
Choose by Brand
RESET SEARCH

CORPORATE GIFTS
MY ACCOUNT

ELUXURY GIFT CERTIFICATE

THE PERFECT GIFT_
For every occasion, eLUXURY is the first name in gifts. Brands you can trust, shipping you can rely on, and a simply elegant presentation. When you think gift, think eLUXURY.

CUSTOMER SERVICE 1.877.890.7171

Items 1 - 10 of 39 Pages 1 | 2 | 3 | 4

eLUXURY FAVORITES

Baccarat
Lucky Butterfly
$125.00

Dior
Chris 47 Watch
$550.00

Michael Kors
Michael Fragrance Gift Set
$168.00

Bvlgari
5 Strand Necklace
$200.00

Fall Exclusives
Cashmere Sidewall/Lined Napa Glove
$125.00

Fall Exclusives
Plaid Cashmere Scarf
$175.00

Santa Maria Novella
Florentine Gift Set
$115.00

Jaqua Girl
Tub Queen
$37.50

Diptyque
Candle Gift Set
$120.00

Dior
Higher 1.7 oz. EDT
$39.50

Items 1 - 10 of 39 Pages 1 | 2 | 3 | 4

Sites such as www.emiliopucci.com and www.johngalliano.com, which are owned by LVMH, have links that enable the user to buy from eLUXURY.

eLUXURY describes itself as 'the ultimate destination for what's hip, hot and hard to find'; and one of its major shareholders is the world's leading luxury products group LVMH (Louis Vuitton Moët Hennessy), which owns many of the world's most prestigious labels. eLUXURY's unique relationship to the brands it carries gives it a sort of 'insider' status, in addition to ensuring many on-line exclusives in the categories of fashion, beauty, gourmet and lifestyle. 'The reason for being a designer', says LVMH's chairman and CEO Bernard Arnault '... is to sell. Fashion is not pure art. It is creativity with the goal of having as many customers as possible wearing the product.'

eLUXURY

WOMEN_ MEN_ HOME_ GOURMET_ BEAUTY_ BRAND SHOPS_

MAGAZINE_ SIGN IN MY LUXURY GIFT FINDER HELP SHOPPING BAG SEARCH GO

Evening chic
John Galliano about
Accessories
SPORTSWEAR
DAYWEAR DAYWEAR DAYWEAR DAYWEAR DAYWEAR DAYWEAR
EVENTS "MUST HAVES"
J G

Credentials | FAQ | Affiliate Program | Customer Service | Legal Terms | Privacy Policy | 

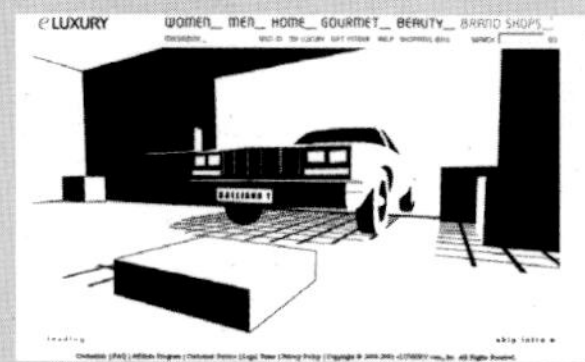

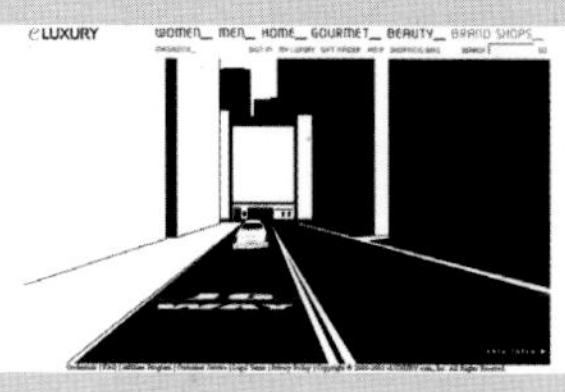

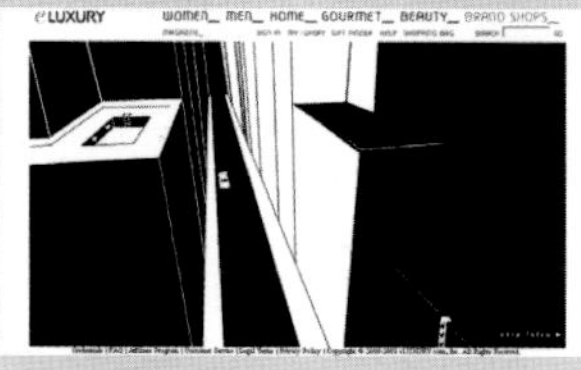

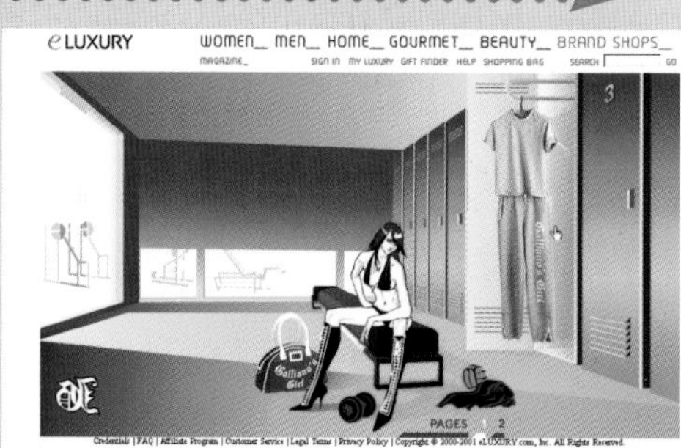


The opening sequence of the Galliano boutique of eLUXURY is seen above, featuring a backwards car chase through the streets of an empty metropolis and Galliano's Girl, a cyber chic (designed by Galliano himself), who is as at home in bias-cut evening dresses as in sportswear with street cred. Designed by Mother, the hip French design agency, the Galliano Girl brand site was launched on eLUXURY on 24 April, 2001, months prior to the launch of Galliano's own site, www.johngalliano.com, in 2002. The site was conceived in the style of a soap opera, explains Mother, with Galliano Girl's antics on eLUXURY forming episode one of a drama that will further unfold on Galliano's own site.

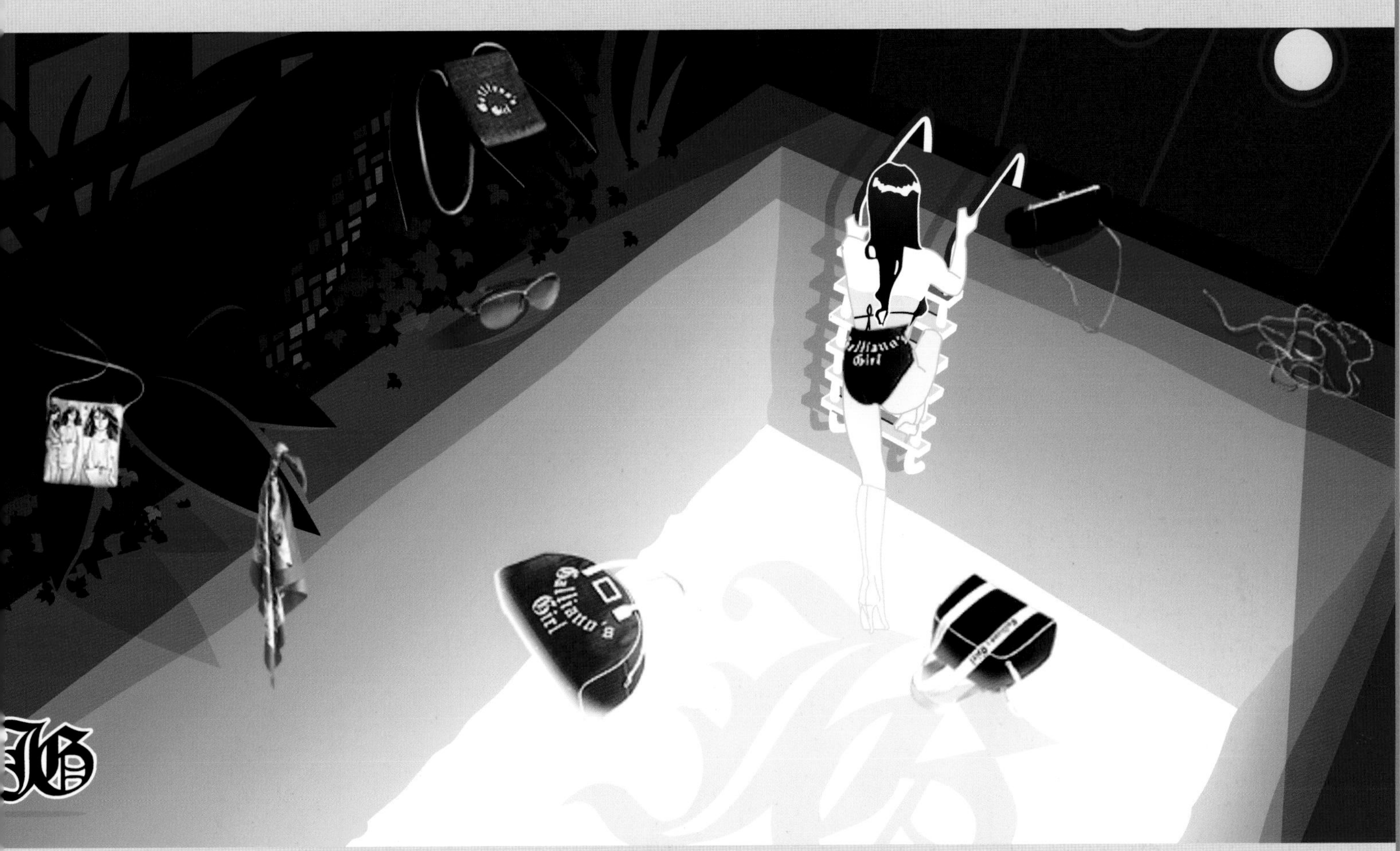

The Galliano Girl brand boutique (where 'Action is the motto!') features evening chic, sportswear, accessories and daywear. Not only is the Galliano Girl collection available exclusively on-line and at eLUXURY, but it was also created by Galliano specifically for the Internet, with features such as 'Web-safe' colours and fabrics, and easy fit garments, broadening its appeal. The Accessories section is seen above. Galliano's Girl climbs out of a pool in her logo maillot, accessories strewn all around her. 'It's kind of like right after the party', explains Galliano. A Product page, right, features the Galliano sling pouch. The accompanying copy promises potential customers: 'You will wonder how you managed before.'

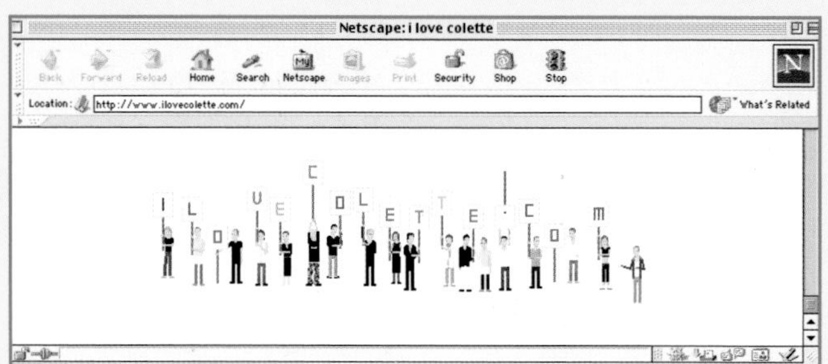


The Home page (left) is seen in detail below. The Top page features links to the sister site, colette.fr, and a pop-up with store and contact information. 'Colette loves' links to the store's trading cards. Web designer Flip Flop Flyin's Craig Robinson has included a myriad of details into the site, such as the Space Invaders icon, which can be seen here wandering above the traffic light (right).

Bottom: Even the store information pop-up is animated with html: flashing pink arrows are literally pulse points, directing love towards Paris.

# www.ilovecolette.com

90

'An oasis of loveliness', is how designer Craig Robinson describes ilovecolette.com. Nothing is for sale on the site, which is 'about the shop and the space' (products can be bought on colette.fr). Instead, ilovecolette happily conjures up the world of Colette. 'It is', says Colette's Sarah, 'fun.'

i ❤ colette
DOWNLOAD COLETTE LOVE!
BONJOUR!
COLETTE
WWW. COLETTE. FR
213 RUE SAINT-HONORÉ 75001 PARIS
Colette loves...
styledesignartfood
J'TAIME COLETTE
DESIGNED WITH LOVE BY FLIP FLOP FLYIN'

i ❤ colette
styledesignartfood

COLETTE
213 RUE SAINT HONORÉ
75001 PARIS FRANCE
T: 0155353390
F: 0155353399
E: info@colette.tm.fr

COLETTE
213 RUE SAINT HONORÉ
75001 PARIS FRANCE
T: 0155353390
F: 0155353399
E: info@colette.tm.fr

Colette's trading cards are a virtual 'who's who' and 'what's what', according to the tastemakers at Colette. Robinson's signature mini-pops, depicting Kate Moss, Nike and designers Viktor & Rolf and Yves Saint Laurent, are shown above. The Style page is seen below and, in detail, above right (the other three sections are Design, Art and Food). 'The whole idea for me', says Robinson, 'was to do something that represented the phrase "I love Colette" and to make the store look like it was alive, not a showroom. I think that was achieved.'

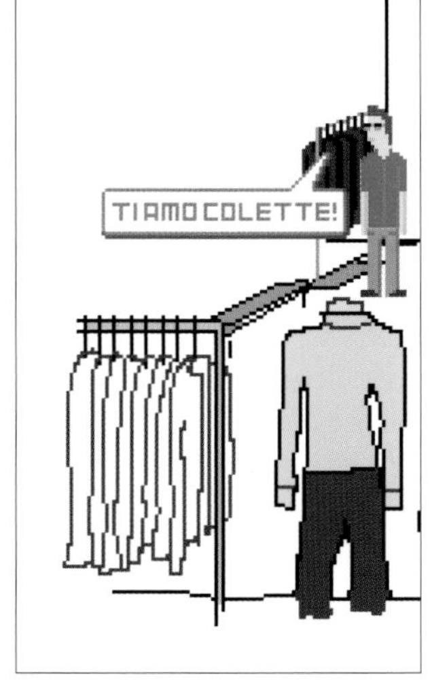
TIAMO COLETTE!

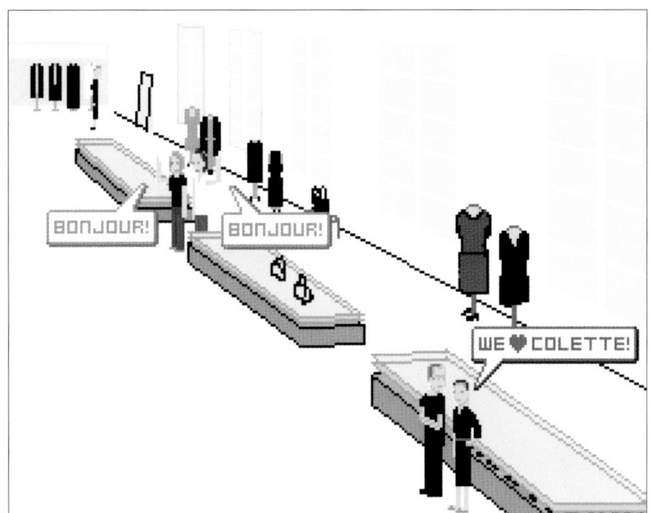
BONJOUR!
BONJOUR!
WE ♥ COLETTE!

J'TAIME COLETTE

i ♥ colette
♥ DOWNLOAD COLETTE LOVE!
WATASHI WA COLETTE GA DAISUKI DESU
J'TAIME COLETTE!
TIAMO COLETTE!
WWW. COLETTE. FR
213 RUE SAINT-HONORÉ 75001 PARIS
Colette loves...
styledesignartfood
J'TAIME COLETTE
DESIGNED WITH LOVE BY FLIP FLOP FLYIN'

www.ilovecolette.com

styledesi

DESIGNED WITH LOVE BY FLIP FLOP FLYIN'

The Gallery, which is reached through the Books and Music sections, is seen on these pages. Past exhibitions have featured the work of designer Raf Simons, illustrator Jean-Philippe Delhomme, the Web design company Mother and graffiti artist Futura.

Left: While a man in the Book section flips pages and muses that he loves Colette, another man (with non-stop wiggly hips) grooves to the music at the CD station.

Above: Visitors at an exhibition are smitten.



The site 'was designed with love' in the course of a single day. After visiting the store, chatting and taking pictures, Robinson went and sat in a park and drew the site almost exactly as it appears here. 'One of the few times', he says, 'ideas arrived fully formed.'

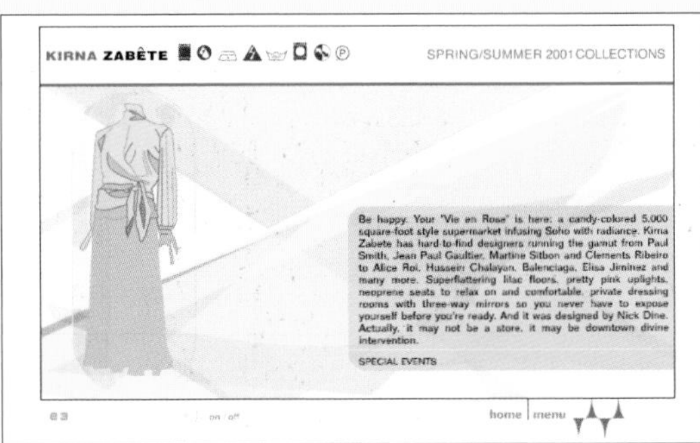

The Home and Top page of the site (left) and a detail of the latter (below), describing the store as 'a candy-colored 5,000 square-foot style supermarket infusing SoHo with radiance'.

# www.kirnazabete.com



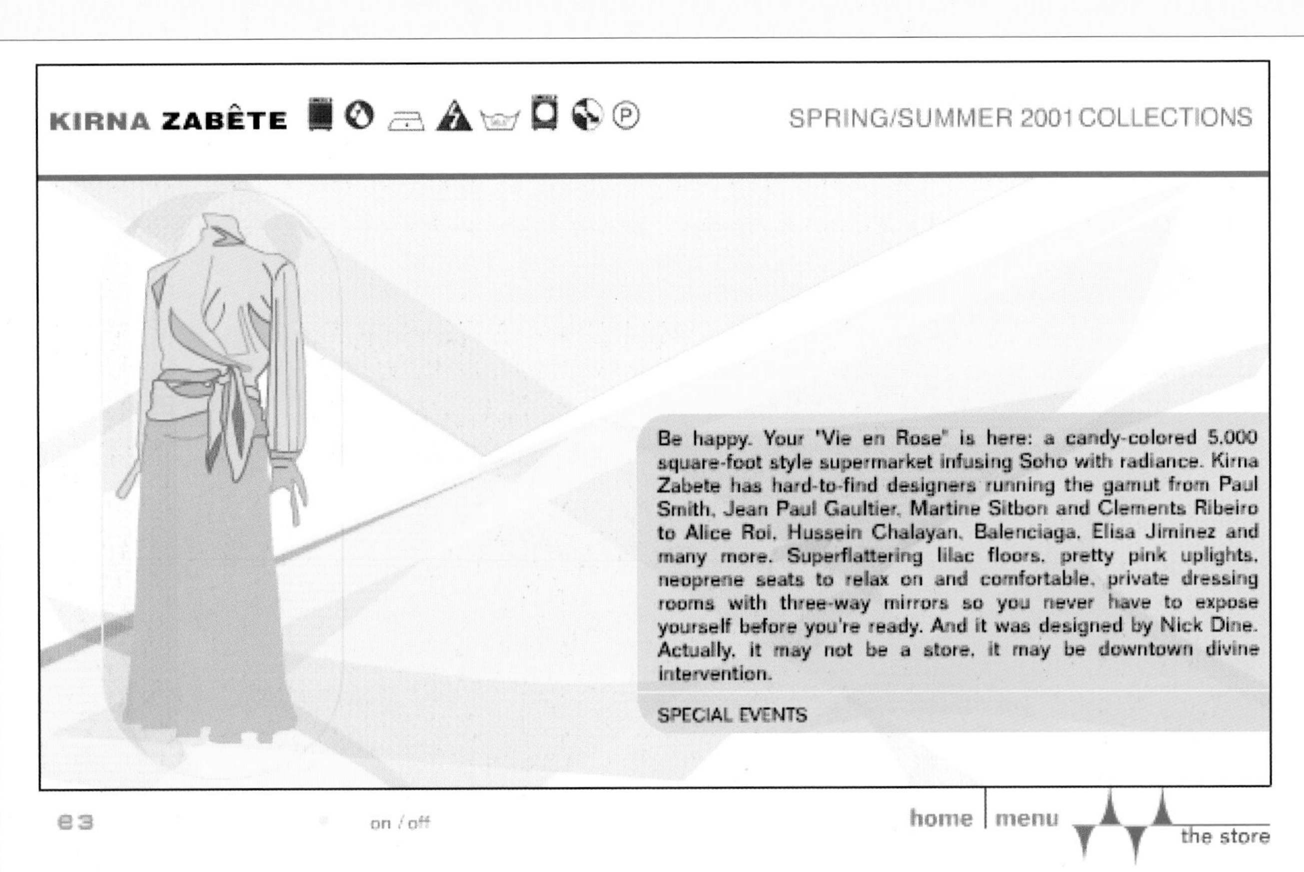

The triangular navigation (above) is inspired by the store's logo. The Top page of the Store section is seen at right. Below: A shot of the entrance, overlaid with animated graphics and accompanied by audio.

'We feel that our store is unique, and that our site reflects the store. It focuses on store design and product – the best elements of Kirna Zâbete', says Sarah Hailes who, with Beth Buccini, co-owns the store. Designed by Engine Three, the site favours catalogue-style shopping over the click-and buy-variety. 'I think fashion is a multi-sensory phenomenon, which is best experienced in real life', says Hailes. 'The Web, however, is a powerful launch pad for information and temptation.'

'We receive international press regularly', says Hailes. 'The site gives people a taste of the flavour of Kirna Zâbete. All pertinent info is also included.' Clockwise from top left: Shots of the store's interior, including 'boyfriend benches' and i-Mac computer stations where customers can play games or check their e-mail.

Opposite: The Top page of the Products page features signature red hang tags. Below, a dynamic horizontal bar features a selection of products. A pop-up of item 04 gives the user an enlarged view of Olivia Morris's tattoo boots and ordering information (via e-mail, phone or fax) is listed above.

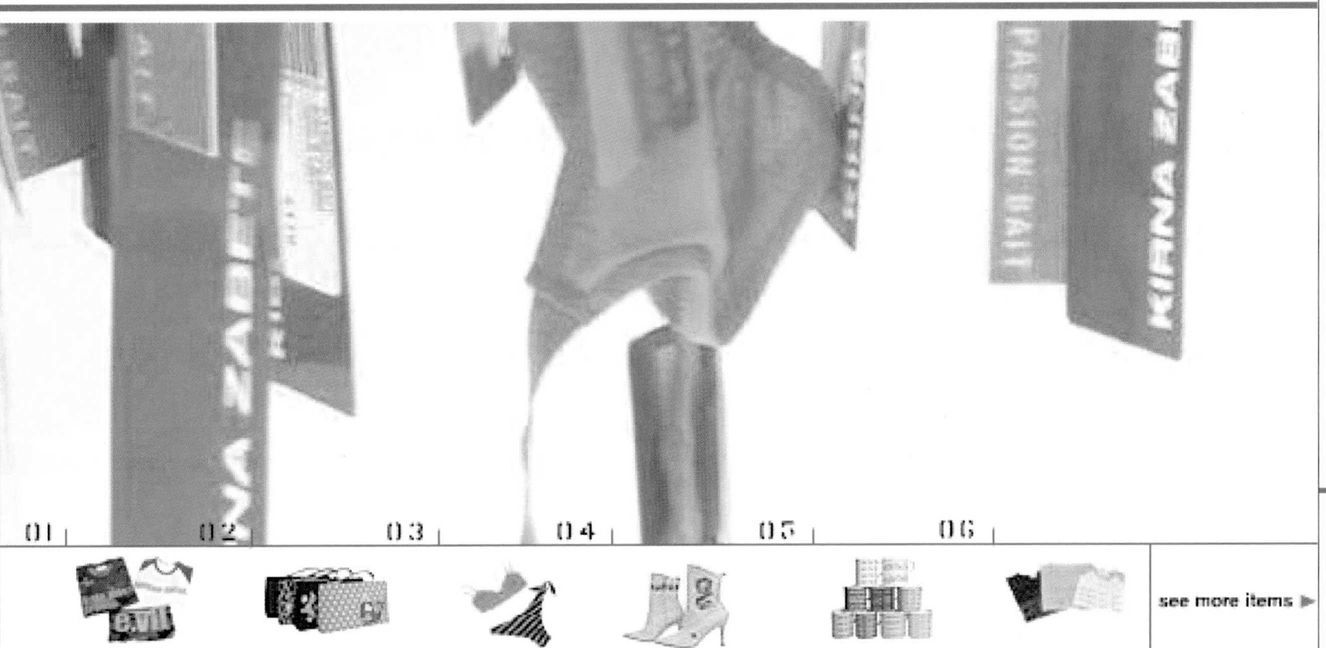

Kirna Zâbete offers 'divine fashion intervention' by specializing in hard-to-find gear for girls and dogs available in a modish, Jim Dine-designed microcosm.

You know you are on a serious shopping site when the Top page (near left) is referred to as the 'storefront'. The Home page is at top left, the Contents page is below left.

# www.net-a-porter.com

'It was always my dream to be able to click on the pictures in a magazine and buy. I think Net-a-Porter is as close as it gets', says Managing Director Natalie Massanet, who was spurred on to found the award-winning site after not finding (high) fashion on-line. Bucking trends, Net-a-Porter has developed the back-end operations and customer service that enable it successfully to cater to a niche market of fashion-savvy customers, who want the latest and the best labels – yesterday. 'It is', says the *Financial Times*, 'doing exactly what most observers have always believed couldn't be done; it is selling cutting-edge fashion over the Web.'

SHEARLING JEAN-STYLE JACKET • CLEMENTS RIBEIRO

Neat fitting camel suede jean style jacket with beige shearling lining and feathered seams. Button front fastening and two front pockets. Button fastenings on cuffs. SEE EDITOR'S NOTE

£845.00* • US$1295**

SIZE CHART AND AVAILABLE SIZES

Click on thumbnails for larger image

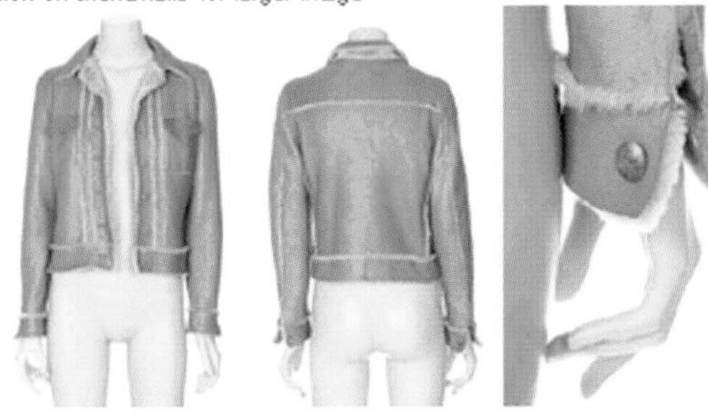

▸ ADD TO MY BASKET

▸ TELL A FRIEND ABOUT THIS ITEM

EDITOR'S NOTE

Worn on the Clements Ribeiro runway with the black chiffon ruffled skirt and studd
Katayone Adeli olive wide ruched pants or Diane von Furstenberg's tweed pants, V
sweater, Jimmy Choo's Viola camel boots and Ursule Beaugeste's camel and brow
Specialist dry clean only

ELL A FRIEND ▸ BASKET ▸ SEARCH ▸ CONTACT US ▸ HELP

FLUFF RUNWAY FIX

OW YOUR SOFTER SIDE THIS
LL IN THE WARMEST SHEARLING
DATS, FUZZY GILETS, AND FLUFFY
TS AND BAGS. HOT STUFF.

Thumbnails, like those above and right, are the e-commerce equivalent of 'working the racks' in a brick-and-mortar store. Net-a-Porter prides itself on bringing its fashion-addicted customers the hottest looks straight from the runway, hence the Runway Fix page (left), combining catwalk images and products shots, from which the customer can 'click & buy'.

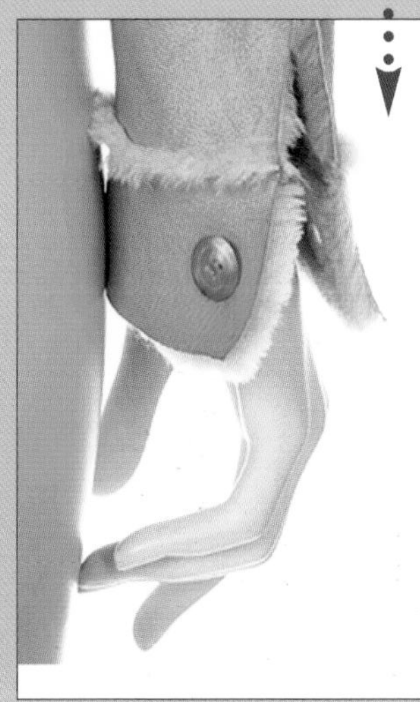

'How many times have you gone shopping with a magazine page in hand?' queries Massanet. Net-a-Porter's fashion editorials are unique and Web-exclusive, eliminating the time between desire and fulfilment. Customers can shop directly from 90 per cent of the site's editorial spreads, which are produced with the same slick professionalism as the most stylish glossy on the newsstand.

BREAK OUT OF THE MOLD.
STAND OUT IN A CROWD.
ALL IT TAKES IS FANTASY AND FLAIR.
THIS IS YOUR BEAUTIFUL LIFE.

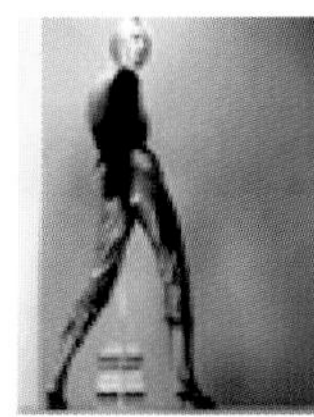

NET-A-PORTER.COM

▸ SIGN IN

▸ RECEIVE EMAIL UPDATE ▸ TELL A FRIEND ▸ BASKET ▸ SEARCH ▸ CONTACT US ▸ HELP ▸ 日本語

HOME

CONTENTS

THE SHOP

ABOUT US

Red jersey dress,
by Eric Bergere
Black glitter wool kimono
coat, by Roland Mouret
Black leather buckle boots,
by Michel Perry

◂ INDEX ▸

▸ RECEIVE EMAIL UPDATE ▸ TELL A FRIEND ▸ BASKET ▸ SEARCH ▸ CONTACT US ▸ HELP ▸ 日本語

BUCKLE BOOTS • MICHEL PERRY

Black leather mid-calf boots with pointed toe, 70mm heel and adjustable silver side buckle. Black zip fastening up inner side. Black and silver herringbone patterned sole. SEE EDITOR'S NOTE

**£345.00* • US$528****

SIZE CHART AND AVAILABLE SIZES

Click on thumbnails for larger image

▸ **ADD TO MY BASKET**

▸ **TELL A FRIEND ABOUT THIS ITEM**

EDITOR'S NOTE

Pure biker chic. Wear with skirts, dresses and jeans - these are the boots to carry you through the season. Please note sizing is French, refer to International size chart in the dropdown menu.

* includes VAT
** approximate value

Reality Bites, opposite and above, features model Eva and was photographed by Barbara Metz and Eve Racine for the Fall 2001 season. When the user clicks on an editorial, an outline appears around the piece selected, which links to the Product page. The process is illustrated on this page (top, bottom left and bottom right). The clean design facilitates shopping. 'I have an allergy to most Web design and a real fondness for all things black, minimalist and stark, hence our packaging and pared-down Website', explains Creative Director Megan Quinn-Newall.

RECEIVE EMAIL UPDATE ▸ TELL A FRIEND ▸ BASKET ▸ SEARCH ▸ CONTACT US ▸ HELP

FASHION FIX

# *Top tan*

CHIC SHADES OF CAMEL, TOFFEE, BUTTER AND BLUSH PROVIDE THE PERFECT BALANCE TO SUMMER'S RIOT OF COLOR. CLAUDIA LEVY GETS INTO NEUTRAL GEAR. PHOTOGRAPHED BY BARBARA METZ AND EVE RACINE.

Clockwise from left :

Rows leather bag with lilac drawstring lining, £197

Anya Hindmarch hair calf bag, £599

Malini Sulaika suede shoulder bag, £202,

Jimmy Choo iguana print high heels, £400

'Women have been making fashion decisions for years by reading magazines,' says Massanet. 'What we've done is taken a magazine experience and shopping and merged them.' The Fashion Fix pages, seen left (Spring 2001) and below (Fall 2000), differ from the Runway Fix pages in featuring product exclusively.

Bohemian (right) is a page taken from the Role Play, which focuses on five style 'archetypes and their shopping lists'. The page design is informed by 'magazine visual vernacular'.

FASHION FIX

# MIX 'N' PATCH

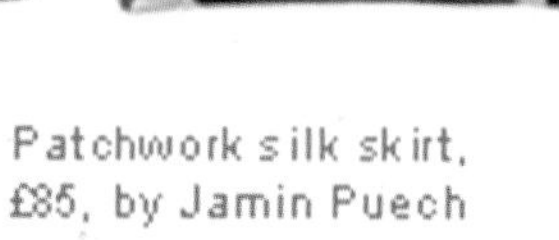

Patchwork silk skirt,
£85, by Jamin Puech

RECEIVE EMAIL UPDATE
TELL A FRIEND
BASKET
SEARCH
CONTACT US
HELP
CLICK & BUY
Bohemian
ROMANTIC AND FLAMBOYANT. THE ETERNAL MAXIMALIST – SHE LAYERS BELTS OVER BLOUSES UNDER COATS OVER SHAWLS, WITH BEADING, RUFFLES AND FRINGING.
MORE IS MOST DEFINITELY MORE.
FAMOUS BOHEMIANS: STEVIE NICKS, HELENA CHRISTENSEN, JADE JAGGER, VANESSA PARADIS.
INDEX
Cacharel, £385 ($590)
Erickson Beamon, £114 ($167)
Erickson Beamon, £185 ($282)
Clements Ribeiro, £645 ($989)
Jimmy Choo, £575 ($820)
Clements Ribeiro, £430 ($658)
Vanessa Bruno, £110 ($167)
Jimmy Choo, £550 ($780)
Jamin Puech, £160 ($245)
Erickson Beamon, £152 ($223)
Cacharel, £185 ($282)
Clements Ribeiro, £485 ($742)
Missoni, £80 ($122)
Les Prairies de Paris, £125 ($191)
Anna Sui, £300 ($459)
Jamin Puech, £190 ($270)

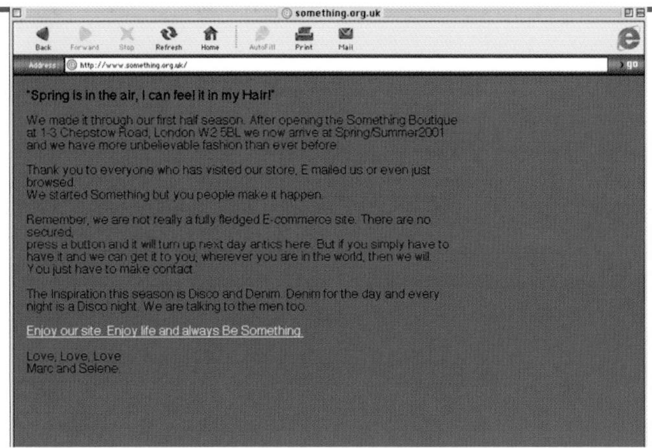


Something.org is a site with an unusual story. It was designed by co-owners Marc Hare and Selene Allen, with Gareth Parkinson of Publicland, to create a real sense of place prior to the opening of the 'brick and mortar' store. Even now, the site retains a separate identity from the store (which was designed in collaboration with David Collins). 'People come into our shop who have visited the Website first and ask us where the lifts are. To many people our internet shop is more real than our real shop', says Hare, adding, with a wink: 'The rent is also cheaper.'

# www.something.org.uk

Something, a select boutique located in London's smart Notting Hill district, is co-owned by Marc Hare and Selene Allen, who apply strict criteria to everything they admit into their universe, always asking: 'On its own, is it something?' The blue and white Home page is seen top left, while the development of the accessories 'floor' is played out, in clockwise fashion, above and right. (That's Hare making a star appearance.)

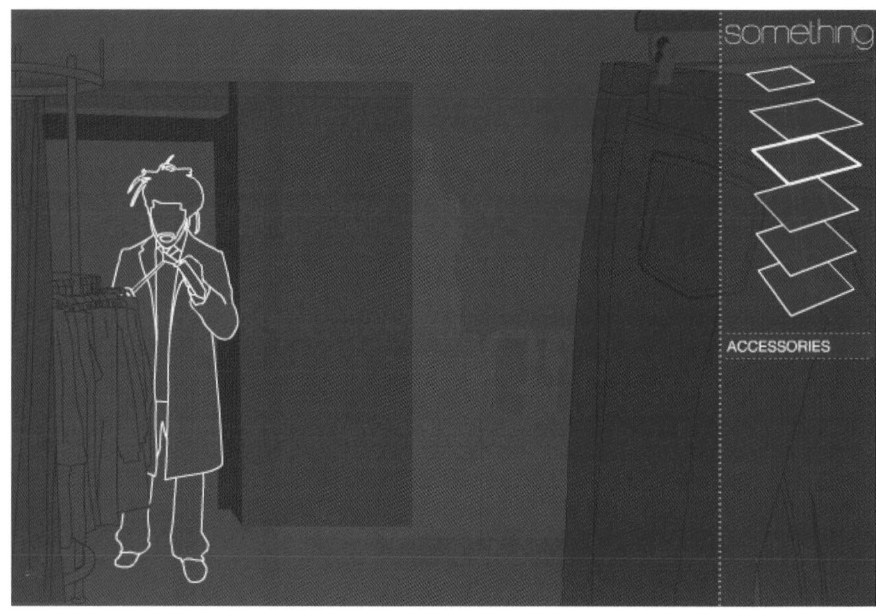

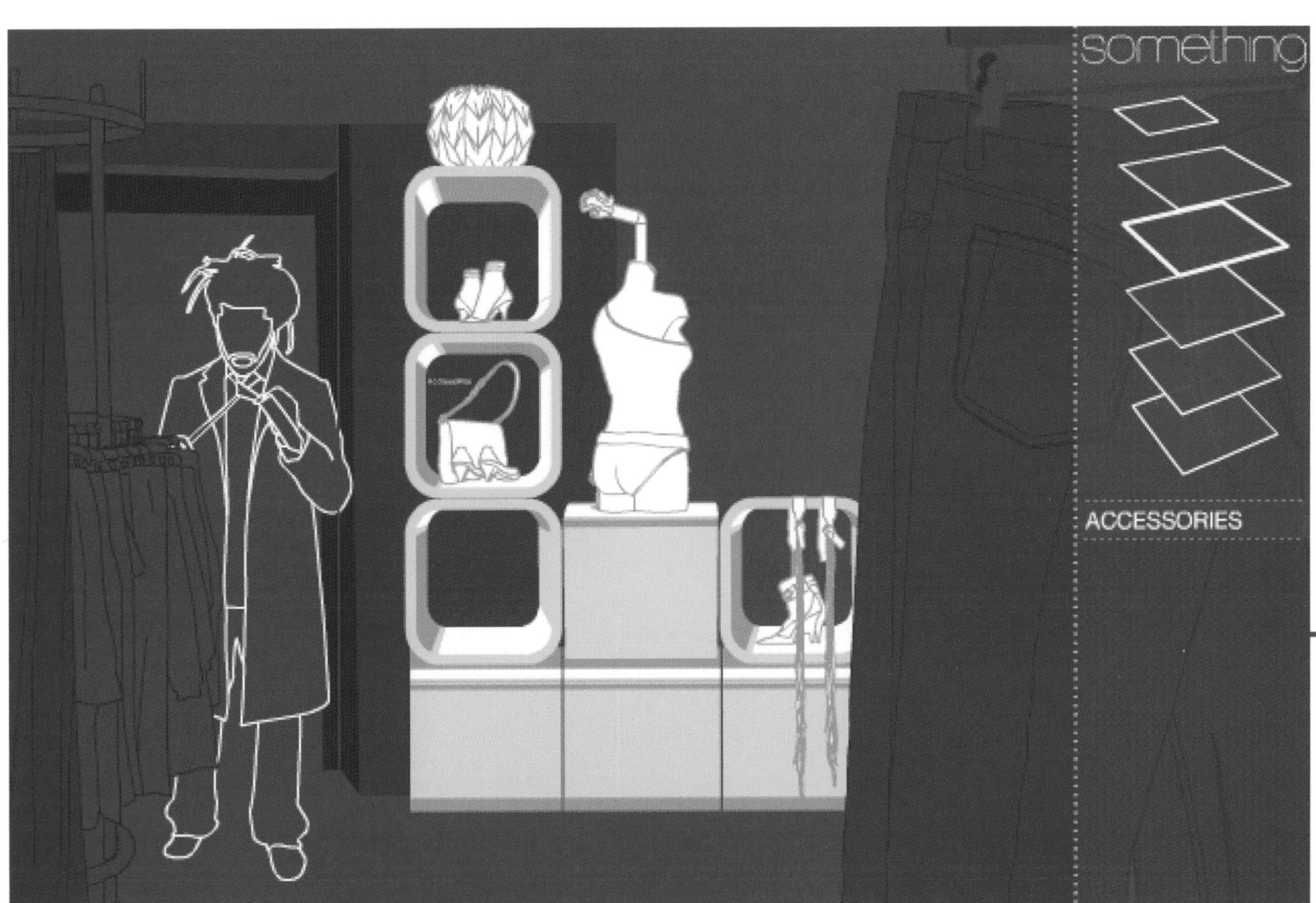
something
ACCESSORIES

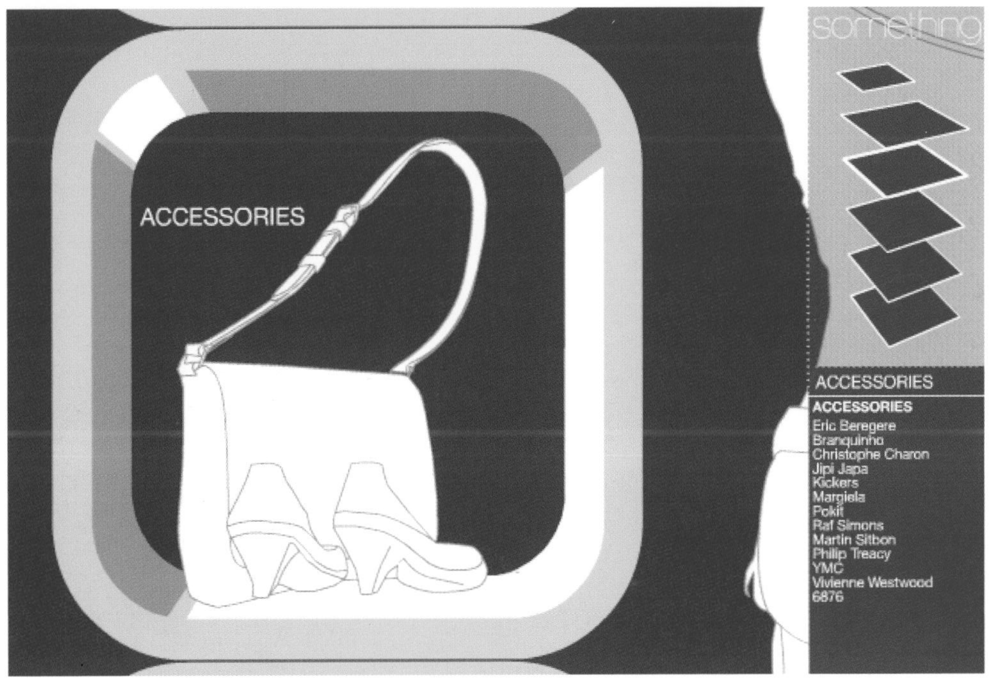
something
ACCESSORIES
ACCESSORIES
ACCESSORIES
Eric Beregere
Branquinho
Christophe Charon
Jipi Japa
Kickers
Margiela
Pokit
Raf Simons
Martin Sitbon
Philip Treacy
YMC
Vivienne Westwood
6876

www.something.org.uk

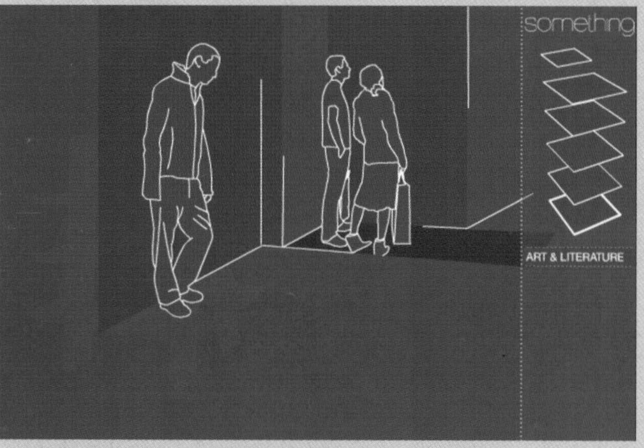


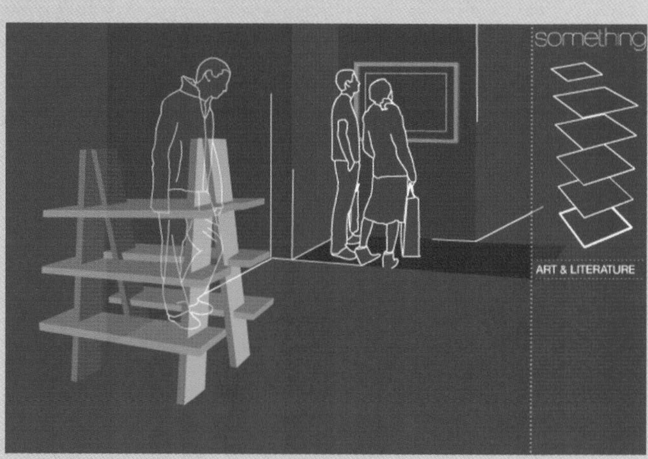

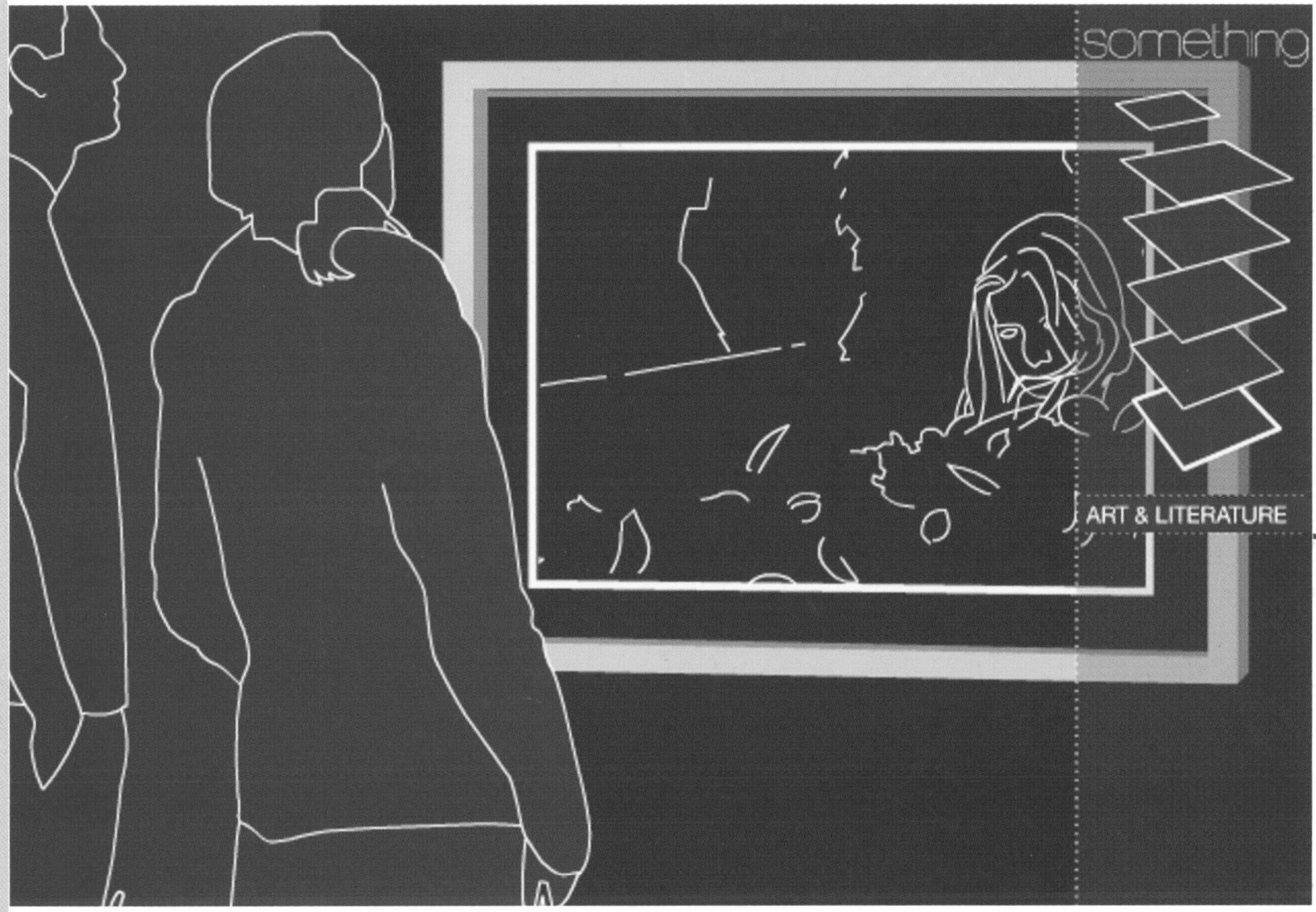


# LITERATURE SELECTION

Users move between floors of the site using a static six-level vertical navigation found on the far right side of each page. A different category of merchandise is featured on every level, from Art & Literature on one to Service on six (where there is a password-only room), with Furniture, Digital, Accessories (where Marc holds court) and Clothing (where Selene reigns) between. The Art & Literature section is accessed from the Home page (opposite, top left). It is seen in two stages of development opposite, bottom left and in detail on this page.

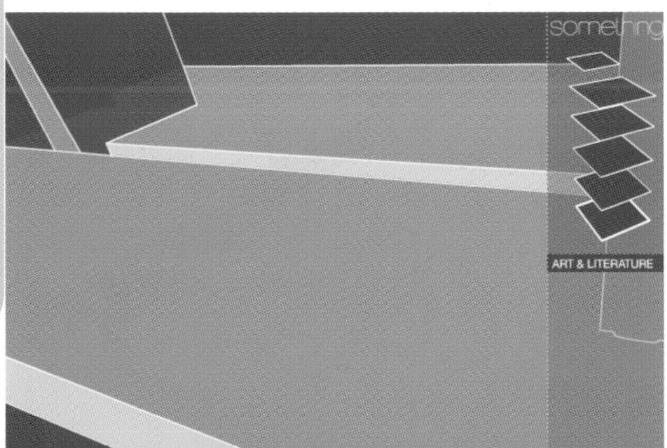


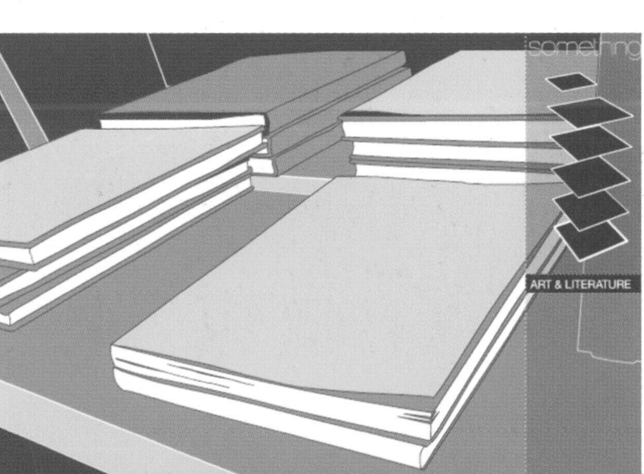

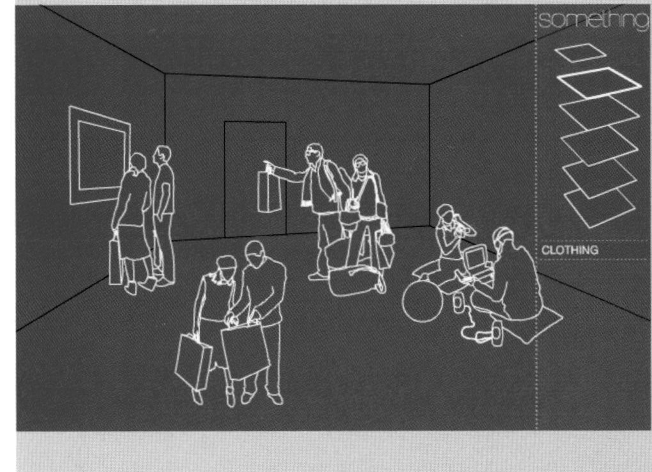
something
CLOTHING

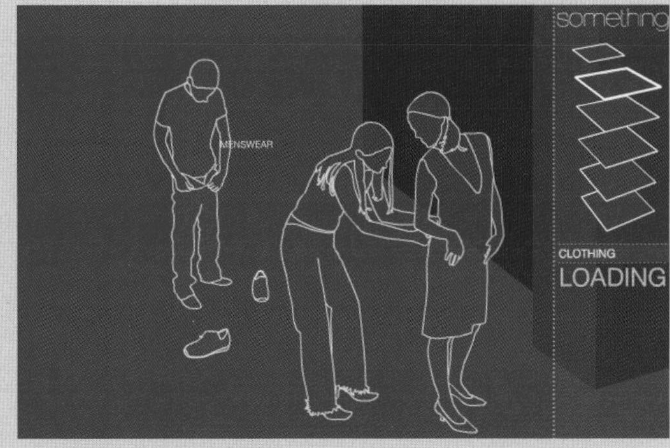
something
MENSWEAR
CLOTHING
LOADING

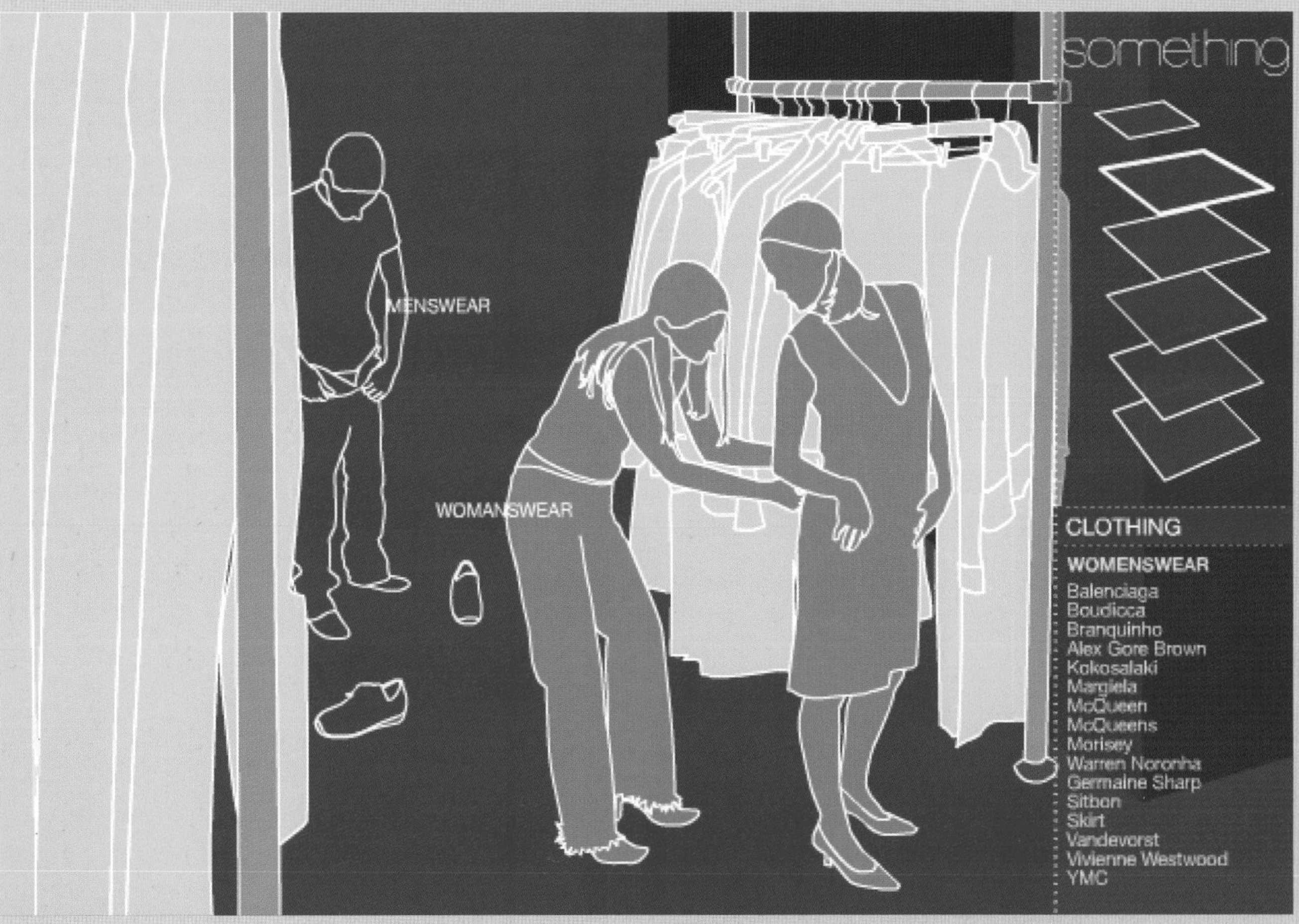
something
MENSWEAR
WOMANSWEAR
CLOTHING
WOMENSWEAR
Balenciaga
Boudicca
Branquinho
Alex Gore Brown
Kokosalaki
Margiela
McQueen
McQueens
Morisey
Warren Noronha
Germaine Sharp
Sitbon
Skirt
Vandevorst
Vivienne Westwood
YMC

Selene is seen fitting a customer in the Clothing section (opposite), which builds in layers while a customer listens to music in the Digital section (this page). 'Everybody should have the ability to zone out to good music', write Hare and Allen (both former DJs). 'We have this section because we would like to do our bit to curb Technophobia. We will concentrate on personal hi-fi in honour of the spirit of Rollergirl....'

'The purpose of our site', concludes Hare, 'is to be able to communicate our shop to anyone anywhere in the world. Also, it is a space where we can play around with how a Website should be. You don't want to sit and read loads of text on a computer screen. We looked at our Website as much from an entertainment point of view as any other.' Rock on.

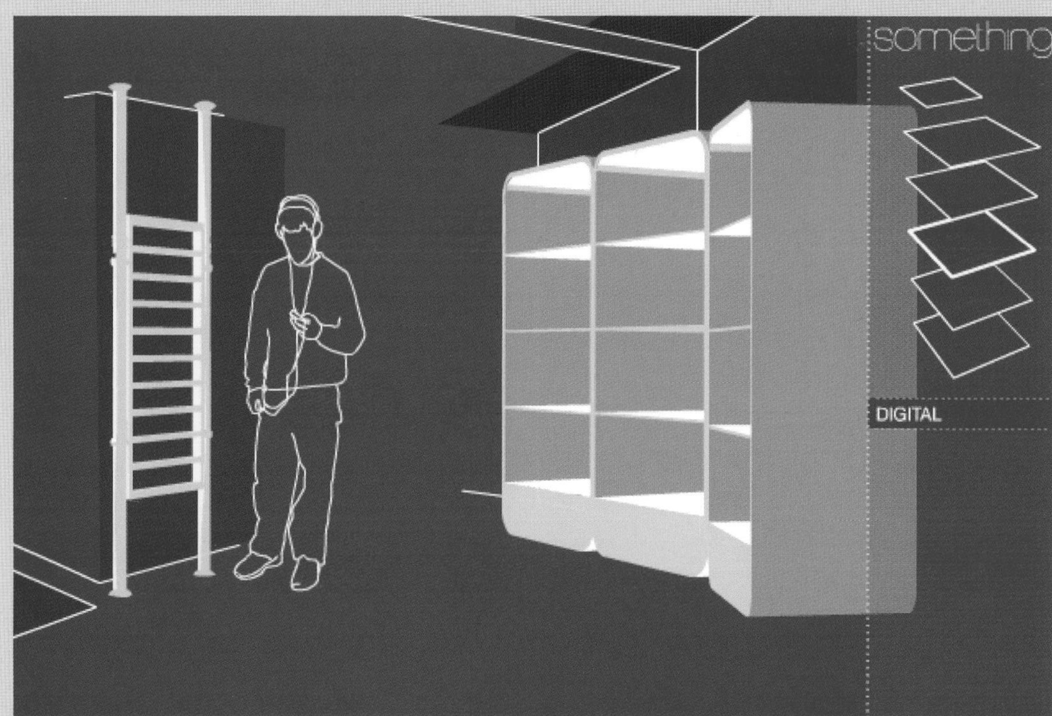


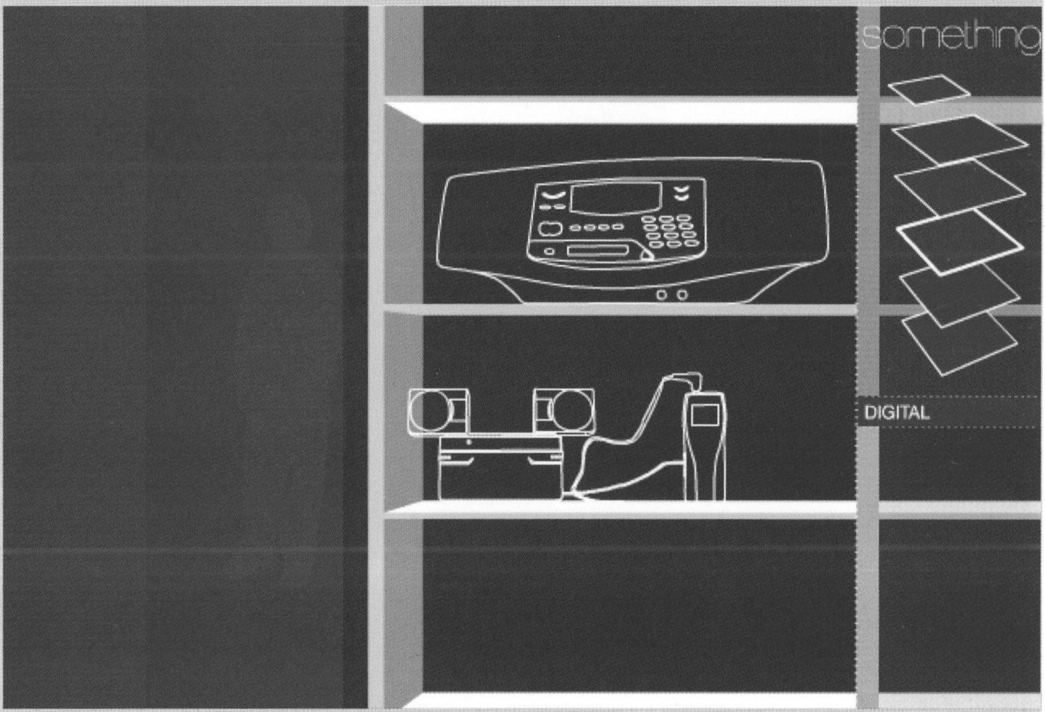

# www.sowear.com

Visitors to the SoWear site can elect to scan the Magazine section, read artists' biographies, consult the Resources and Classified sections or pose questions in the forums or shop. Accessories, men's and women's wear are available. In addition to category, shoppers can view merchandise by designer or type (tops, jackets, etc.).

Top left: The Home page.

Above: A detail of the Shop by Designer Top page.

Left: The ATK Designer page. There are links to various types of information from the Designer page, including a portfolio of images selected by the designers to show their wares in more detail and/or express their aesthetic.

Bottom right: ATK's Portfolio page, seen in full and in detail.

Top right: ATK's charity T-shirt in full and in detail.

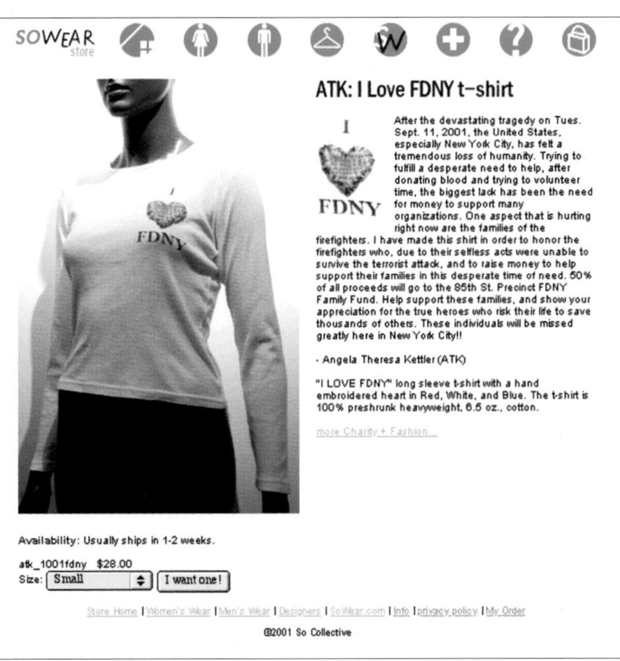


SoWear is not just about shopping. Since most of the designers are unknown (and come from all over the world), biographical, store and sizing information for each of them can be accessed from the Designer page by clicking on directionals, such as those seen below.

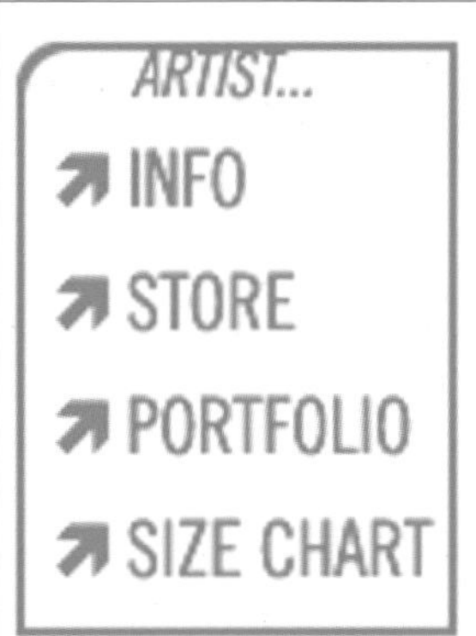




'SoWear is a fashion collective dedicated to promoting and helping emerging talents in fashion', explains Jason Yang, who founded the site. By establishing a showroom in 2001, Yang now services both the individual consumer and the wholesaler. 'About 70 to 90 per cent of our merchandise at any time is not available anywhere else, on the Web or in stores', says Yang. 'I have designers from all around the world and many have never been heard of by anyone. We offer many one-of-a-kind and handmade items.'

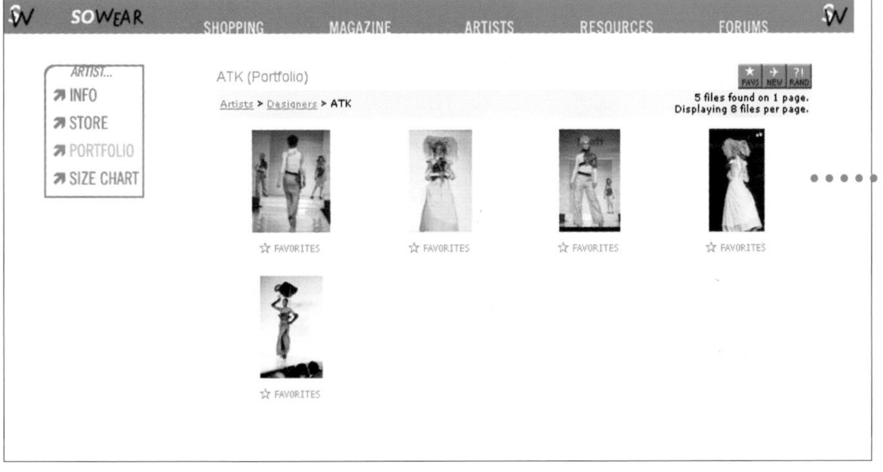

SoWear went live in February 2000 with ten artists and this has now increased to more than two hundred. Each section of the site 'cross-pollinates' with others, aiding and abetting emerging fashion *artists*. Stylists and photographers pull pieces from designers in the shop to create editorials for the Magazine section, which, in turn, encourages sales.

Right: The Product page for Spanish-born and New York-based designer Sylvia Lloses, with a pop-up inset of her 'Gogol' jeans, named after a popular local band (Gogol Bordello).

SHOPPING MAGAZINE ARTISTS RESOURCES FORUMS

Artists > Designers > Sylvia Lloses

5 files found on 1 page.
Displaying 8 files per page.

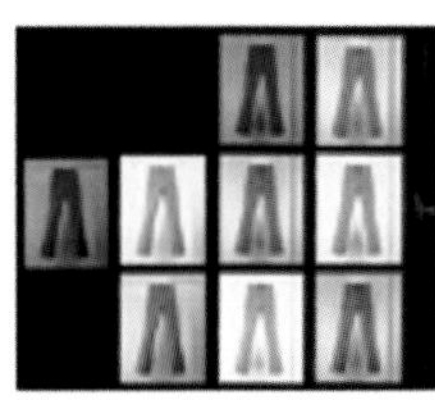

☆ FAVORITES

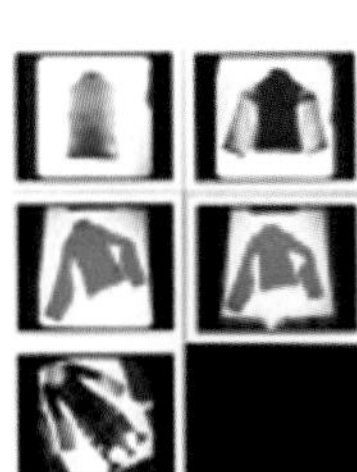

☆ FAVORITES

☆ FAVORITES

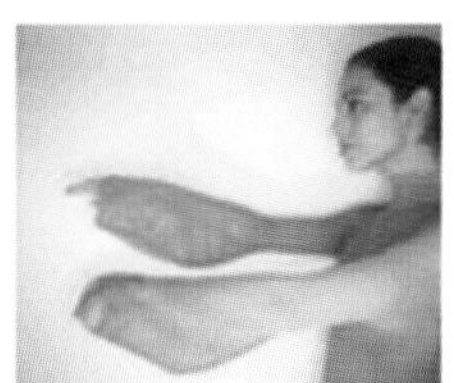

☆ FAVORITES

Sylvia Lloses (look2)

Artists > Designers > Sylvia Lloses > look2

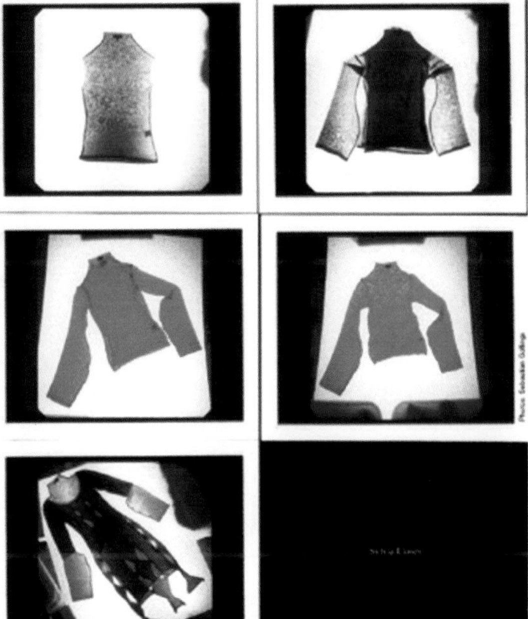

☆ FAVORITES

Return to Thumbnail View
Send As A Postcard

Lloses's Portfolio page, above, and a detail, left. Yang hopes not only to 'tie desire with fulfilment' throughout the site, but to create a unique and personal experience for the viewer. It is his hope that by bypassing the media filter, the Web will create a greater awareness of global trends and a desire for things outside the mainstream, which, in turn, will help young designers.

Left: The Home page. STYLE.com is updated daily from Monday to Friday. The contents include fashion shows, trends, shopping, and people & parties. Below: The Shop Top page from Spring 2001, with horizontal and vertical navigation.

# www.style.com

The on-line home of *Vogue* and *W* magazines, STYLE.com has set the industry standard for fashion show coverage. STYLE also redefined shopping on the Web through the establishment of a ground-breaking, year-long, strategic partnership with the department store Neiman Marcus. The resulting co-branded Store on STYLE.com created a direct link between editorial and commerce (via the *As Seen in Vogue* feature, for example), with looks chosen by in-house merchandisers. Neiman Marcus handled customer service, inventory management, shipping and returns.

The Store's Fall 2001 and Spring 2001 Top pages, above and right. Some of the ways users could navigate the Store were by: Hit List; Designers; and Category. For both seasons a print catalogue was produced and mailed, driving additional traffic to the Store.

Right: The user was able to access this page in the Spring 2001 Store via a category search (sunglasses), a designer search (Oliver Peoples) or via the Troop Detail Trends page (seen opposite, below). Below: The Jean Paul Gaultier Designer page from the Fall 2001 Store, including details of the merchandise. Users clicked to pop-up slideshows from this page.

Trend pages from the Summer 2001 and Spring 2001 Store, above and left. The most contextual and editorial elements in the Store, Trend Shopping pages created visual stories around a current theme. Hit List pages often had a subliminal 'how-to' element, as they built a look across categories. More importantly, they expressed editorial authority in the most direct way. Employing the coy didacticism that marks fashion-speak, they informed the consumer of what was currently important and desirable, what was not only 'on trend' but 'in style'.

At the same time that the Store featured the Troop Detail Trend page, military looks appeared in the Fashion Shows section of the site. STYLE's editors and merchandisers collaborated, so that e-commerce and editorial could best co-exist and so that the user could act immediately on what had been read, literally going from runway to reality with the click of a mouse – supported by the lionized authority of *Vogue* and *W*.

# fashion talk

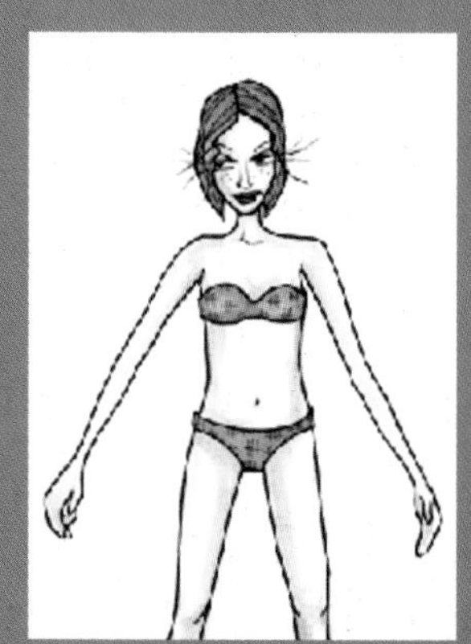

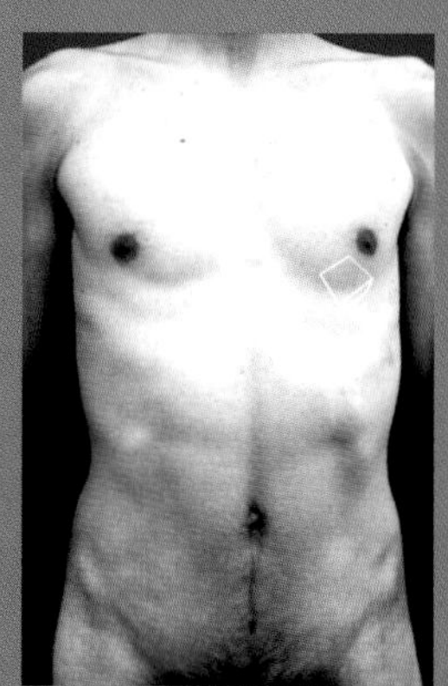

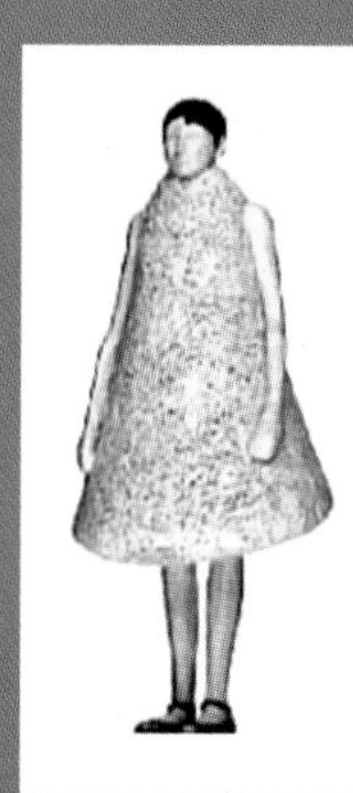

www.2fanzine.com.br

www.dresslab.com

www.hintmag.com

www.itfashion.com

www.nylonmag.com

www.showstudio.com

www.vogue.co.jp

www.zoozoom.com

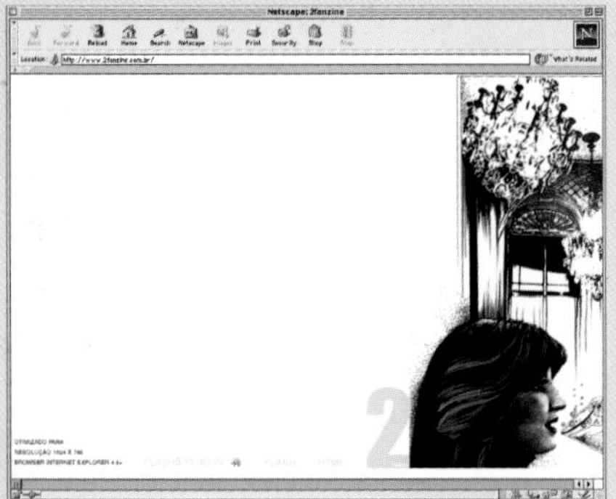

Left: 2fanzine's illustrated Home page.
Below: The Top page in three states – the mission statement (left), the mission statement with 'adhesives' (bottom left) and with 'adhesives' applied (below right).

Right: Festa, a multimedia editorial (collage and illustration) by Fabia Bercsek, accessed from the Top page and displayed opposite.

# www.2fanzine.com.br

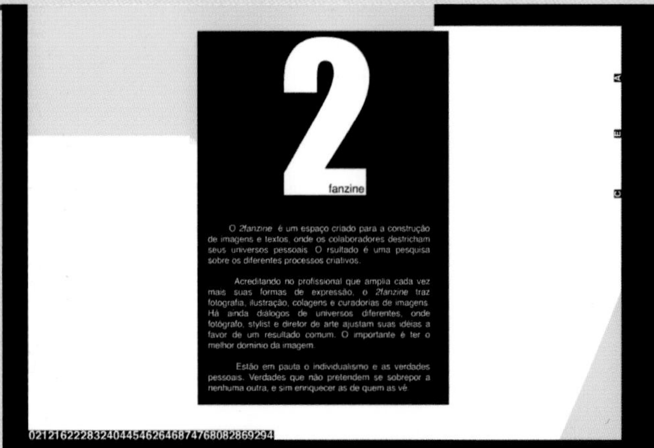


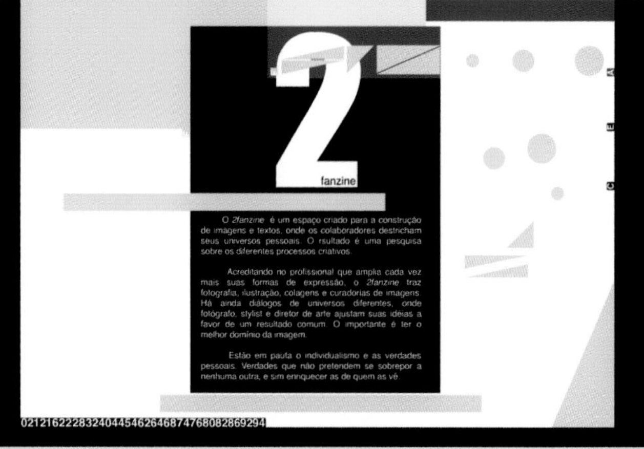

2fanzine.com is the electronic version of 2fanzine, a non-commercial magazine printed in editions of 1000 and freely distributed in Brazil. In print, 2fanzine can be customized with coloured geometric adhesives, an idea that has been carried over to the electronic version. The site is designed to be a 'creative space' where people can engage freely in creative dialogue and give expression to their personal universes through collaborations and using various media.

FESTA
ilustração FABIA BERCSEK

FESTA
ilustração FABIA BERCSEK
02121622283240445462646874768082869294

FESTA
ilustração FABIA BERCSEK
02121622283240445462646874768082869294
C
E
A
R
P

É a cumplicidade o ponto forte do processo criativo em casal. O convívio contínuo cria uma espécie de consciência comum, cheia de códigos próprios. Construindo imagens juntos, eles acionam naturalmente essa consciência, um complementando o outro. Emilene e Gustavo chegam a um resultado só, mas dentro dele dialogam os universos dos dois.

Emilene fez as fotos para seu trabalho de graduação na Faculdade Santa Marcelina, em 99, onde reuniu todas as suas vontades e, pela primeira vez, transformou-as em imagem. Fez um desfile, uma tese e o trabalho fotográfico. Vestiu as roupas da coleção e fotografou-se em um motel, construindo a imagem feminina em que acredita: silhuetas absurdas

EMILENE GALENDE e GUSTAVO MENEGAZZO

C E A

02121622283240445462646874768082869294

B P



www.2fanzine.com.br

Lucia Dossin, Dudu Bertholini and Kleber Matheus, founders of both the magazine and the site, see the Web as a 'powerful communication tool' that allows them to share their work with, and to access information from, others around the world. 'There is something really interesting about the Web', they say; 'the user can also be the producer. At the same time you "consume" information, you are also allowed to transform it into something new to be "consumed" by someone else.'

The editorial on this page is a collaboration between Emilene Galende, a photographer, and Gustavo Menegazzo, an architect and interior designer. Menegazzo juxtaposes Art Nouveau-style calligraphics with Galende's black and white photographs, creating an exciting 'reveal/conceal' tension that draws the eye around the elegant swirls and deeper into the photograph.

02121622283240445462646874768082869294

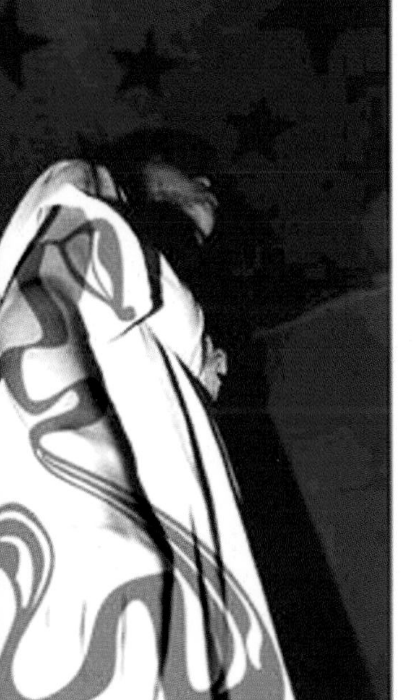

C

EMILENE GALENDE e GUSTAVO MENEGAZZO

R PROXIMA

Three pages from Galende and Menegazzo's editorial are displayed here. The text (which scrolls up and down) speaks about the artists. Users move from page to page using the subtle 'R' 'P' navigation, seen at the bottom right of the Web page.

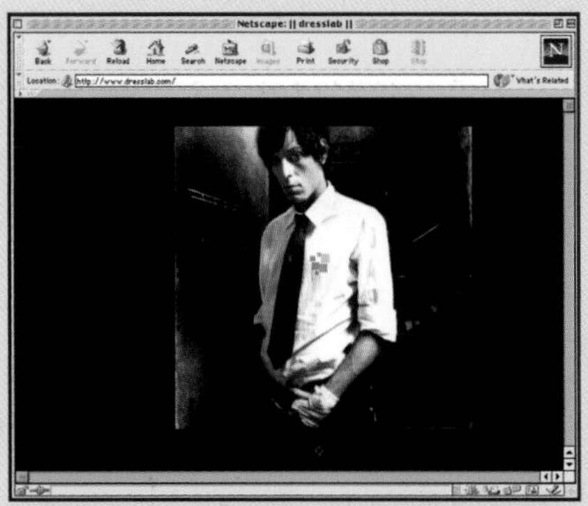


Dresslab's Home page, seen here in various states, gives new definition to *high* fashion. The diagnosis? Fashion addiction. To enter the site the user must take aim through a scope and crosshairs (seen on the black ground at far right) and shoot at the model's beating heart. Dresslab has five sections: See; Play; Lab; Shop; Talk. The inset, opposite, below, shows the navigation when See is selected.

# www.dresslab.com

Dresslab's founders, Jordi Belda, Alex Segura and Eduardo Nofuentes, describe it as: 'an interactive, dynamic and audiovisual magazine f-zine that covers the topics of fashion-art-music-and-everything-in-between'. Equal importance is given to the content – fashion – and to the media by which it is communicated so vibrantly – photography, graphic design, animation and music. Dresslab is a 'playground', say its founders, where 'numedia – nuperspectives – nuliberty' are explored and enjoyed.

Conceived of as a lab, Dresslab's content is comprised of in-house work and outside submissions (both unsolicited and commissioned). Play is an important theme on the site and is built into its functionality through interactivity and entertainment.

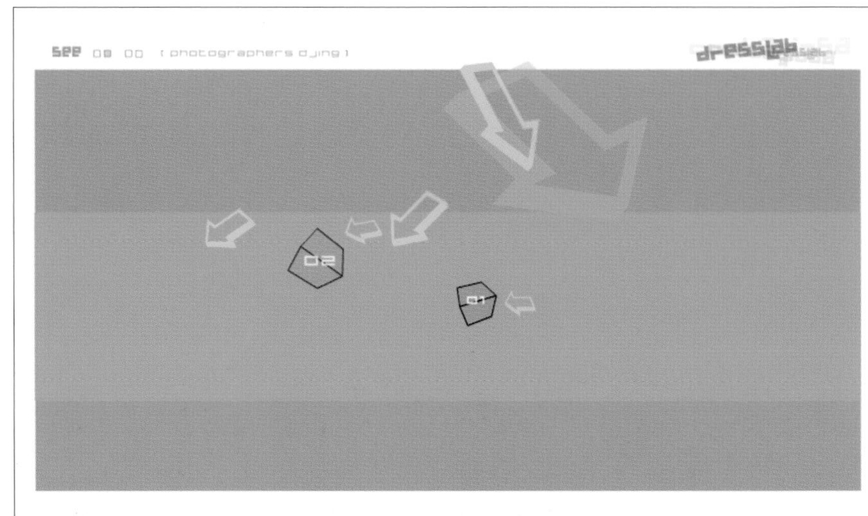


In a broader sense, the style and attitude of the site are clearly an expression of the real joy that Dresslab and its contributors find in playing with a new medium.

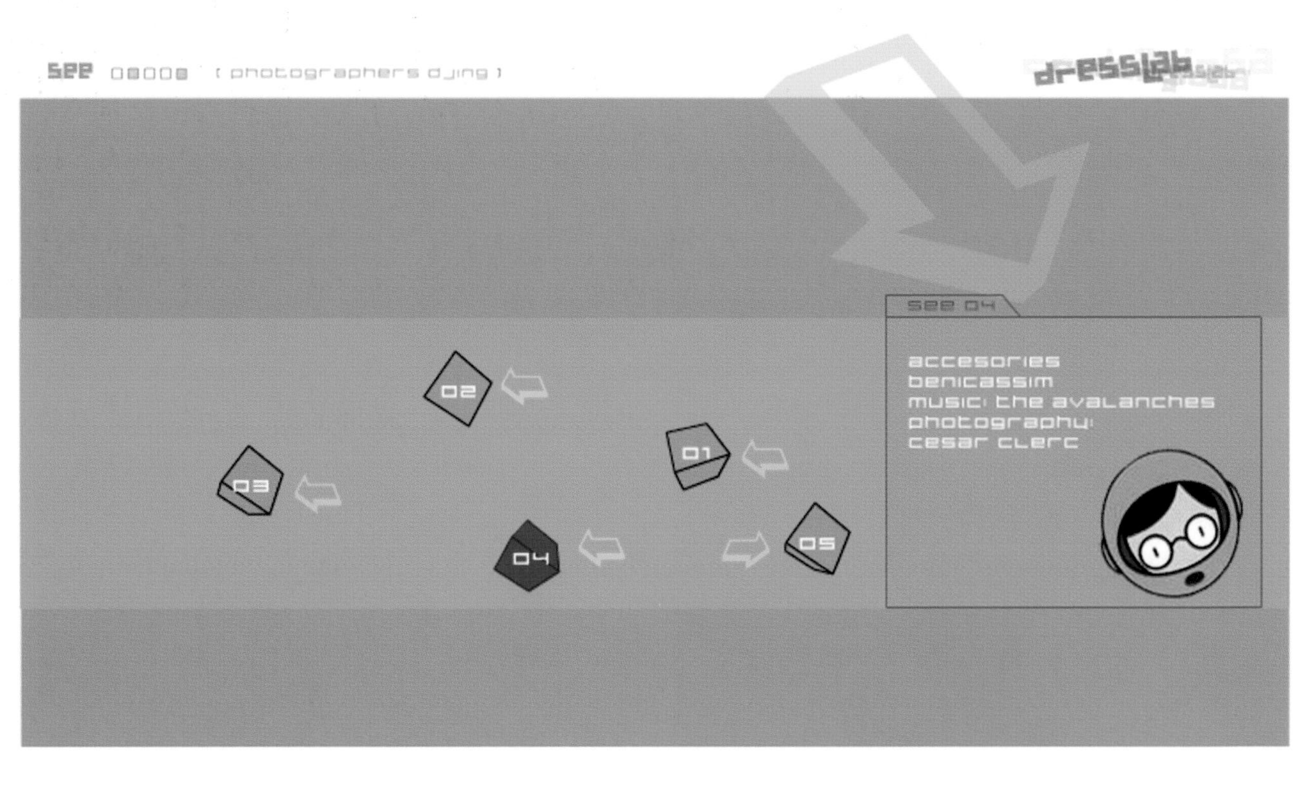

Opposite, above and below: The Top page of the See section, in two states of development.

The full title of the site's first section is: See: Photographers DJing. The title evokes a sense of play – and of cool – and hints at Dresslab's emphasis on pop culture and the 'real' fashion mix. This is well demonstrated by Benicassim's accessories feature, BNCSM2001_ACCSRS, a series of photographs by Cesar Clerc shot on the street and in the clubs of Barcelona. The accompanying soundtrack is *Since I Left You* by The Avalanches.

'Dresslab is not like a plain fashion magazine that covers the latest trends', say its founders. 'It's more like a playground for artists and content providers to give their opinions, and critiques the world and culture in, around, and behind "fashion". Dresslab is a place to renew and recycle old ideas and to get fresh perspectives.' The Lab section explores Life beyond Fashion with a series of pioneering 'installations' of stylish, interactive Web design. The Lab Top page is seen below.

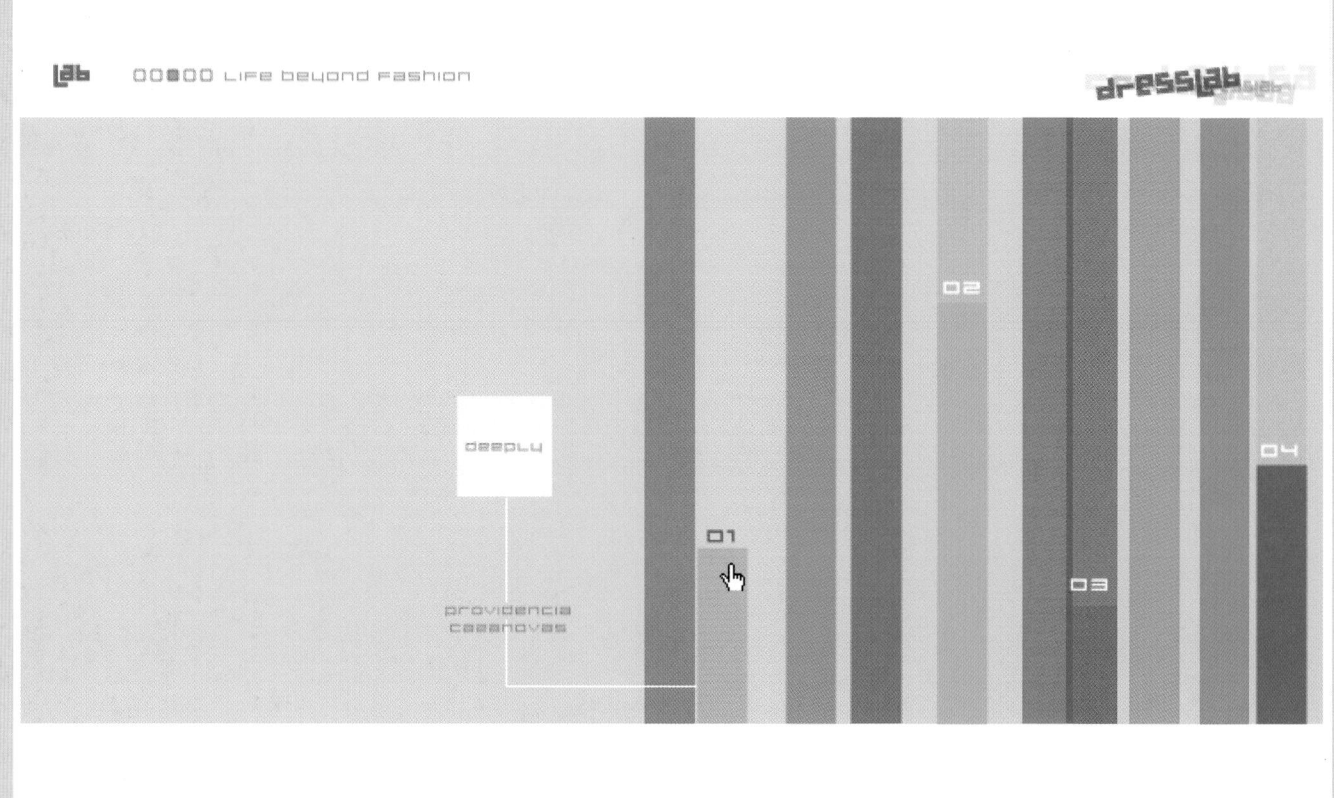

Right: Geometry meets anatomy in Providencia Casanova's 'installation', Deeply. Users are given the following directions: 1) 'drag the objects'; 2) 'drop it on the body'; 3) 'experiment: it's a lab'.
Sonia Soms's 'Set 4' (middle, left and right) is composed of four cubes, each with four settings and four music selections that the user can activate in a staggering number of combinations for a multi-sensory experience.

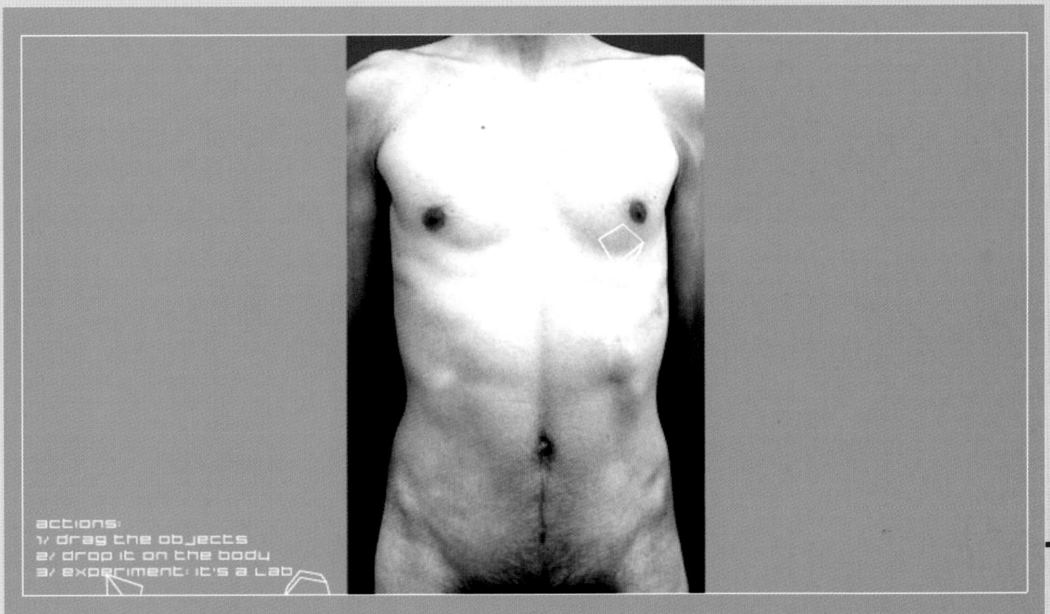




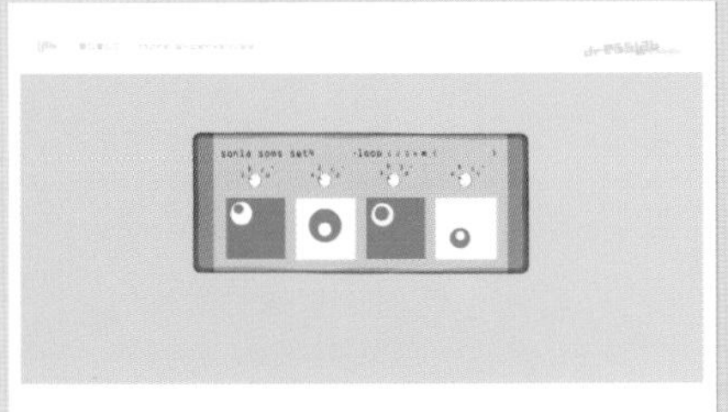

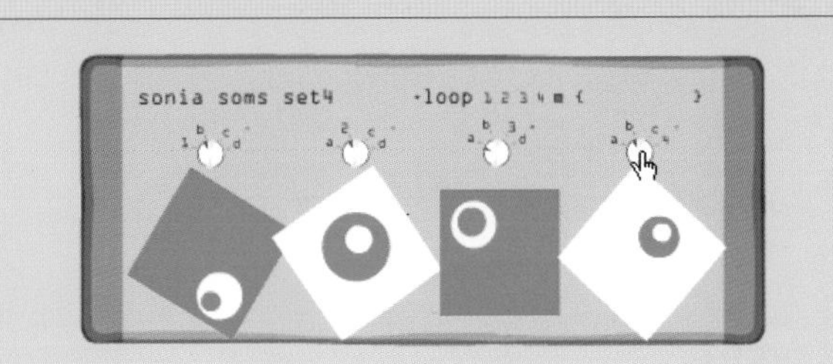


The title of the fourth section of the site, Shop: Increase Your Targets, continues the theme of taking aim and firing that plays throughout the site via the crosshair navigation. In this ever-expanding section, users can select cities from the Top page to access information and visuals on hot shops.

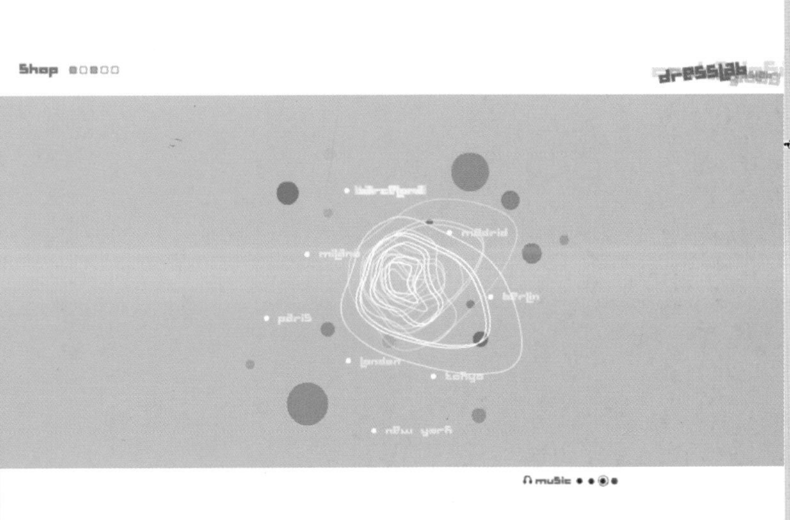

'Fashion is ideally suited for the Web, both in saleability and the allure of multimedia, but a large section of the fashion industry still chooses to remain ignorant of the Web', says Hint's editor-in-chief and creative director, Lee Carter. Having embraced this new medium, Hint has become an award-winning site whose reach, states Carter, 'is farther than most print fashion magazines, ultimately reaching more readers worldwide'. Provocative and irreverent, Hint has become an industry essential.

# www.hintmag.com



Hint's Home page (above) and Contents page (right). The fashion community is addicted to the Chic Happens column, Hint's weekly gossip feature. Other columns include Shop Tart and Model Mania.

'Since its beginning', Carter says, 'Hint has been a pioneer of fashion on the Web in both style and substance, and because we're independently owned we've allowed ourselves to remain risk-takers.' Hidden Places – an editorial photographed by Mika Nakanishi, featuring garments by designers including Missoni and Alice Roi and with audio by Björk – is an example of Hint's forward-looking aesthetics. The feature (shown opposite) proceeds from top left down to middle, across, and then from bottom left to right.

SC

NEXT >>
DRESSES BY JUNYA WATANABE
TIGHTS BY HUE
WHITE SHOES BY FAUSE HAUTEN
TURQUOISE LACE SHOES BY VICTOR DE SOUZA

NEXT >>
TURTLENECK BY ALICE ROI
RUFFLE SKIRT BY MARKUS LUPFER
TIGHTS BY WOLFORD
LEATHER BALLET FLATS BY SIGERSON MORRISON

Hint's editorial fashion coverage takes many forms. Screen shots and details from Morrow is Today, a Flash-enhanced interview with British designer Hamish Morrow, are seen on this page. 'At its core, Hint is a fashion magazine, not unlike any other with photo shoots, gossip pages, etc.', says Lee Carter. 'But unlike glossies', he continues, 'Hint offers slick multi-media interactivity and an unparalleled global community of fashion *freaks*, and I mean freaks, devoted to pushing fashion ever forward.'

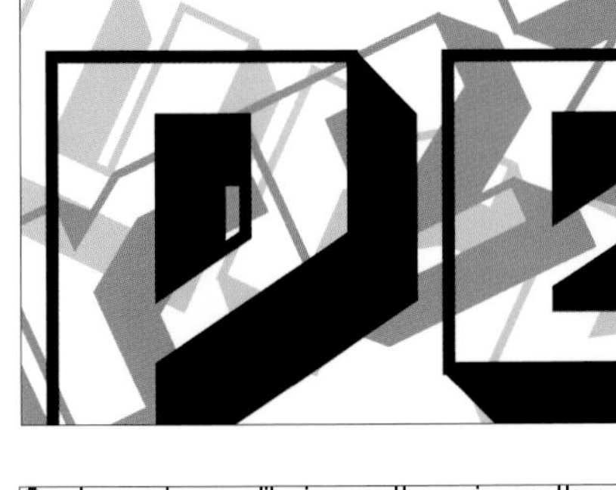

Supernova, a feature on young designers, is found in Hint's Columns section. Two pages from Lee Carter's profile on the New York label 'People Used to Dream about the Future' (designed by Adrien Cowen and Diva Pittala) appear below and left.

Card-carrying egalitarians -- the pair say they left Europe to escape its outdated notions of snobbery and entitlement -- People are more likely to be influenced by anti-globalization demonstrations on the continent than by the mercurial conceits and vanities of the fashion industry at large. "We're not snobs," says Cowen. "In an abstract way, we want our work to reflect social and political issues, to be relevant somehow. Trends in fashion mean nothing to us. Like 'retro,' which we see as a refusal or inability to design something new. The future is the present."

"Trends in fashion mean nothing to us."

# www.itfashion.com

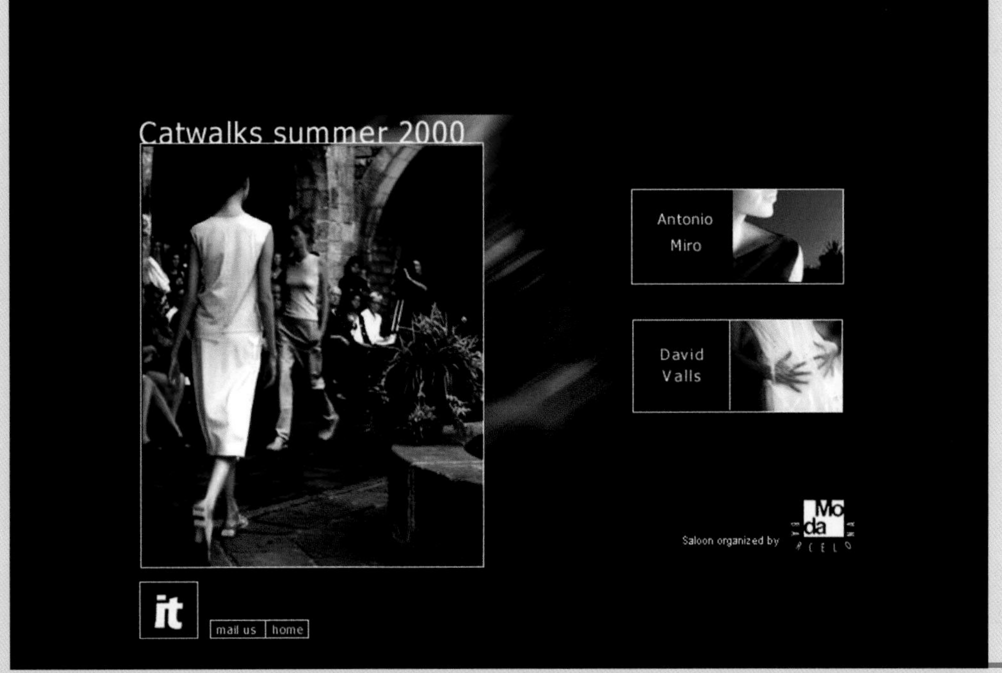


Launched in January 1999, It Fashion is now in its tenth volume. Volume 1, Missing the Summer, is seen opposite, middle, while the Top pages of Volume 10 are seen opposite, top left and those of Volume 3, Girls of Summer, are seen above each other, opposite.

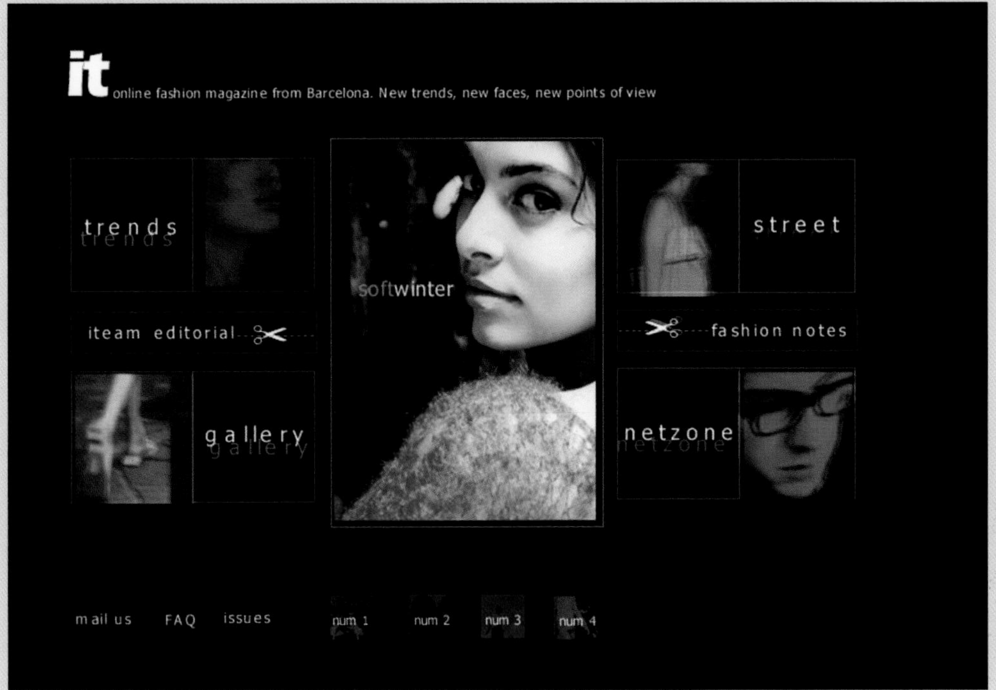


Above: Home page of Volume 4, Catwalks Summer 2000.
Left: Home page of Volume 5, Soft Winter.
Below: A pop-up from Volume 9.

Estel Vilaseca, Estel Munné and Mireia Sabanés founded It Fashion in 1999 when they were all full-time students. Their philosophy: 'Be ourselves.' Their mission: 'to show a different face of fashion, a vision of fashion that is more accessible than commercial and closer to the streets, regular people and daily life.' In short, to find 'it'. While the iteam affirms the importance of fashion magazines, they believe that the Web offers equality of opportunity for everyone, and thus encourages 'a more heterogeneous, multicultural and extensive vision of fashion'. 'The Internet', they say, 'has given us the possibility of realizing our dream: contact with people of the world.'

itfashion
trends, ideas & netcoolhunting
IT postcards
this IT issue
collaborations
iteam
suscription/mailing
la casita de wendy- summer 2001
elisa amann - summer 2001
lydia delgado - summer 2001
catwalk
catwalk
scarapbook
perfiles
memuevo
netzone

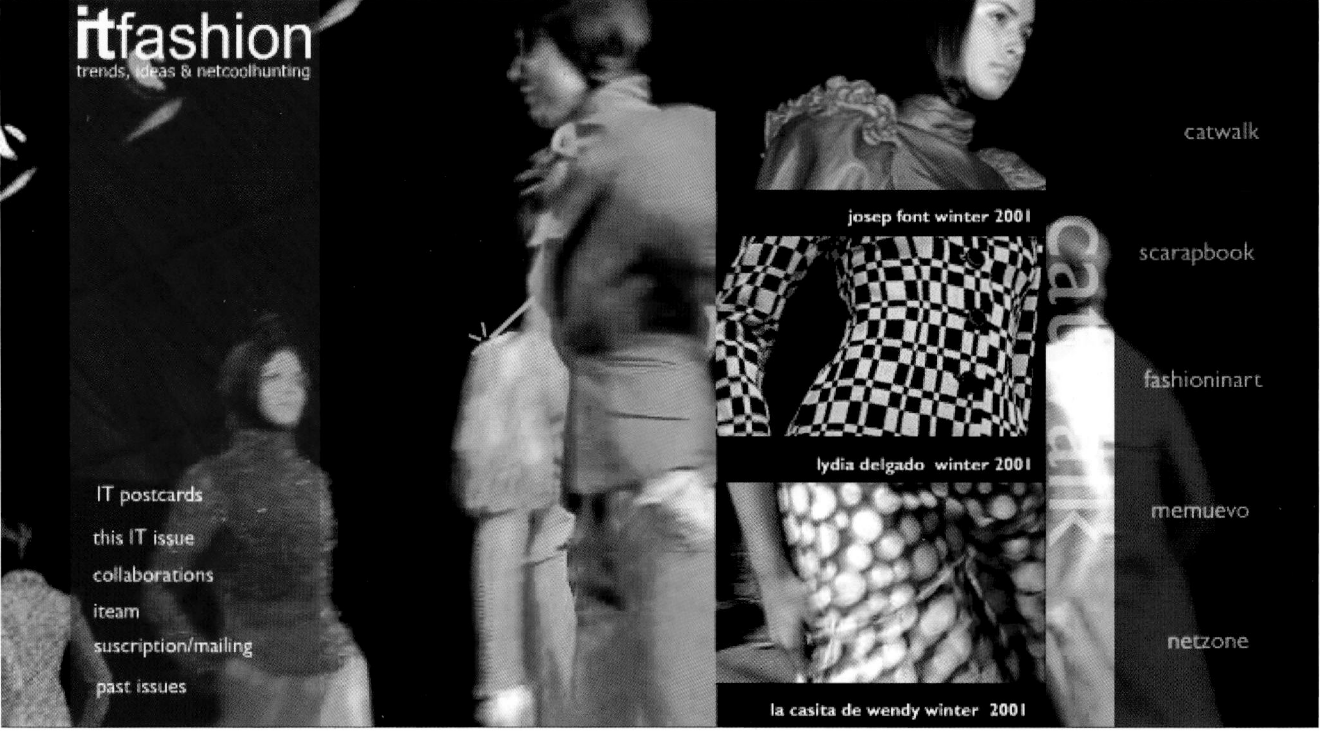

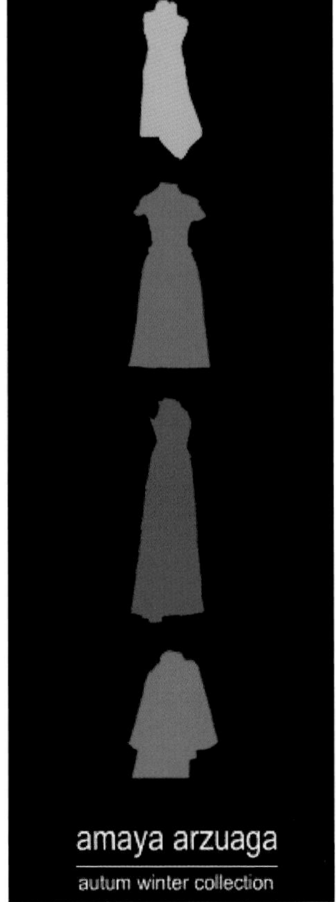


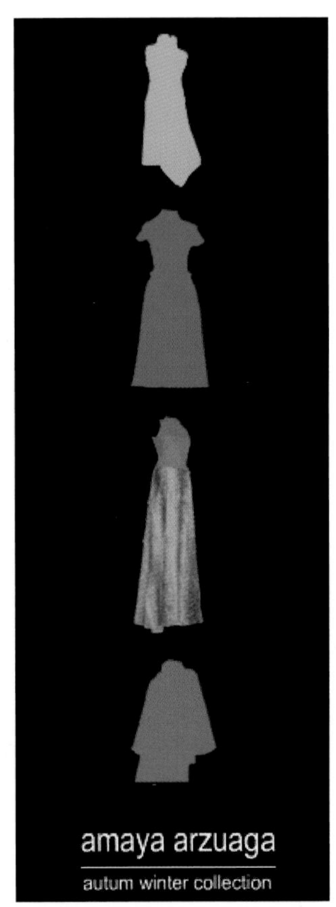


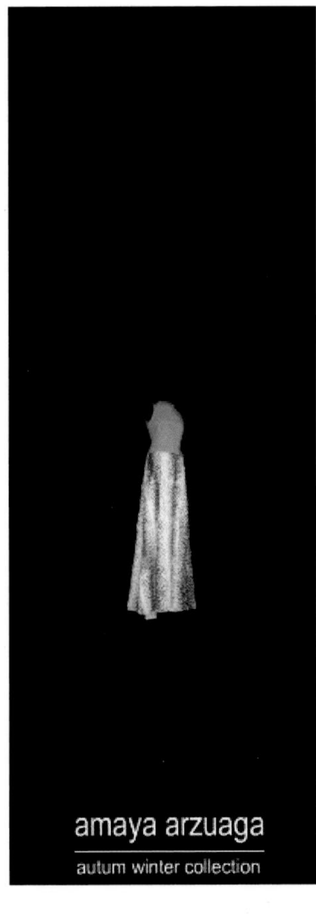


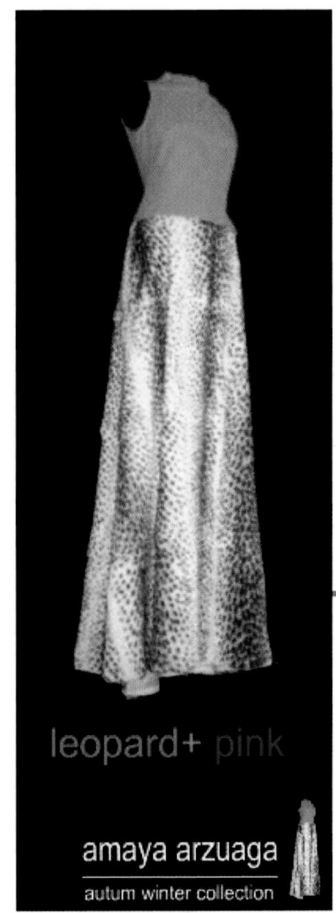

Left: The catwalk Top pages from Volume 9, Summer 2001 (top) and Volume 10, Winter 2001 (bottom). Both feature Spanish designers who show in Barcelona. Above: An inventive It editorial of Amaya Arzuaga's Fall 2000 collection from Volume 8. Below: An editorial of Lydia Delgado's Fall 2001 fashions. The various boxes are in continuous rotation, creating an ever-changing view of the designer's work.

As little girls, the iteam dreamed of being fashion editors. The Web has enabled them to actualize their desires, something they could never afford to do in print. 'The budget of the magazine', they say, 'is zero pesetas and the result is the fruit of disinterested collaborations, ideas and illusion.'

Barcelona is the fashion capital of Spain and hosts its own fashion week. It Fashion lavishes creative attention on its coverage of these shows. Josep Font's Fall 2001 show, designed by Estel Vilaseca, is seen here (top left). 'Trends, Ideas and Net Cool hunting' – It Fashion's tag line and subject matter are reflected in the Tiles page (bottom left), a collage of images from international fashion magazines.

The iteam designs and creates all of the site's content – sometimes 'with a little help from [its] friends'. Jordi Sabanés photographed the two editorials at right. The first, a summer story from Girls of Summer, Volume 3, runs across the page, top right. The second, from Volume 5, Soft Winter (with a wonderful visual navigation), is laid out clockwise from middle, right.

it
reports
gallery
faces
pola st
trends
tiles
ranking
links
girls of summer
1
2
3
4
5
6

PHOTOS by Jordi Sabanes
gallery
trends
street
netzone
it

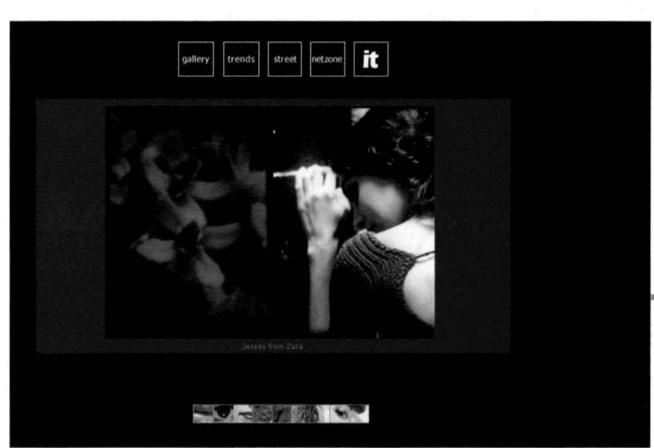
gallery
trends
street
netzone
it

gallery
trends
street
netzone
it
Dress from ZuZa

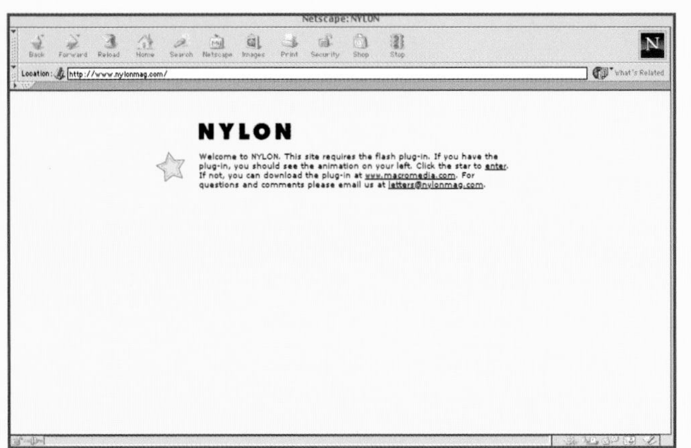


'Nylon', says publisher Marvin Scott Jarrett, 'is an independent magazine for intelligent women who care about their personal style'. Designed by Flashlight Media, nylonmag.com was conceived as a complement to, rather than as a substitute for, the print version. Highly interactive, the site stands on its own, while maintaining the look and feel of the print magazine.

# www.nylonmag.com

Nylon 5's Top page. The user is encouraged to click on various sections of the Home page by a hip girl guide, who 'voices' her comments, and by 'hot' spots that colour in or change pattern as the mouse runs over them. If the user clicks on the star-patterned bed cover, for example, the month's horoscopes appear.

Cover girls: Danita Angell as envisioned by Kaws (Nylon 3), left, and Björk (Nylon 5), below.

This spread demonstrates the functionality of the Nylon 5 Top page. When the mouse rolls over the illustrated model's T-shirt, she declares: 'There's room in everyone's closet for another tshirt.' When the drawn T-shirt is clicked, the pop-up, below, appears.

Opposite: The Top pages and first spread of Giddyup, a fashion editorial photographed by Clang from Nylon 5.

NYLON

select

giddyup

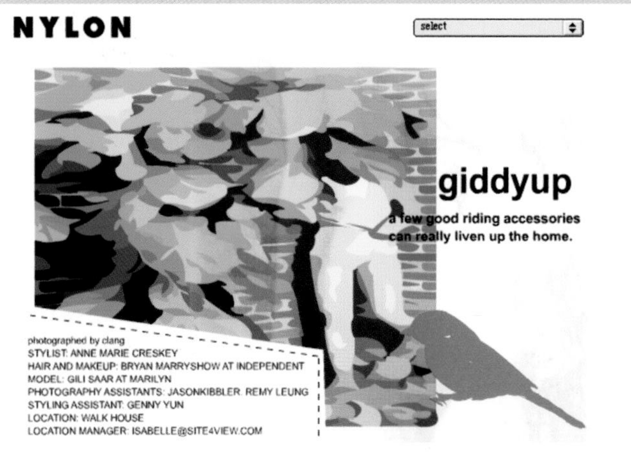


NYLON

select

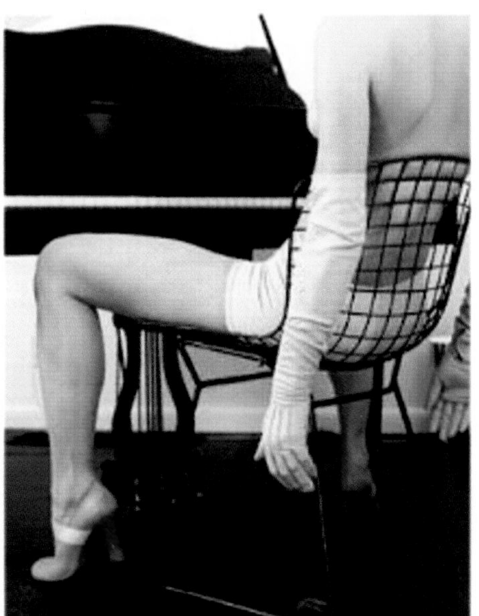

GLOVES BY PRADA,
PANTIES BY DKNY,
SHOES AF VANDEVORST

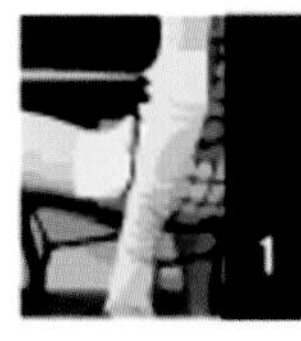

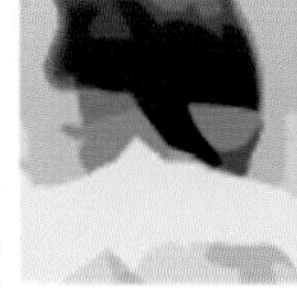

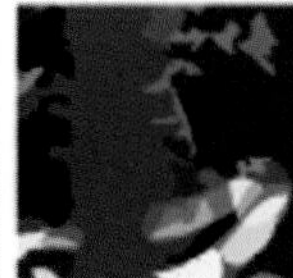
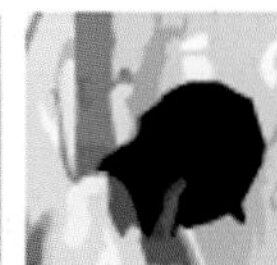

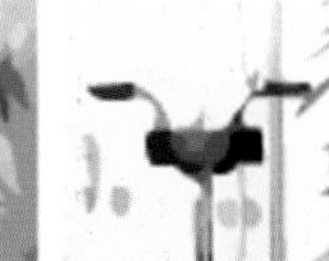
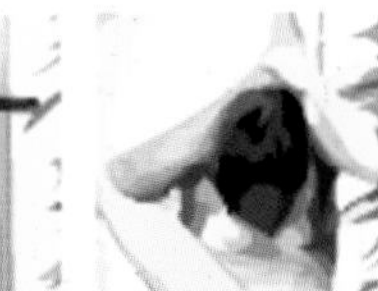

Dress Me Up is a charming example of nylonmag.com's interactivity. Illustrated by Heather Hernon, this virtual doll can be dressed up in pieces from designers as varied as Prada and Eley Kishimoto. The series is from Nylon 4.

Opposite: Loud and Proud, an editorial feature from Nylon 4, was photographed by Marcelo Krasilcic and features graphic clothing by Junya Wantanabe, modelled by Juliana McCarthy.

ALL CLOTHING BY
COMMES DES GARCONS,
NECKLACE BY BLESS.

ALL CLOTHING BY
COMMES DES GARCONS.

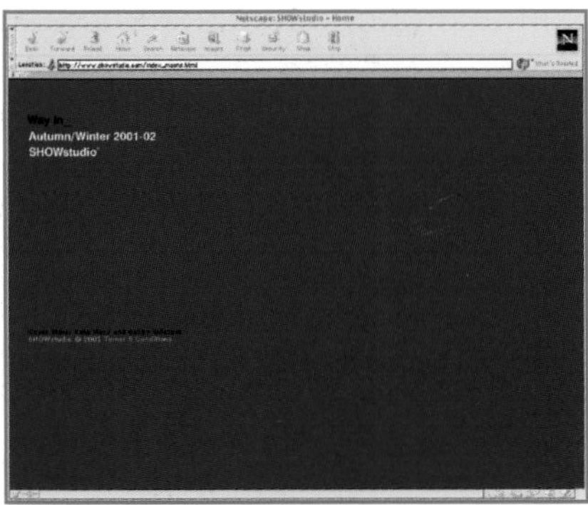

On SHOWstudio the Web page is a blank canvas, an invitation to creativity. Founded by photographer Nick Knight, the site defines itself as a 'pioneering fashion multimedia workshop that invites creatives from the fields of fashion, design, music and the visual arts to make new work for its online group show'. The site is unlike any other in that it is a virtual ground zero, founded by, and featuring the work of, the insiders who create the fashion and fashion images followed by the rest of the media. Moreover, on SHOWstudio, fashion – which 'is about speed of change', according to Knight – is united with new technologies in ways that capture uniquely the 'immediacy' of fashion.

# www.showstudio.com

SHOWstudio is a pioneering fashion multimedia workshop that invites creatives from the fields of **fashion, design, music** and the **visual arts** to make new work for its online group show.

**SHOWstudio**©

**Home** | About | Site Guide | Contact | Requirements | FAQ+Help

**Now Showing**
Latest projects Autumn 2001

**Archive**
Browse past projects

**Coming Up**
Forthcoming projects and events

**Shop**
Limited edition box set

**e-Mailing List**
Subscribe to our e-mail newsletter

**Resources**
Links, contacts and artist profiles

**Now Showing**

**Angel**
**Nick Knight/Alexander McQueen/ Björk/Danny Brown**
Spellbinding sound and image project generated from Nick Knight and Alexander McQueen's installation for *La Beauté* in Avignon, with an exclusive Björk soundtrack.
Texts + Image Download + Movie + Documentary + Interactive

**Stormtrooper In Drag**
**Jason Evans**
This is not a love song. Jason Evans dresses up to test the parameters of identity and propriety.
Movie + Text

**Mackness Test**
Whereas the Rorschach test reveals aspects of the personality by asking patients to describe configurations of inkblots, The Mackness Test unlocks the key components of your character and generates the visual imprint of your psyche.
Test + Results

**Pagan Poetry**
**Björk/Nick Knight/Insert Silence/ Paul Barnes**

**SHOWstudio**©

Home

014 GIVENCHY COUTURE  Movie

## GIVENCHY COUTURE

**PHOTOGRAPHY Nick Knight**
**STYLING Katy England at Smile**
**LIGHTS SUITS by Alexander McQueen for Givenchy Autumn/Winter 2000 Haute Couture**

FILM & SOUND EDIT Adam Mufti
MODEL Kim Iglinsky at Storm & Eleanore at IMG Models
HAIR Sam McKnight at Premier
MAKE-UP Val Garland at Untitled
MANICURIST Natalie Collins for Amalgamated Talent

Shot at Metro Studios, London

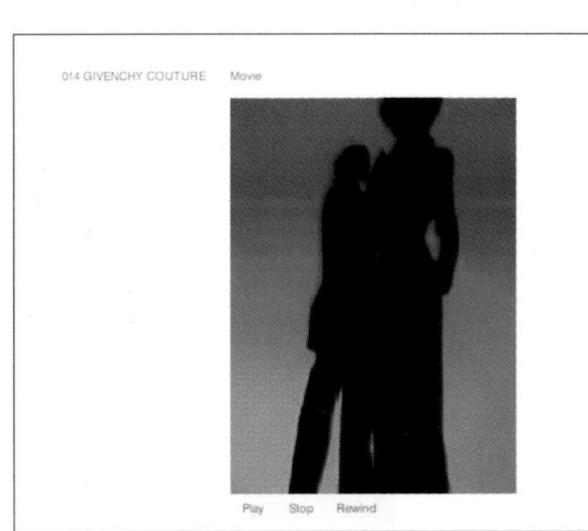

Givenchy Couture is a collaborative project between Nick Knight and Alexander McQueen that offers an abstract and contemporary take on haute couture, fashion's oldest and most elite institution. The addition of Web animation and cinematic lighting creates a product that forces the viewer to abandon any preconceptions of how couture is presented and of the traditional role of photographer and designer.

Right : A detail of Sweet's interactive section. Many of SHOWstudio's shots are conceived with the interactive element and the user/audience in mind.

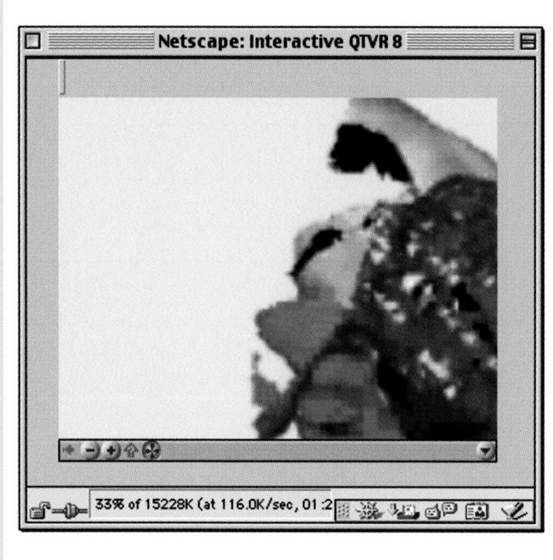


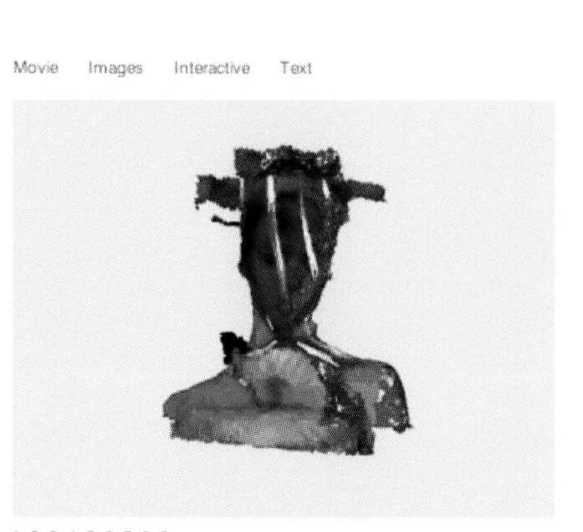

# SWEET

**DIRECTION & 3D PHOTOGRAPHY Nick Knight**
**COSTUMES Jane How at Katy Barker**

ANIMATION DIRECTION Dominic Wright at Createc
HAIR Sam McKnight at Premier
MAKE-UP Val Garland at Untitled
MODELS Viven Solari at Models One, Marleen Berkova at Nathalie
TEXT Susannah Frankel

Animation Production by Peter Martin at Createc
Music written by Adem Ilhan, Kieran Hebden, Samuel Jeffers
Used by kind permission of Universal/MCA Music ltd.

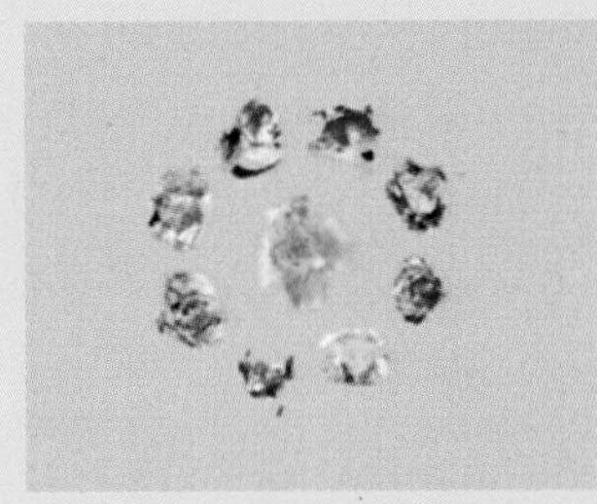

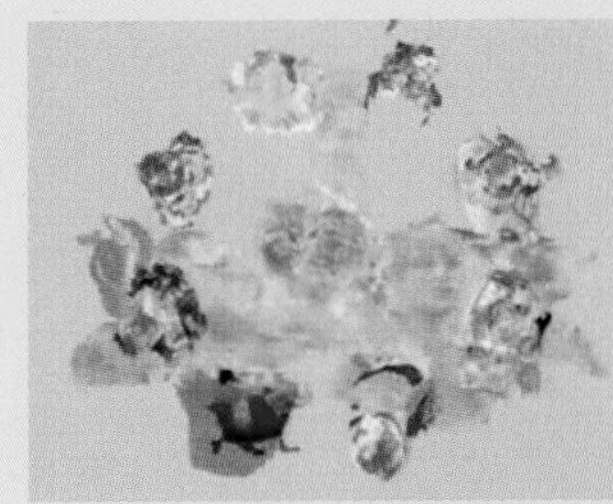

Sweet is a surreal video fantasy created by Nick Knight and Jane How and shot using 3D photography. The video features cupcake-cuties, who swirl and bloom to a soundtrack that is at once eerie and treacle-sweet. Like many SHOWstudio projects, Sweet has several components, including text and an interactive section allowing the manipulation of stills using Quick Time VR technology.

Top and bottom: Stills from the video, which finishes much as it starts, in ring-around-the-roses fashion.

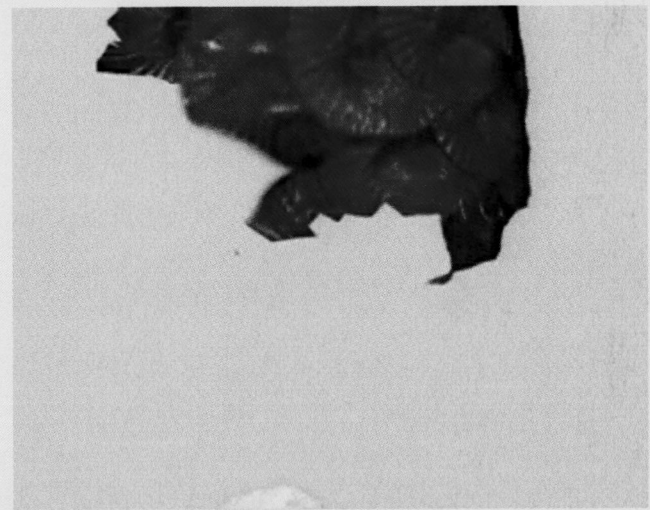

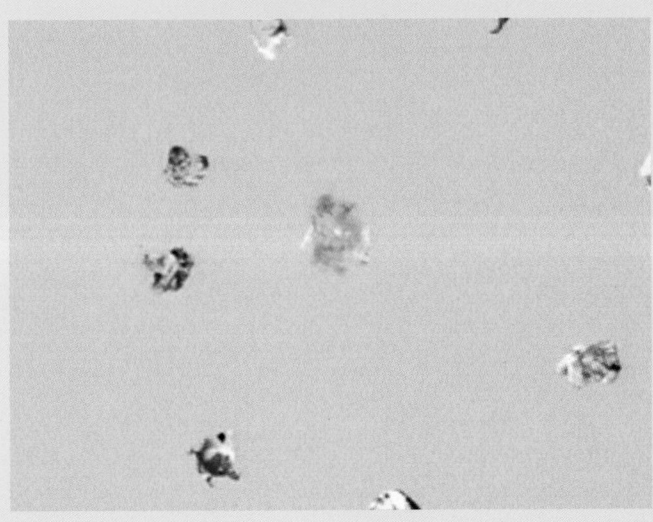

SHOWstudio©

Home

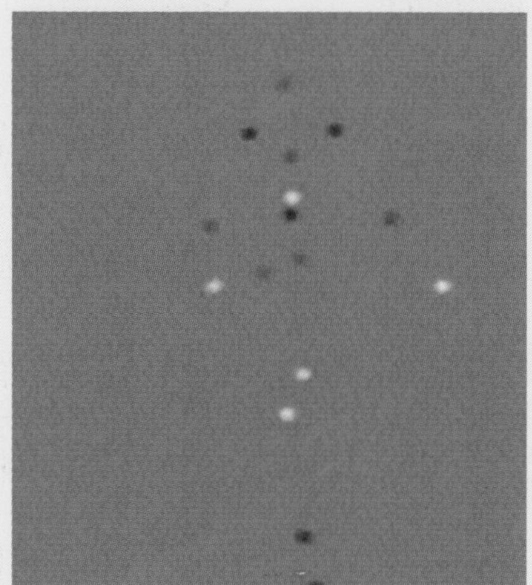

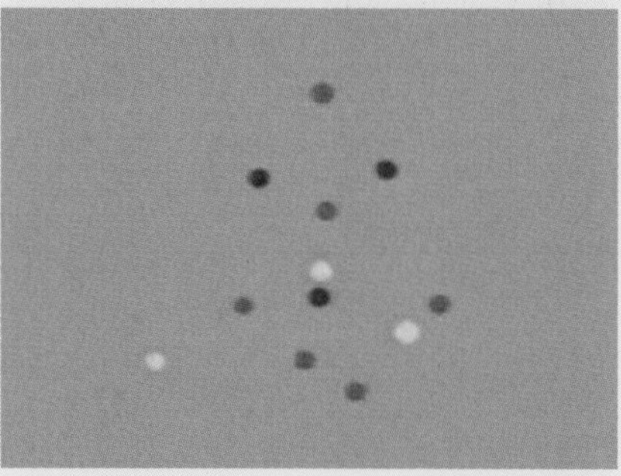

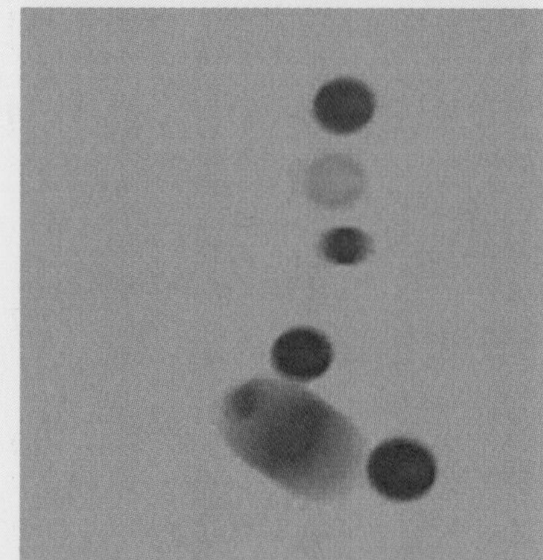

004 J WALK Movie Text

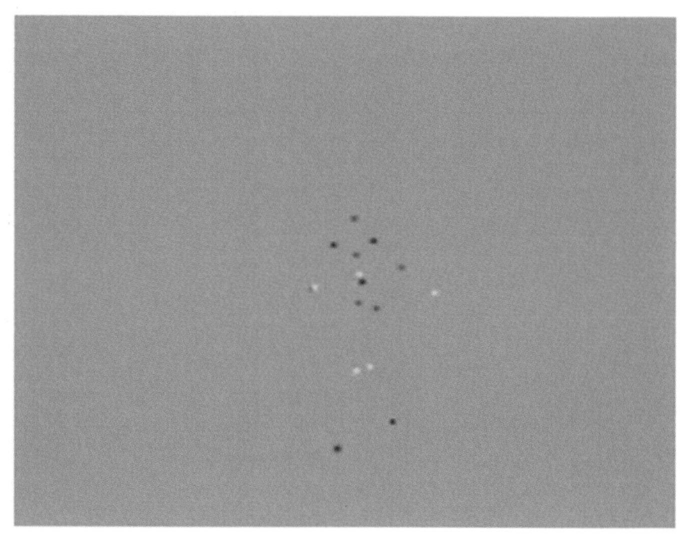

Play Stop Rewind

004 J WALK Movie Text

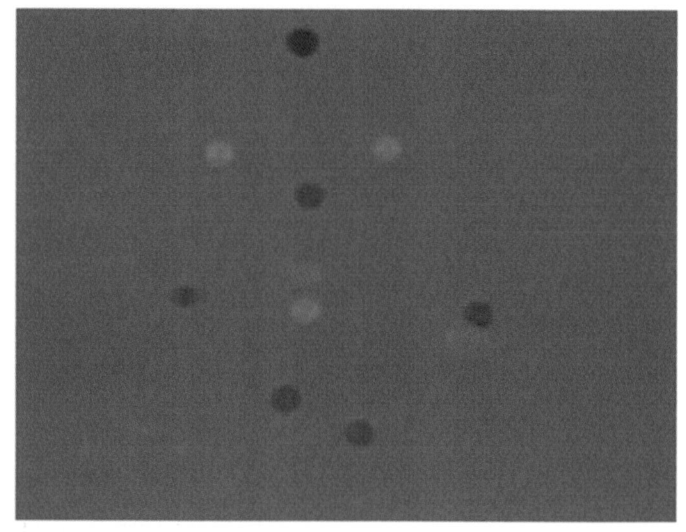

Play Stop Rewind

J. Walk was shot by Nick Knight using a motion capture rig that recorded J. Alexander's walk as he moved in a black body suit, to which dots of white fabric were attached. Alexander is famous for teaching models how to 'walk the walk'. The movie is accompanied by an interview with the charismatic Alexander by Marion Hume.

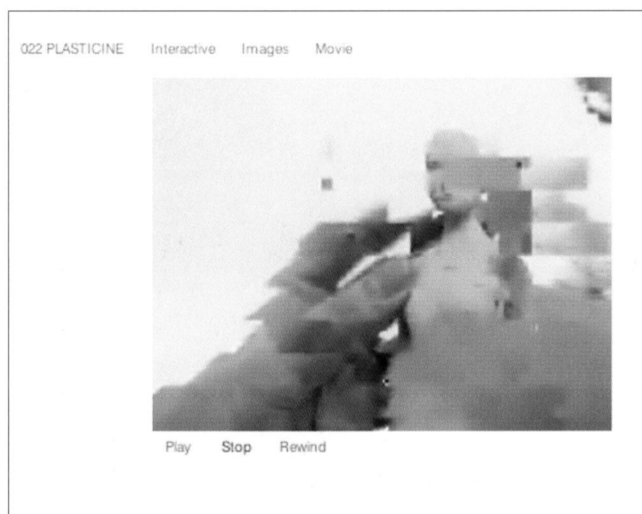

Conceived and directed by Nick Knight, Plasticine features clay figurines by Lone Sigurdsson. On this page are stills from the artful 'behind-the-scenes' movie that shows Sigurdsson in the process of creating the figures.

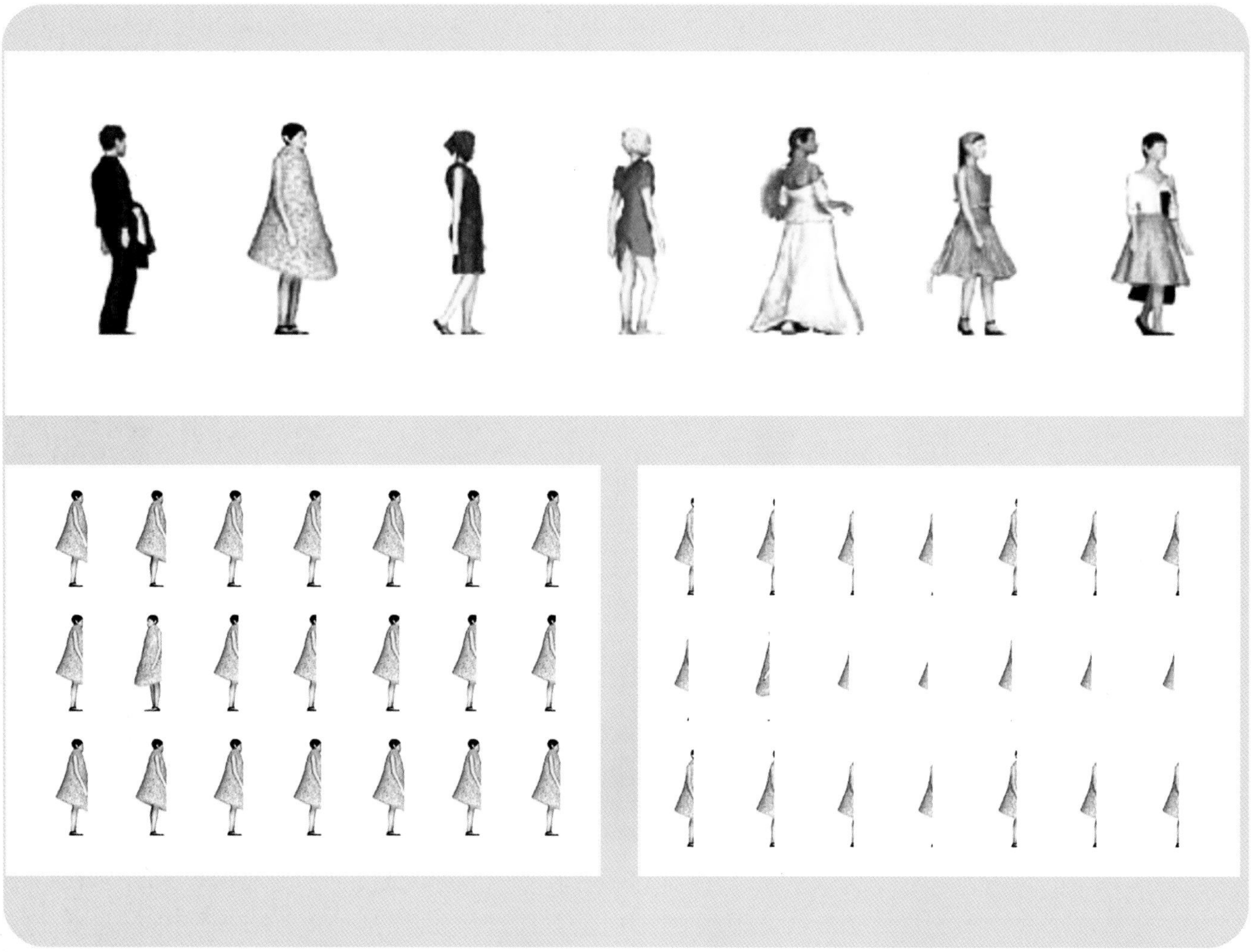

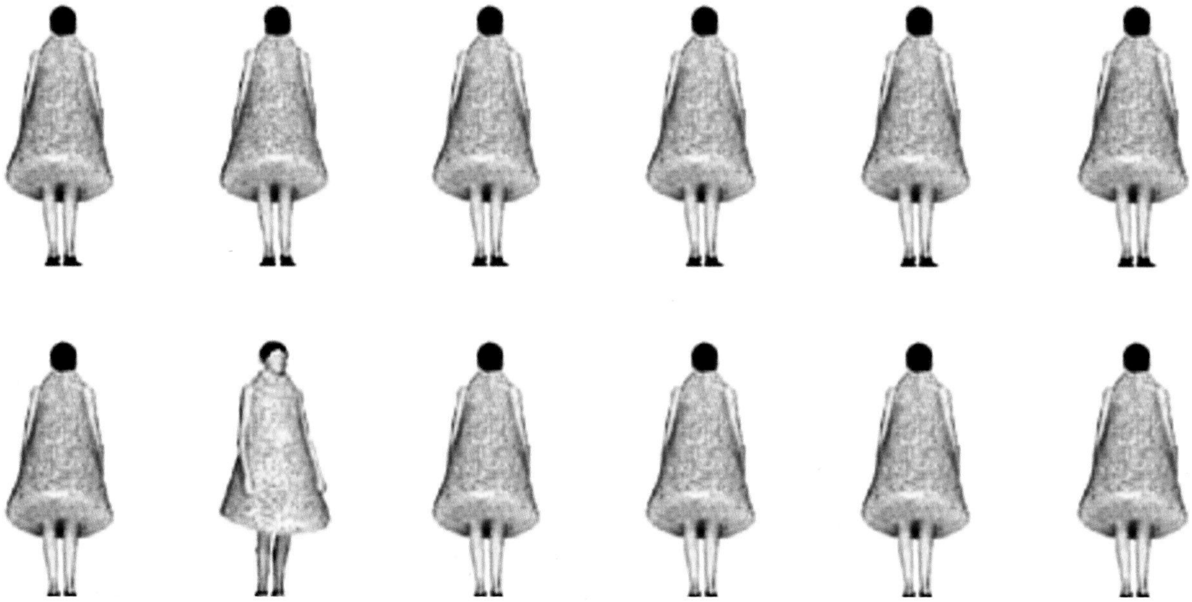

Top left: The complete 'collection' of figurines. The circulation of the model in Hussein Chalayan's pink tulle dress is traced on these pages. Each angle of her top-like 360-degree rotation is captured.

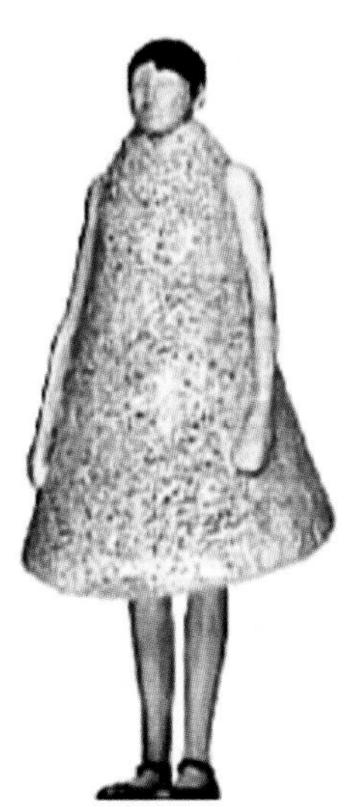

'Fashion shoots are performances', says Nick Knight. Web technologies such as the Web Cam allow SHOWstudio to 'open things up'. On 10 and 11 December 2001 the site staged Sleep, the first ever global, live fashion shoot. Users could log on from midnight to watch fully dressed and styled top models sleep (in real-time) in rooms at the London Metropolitan Hotel. For this, a one-time-only event, intimate stills and video record and preserve moments of the live installation on the site. Knight's shots of elegantly dishevelled and sleeping Storm models Elise Crombez, Natasha Prince, Devon Aoki and Zora Star are shown, from left to right, below.



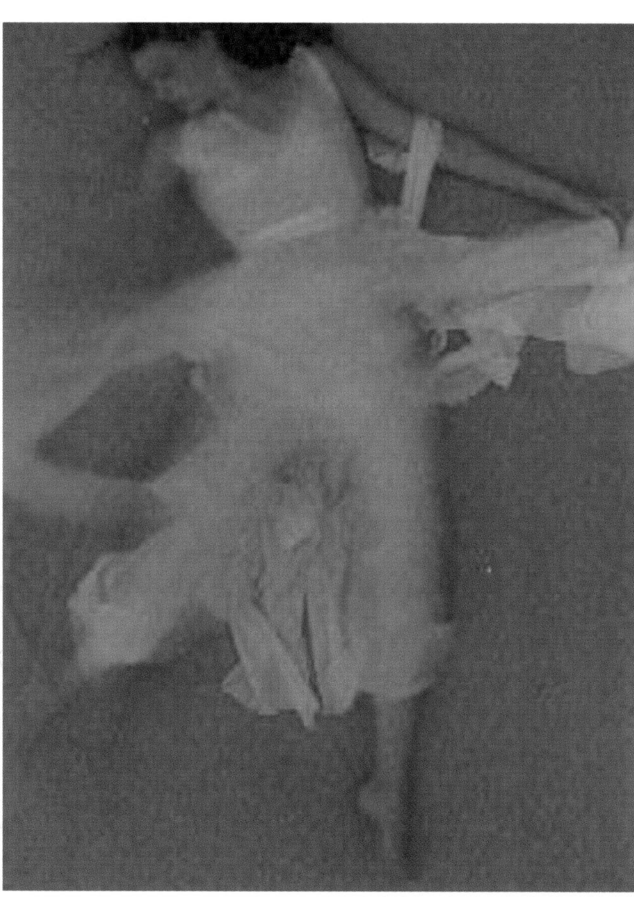

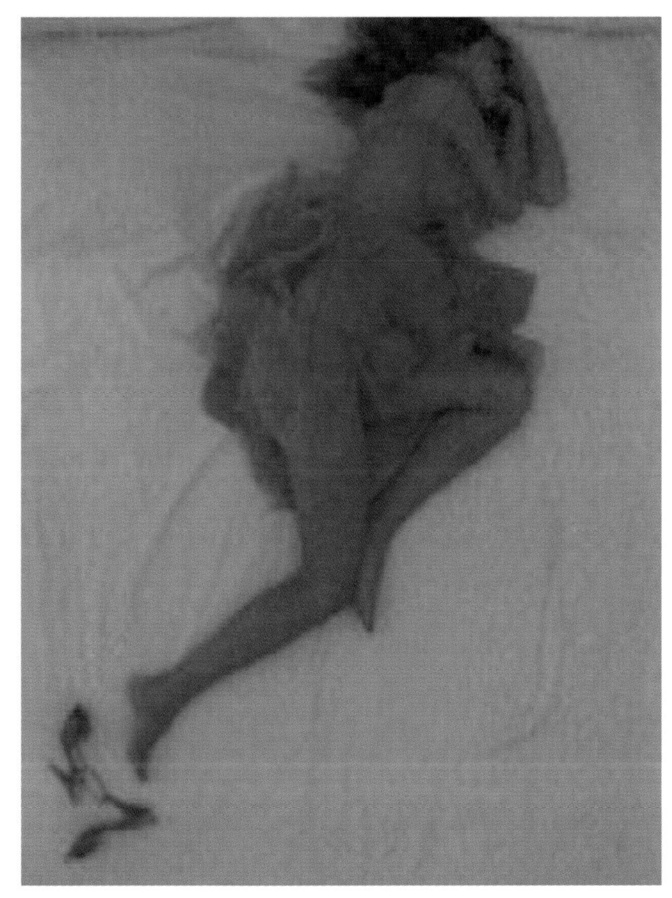

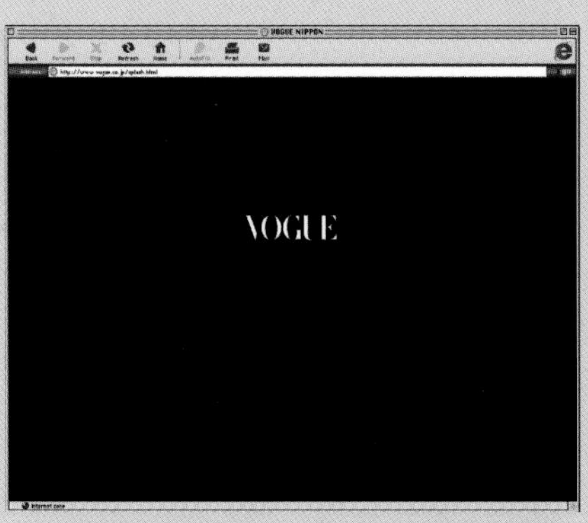


# www.vogue.co.jp

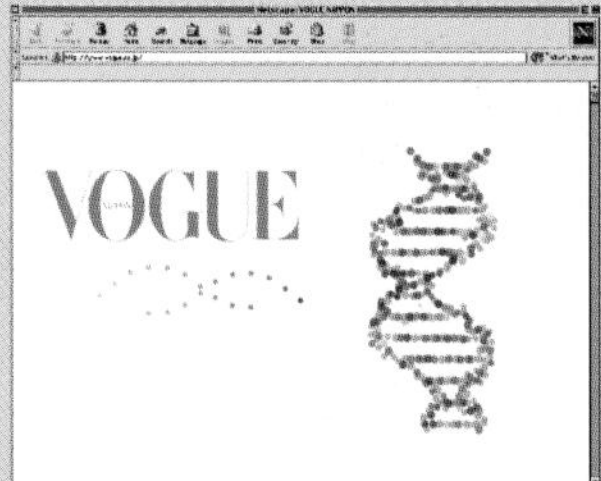


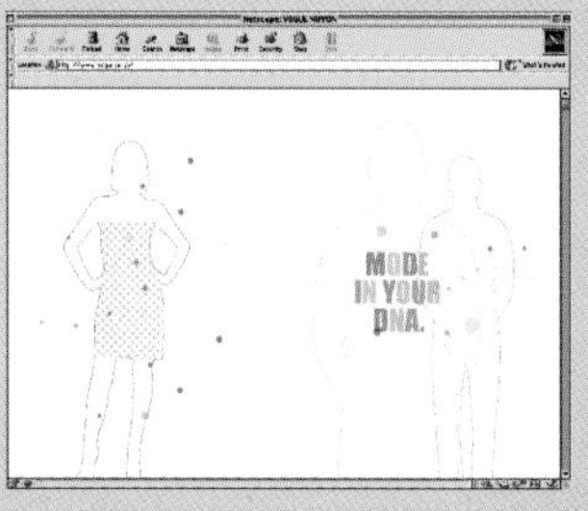


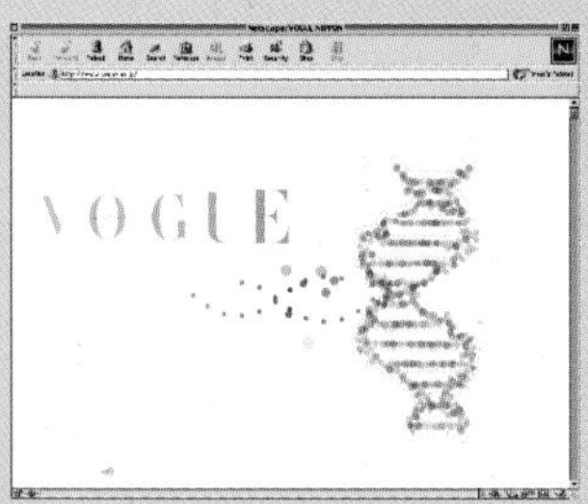


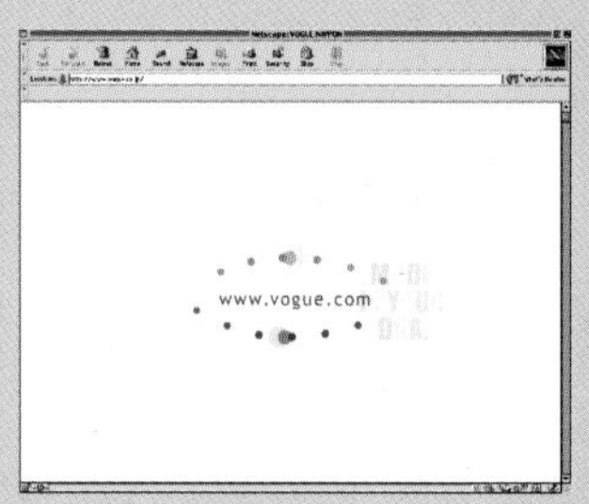


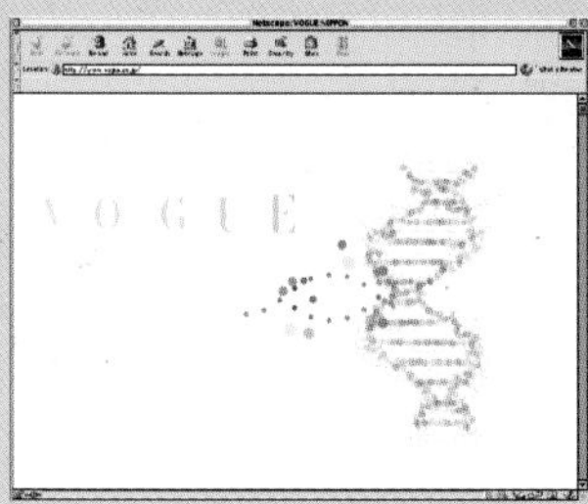

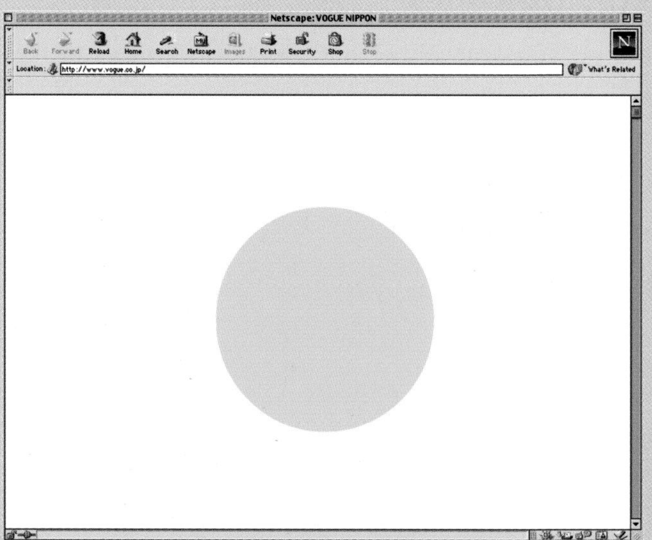


*Mode in your DNA*, the Flash movie that introduces the *Vogue Nippon* site, reinforces the vitality of the *Vogue* brand and its essential association with fashion (from its origin forward), as well as its (new) connection with Japan. A selection of screens is shown at left, moving from a gene helix (top left) to the Japanese flag (above).

The site's contents include fashion show coverage, profiles and lifestyle features, teaser content from the latest issue and a special feature – Experience vogue.com at vogue.co.jp – from which the images in this interactive section are taken. Images from the September 2001 issue of the print magazine are used to introduce: 'New concept: future'.

Right, clockwise from top left: The Feature Top page; the introduction to the Experience section; the introduction in two states, featuring images from Sexy Special, an editorial shot by Raymond Meier featuring model Roos van Bosstraeten from the September 2001 issue.

Vogue.co.jp has the task of introducing *Vogue* – the concept and magazine – to Japan. It exists 'to integrate magazine and Web contents, enabling readers and users to experience the quality of *Vogue Nippon*'. One of its functions is to serve as a 'teaser', luring users to part with their yen and pick up a magazine. The site went live in November 2000 after the launch of the magazine in Japan in September 1999. The designers at Y.K.CondeNet.jp have built an interactive site around the belief that 'the Web is able to let users experience the power, inspiration and energy of fashion, enabling them to explore and find their own style'.

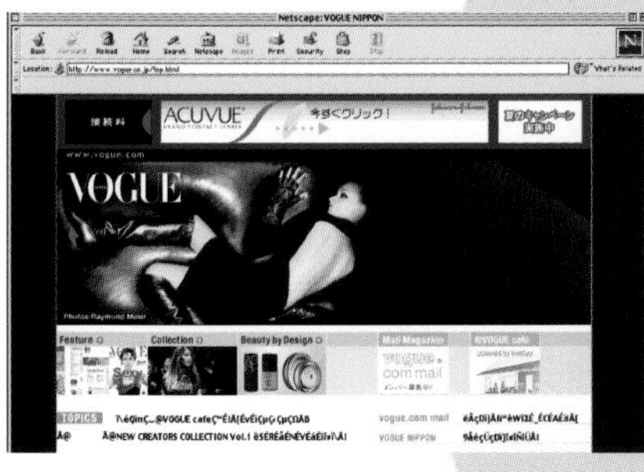


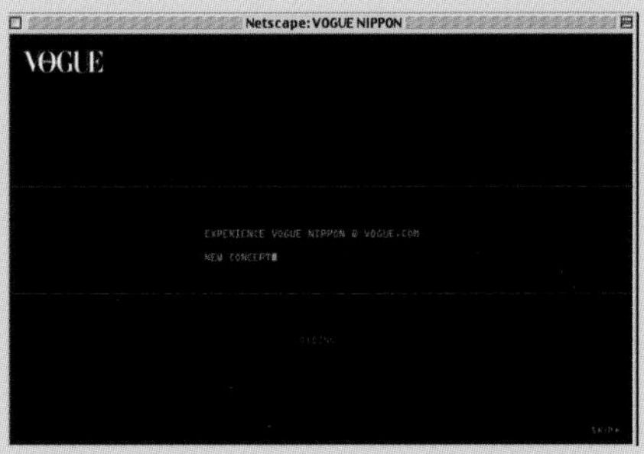

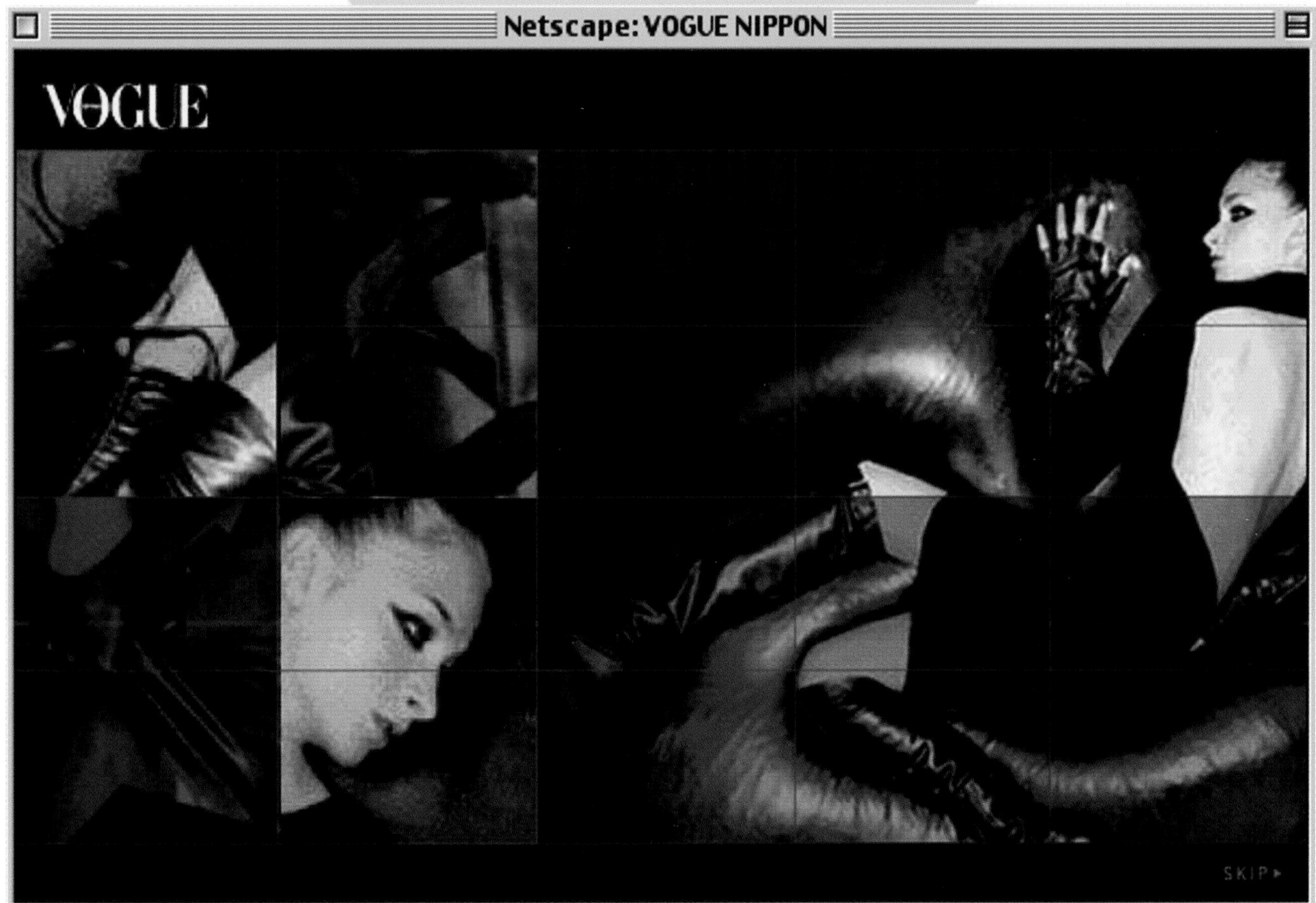

Style, a Flash collage focusing on beauty, seen in a changing state (above) and resolved (right). The images of Guinevere Van Seenus, made up by various make-up artists and shot by Michael Thompson, were taken from an editorial entitled 'What is modern beauty?'

Left: A Flash collage of the She-Vogue! editorial, featuring Christian Dior clothing created by Gogh Imaizumi and hitomi and photographed by Shuichi Maiyama.
Below: Thumbnails of the entire September 2001 issue.

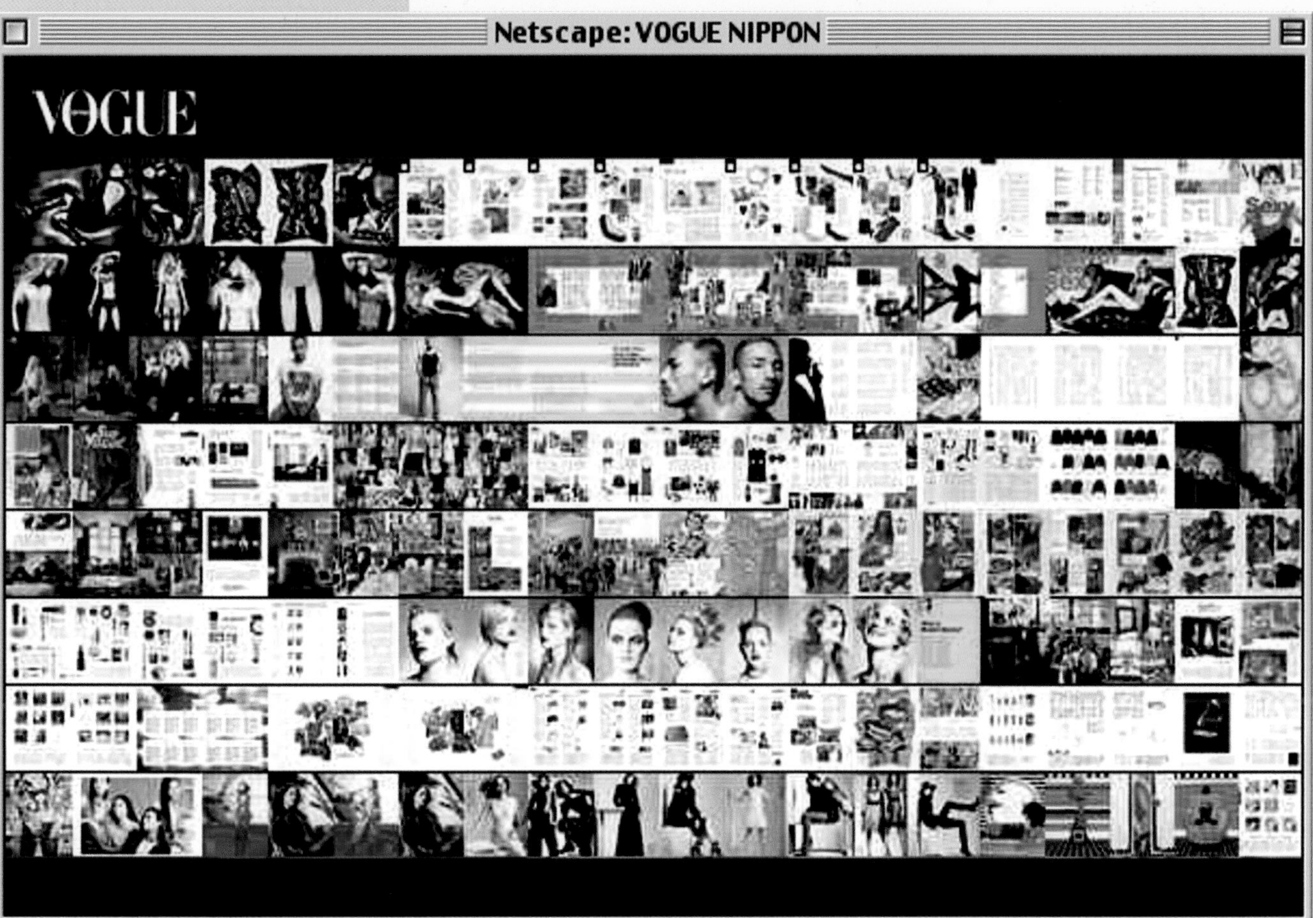

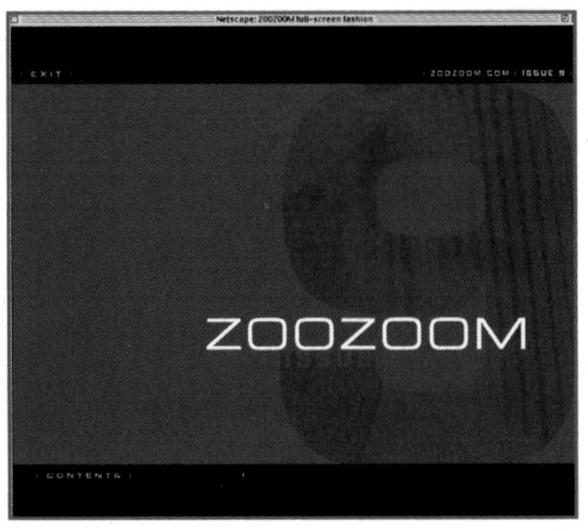

The development of Issue 9's Home page is traced on this page, clockwise from top left. Right: The Home page for Issue 8, displaying ZooZoom's signature overlay navigation with 'TV' screen. It shows that the Bruce story has been selected (pages of which appear below right).

# www.zoozoom.com

| EXIT | ZOOZOOM.COM | ISSUE 9

ZOOZOOM

> full-screen fashion <

| CONTENTS |

ZooZoom 'monitors, records and creates' original and provocative content using 'cutting-edge photography and fine art'. Every issue contains fashion and beauty editorials, designer profiles and art features. Unlike most print magazines, ZooZoom offers the user the opportunity to enjoy 'pure' images, before text, credits and product information are juxtaposed upon them.

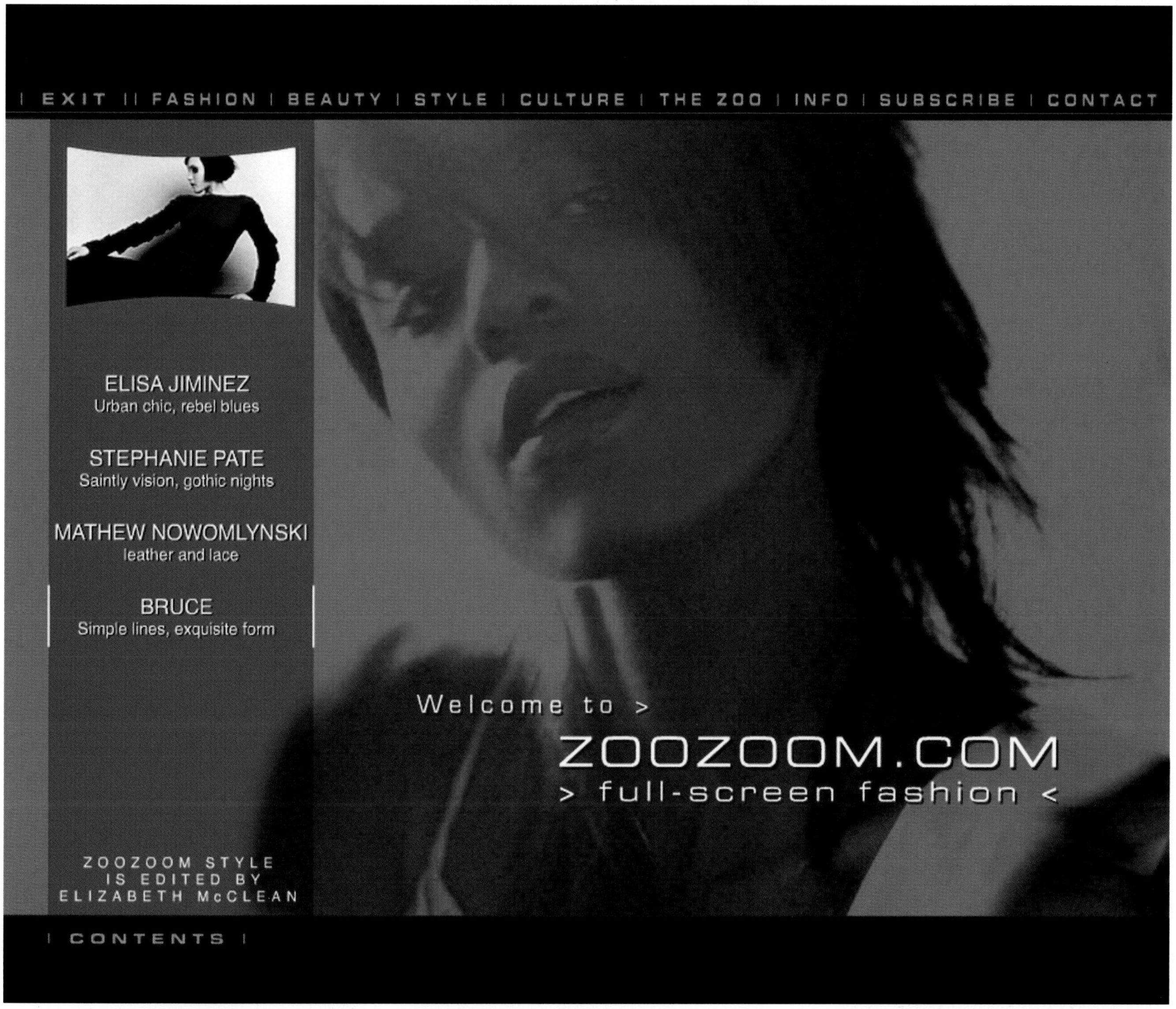

| EXIT || FASHION | BEAUTY | STYLE | CULTURE | THE ZOO | INFO | SUBSCRIBE | CONTACT

ELISA JIMINEZ
Urban chic, rebel blues

STEPHANIE PATE
Saintly vision, gothic nights

MATHEW NOWOMLYNSKI
leather and lace

BRUCE
Simple lines, exquisite form

Welcome to >
ZOOZOOM.COM
> full-screen fashion <

ZOOZOOM STYLE
IS EDITED BY
ELIZABETH McCLEAN

| CONTENTS |

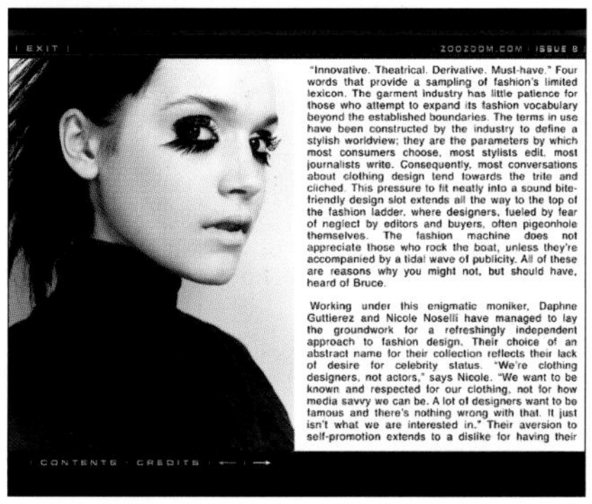


"Innovative. Theatrical. Derivative. Must-have." Four words that provide a sampling of fashion's limited lexicon. The garment industry has little patience for those who attempt to expand its fashion vocabulary beyond the established boundaries. The terms in use have been constructed by the industry to define a stylish worldview; they are the parameters by which most consumers choose, most stylists edit, most journalists write. Consequently, most conversations about clothing design tend towards the trite and cliched. This pressure to fit neatly into a sound bite-friendly design slot extends all the way to the top of the fashion ladder, where designers, fueled by fear of neglect by editors and buyers, often pigeonhole themselves. The fashion machine does not appreciate those who rock the boat, unless they're accompanied by a tidal wave of publicity. All of these are reasons why you might not, but should have, heard of Bruce.

Working under this enigmatic moniker, Daphne Guttierez and Nicole Noselli have managed to lay the groundwork for a refreshingly independent approach to fashion design. Their choice of an abstract name for their collection reflects their lack of desire for celebrity status. "We're clothing designers, not actors," says Nicole. "We want to be known and respected for our clothing, not for how media savvy we can be. A lot of designers want to be famous and there's nothing wrong with that. It just isn't what we are interested in." Their aversion to self-promotion extends to a dislike for having their

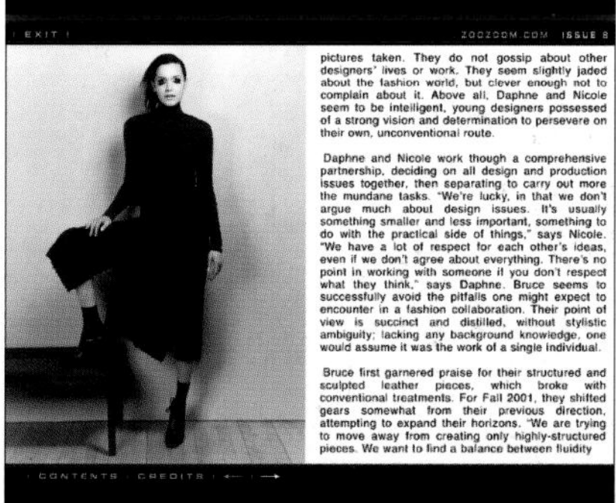


pictures taken. They do not gossip about other designers' lives or work. They seem slightly jaded about the fashion world, but clever enough not to complain about it. Above all, Daphne and Nicole seem to be intelligent, young designers possessed of a strong vision and determination to persevere on their own, unconventional route.

Daphne and Nicole work though a comprehensive partnership, deciding on all design and production issues together, then separating to carry out more the mundane tasks. "We're lucky, in that we don't argue much about design issues. It's usually something smaller and less important, something to do with the practical side of things," says Nicole. "We have a lot of respect for each other's ideas, even if we don't agree about everything. There's no point in working with someone if you don't respect what they think," says Daphne. Bruce seems to successfully avoid the pitfalls one might expect to encounter in a fashion collaboration. Their point of view is succinct and distilled, without stylistic ambiguity; lacking any background knowledge, one would assume it was the work of a single individual.

Bruce first garnered praise for their structured and sculpted leather pieces, which broke with conventional treatments. For Fall 2001, they shifted gears somewhat from their previous direction, attempting to expand their horizons. "We are trying to move away from creating only highly-structured pieces. We want to find a balance between fluidity

Inspected By…, a lingerie editorial photographed by Sabine Liewald, appeared in ZooZoom's eighth issue. One of ZooZoom's unique selling points is the way in which credits are handled. While product information is juxtaposed upon almost all fashion photography in print, on ZooZoom editorial images exist in two states: with and without credits. 'Pure' images are the first to appear in their full-screen glory – sans credits – as below left. When the user clicks to proceed to the next page, credits are juxtaposed upon the 'clean' image. The primacy of the image is thus celebrated and respected. On ZooZoom the image alone creates desire (for information/identification/possession), free from any preconceived associations with labels and price points.

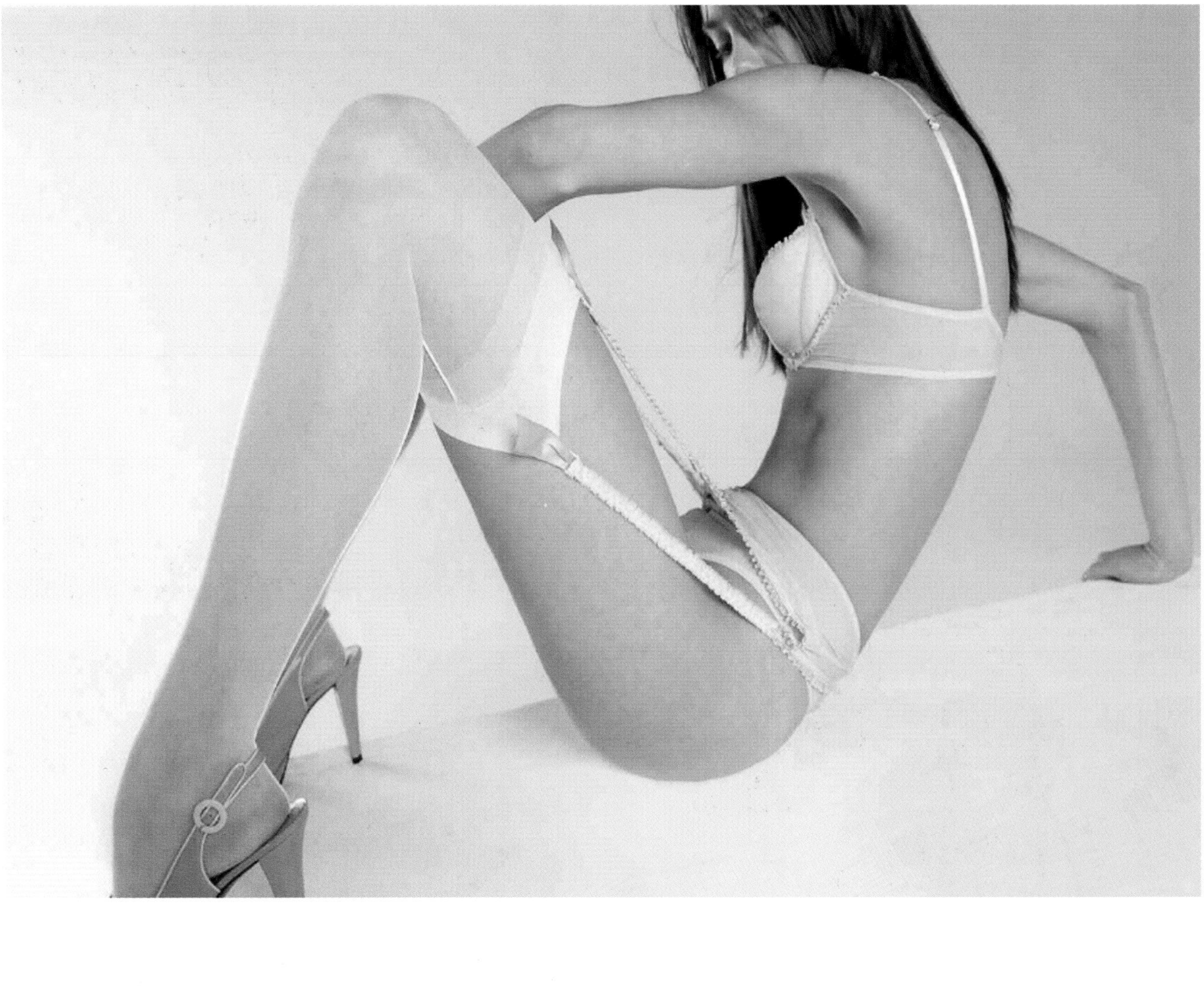

The 'pure' image (left) and with product information (inset).

# take the high road

PHOTOGRAPHY BY KAREN DETRICK

Take the High Road, photographed by Karen Detrick, is a moody road trip of an editorial from ZooZoom's eighth issue.

Detrick's photographs, which emphasize the open expanses of the American road, showcase the advantage of text-free shots. The final page of every editorial lists all members of the creative team. The user can click on any name for contact information, and in many cases can link directly to the creative's e-mail to send a message.

| EXIT | | ZOOZOOM.COM | ISSUE 9 |

take the high road

photography
KAREN DETRICK
fashion editor
SARAH MCGOVERN
makeup
ANDIE MARKOE-BYRNE
hair
MIKI MORI
model
KATE DAVIS
film processing
DIA POSITIVE
color prints
BOND ST PRINT LAB
thanks
DOROTHY COWFIELD
AND CHARLES REIDY

*For contact information please click the artists name above*

*click credits to close*

| CONTENTS | CREDITS | ⟵ | ⟶

These dreamy stills are extracted from a designer profile photographed by Karen Pearson, featuring New York label United Bamboo.

| EXIT |
| ZOOZOOM.COM | ISSUE 9
| CONTENTS | CREDITS | ← | →

## 2FANZINE
**www.2fanzine.com.br**

established: September 2001
location: São Paulo
language: Portuguese
plug-ins: Flash 5, JavaScript enabled browser
designed by: Lucia Dossin
contact: lucia.lugaralgum.com
programmed by: Lucia Dossin
contact:
Praça Franklin Roosevelt 104, ap 51
01303 20 São Paulo SP, Brazil
t: +55 (0)11 3159 4691/ 9762 9857
f: +55 (0)11 3159 4691
e: ludosson@excite.com

pp. 122–5

## A.P.C.
**www.apc.fr**

established: 1996
location: Paris
plug-ins: Flash, Real Player
Languages: French, English and Japanese
e-commerce: International
contact: Rik Bas Backer
e: rikbb@wanadoo.fr
programmed by: Log Access
contact:
39, rue Madame
75006 Paris
t: +33 (0)1 44 39 87 87
f: +33 (0)1 44 39 87 95
e: info@apc.fr

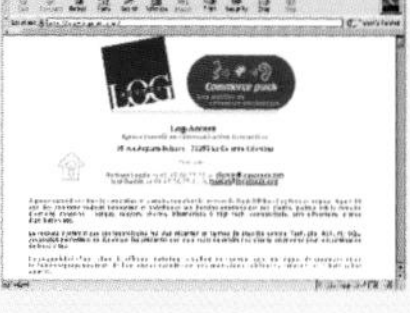

## LOG ACCESS
**www.logaccess.com**

contact:
35, rue Auguste Buisson
92250 La Garenne-Colombes
Paris
t: +33 (0)1 47 86 97 90

pp. 78–81

## ALEXANDRE HERCHCOVITCH
**www.uol.com.br/herchcovitch**

established: 2000
location: São Paulo
languages: Portuguese and English
plug-ins: Flash 5
designed by: Rodrigo Teco and João Paulo Martins at Grafikonstruct
programmed by: Fernando Ballesteros at Grafikonstruct
awards:
Amni Spot
Site of the week, domus.it
Web Design Index, 2001
contact Brazil:
Fanny Oster
Marketing Mix
Rua da consolação, 3367
cj 8182, 01416 001 São Paulo, Brazil
t: +55 (0)11 3088 4493
e: fanny@mktmix.com.br
contact Brazil:
Tânia Otranto
t: +55 (0)11 3167 1544
f: +55 (0)11 3167 2848
e: herchcovitch@uol.com.br
contact Paris:
Kuki de Salvertes-Girault-Totem
t: +33 (0)1 49 23 79 79
f: +33 (0)1 49 23 79 90

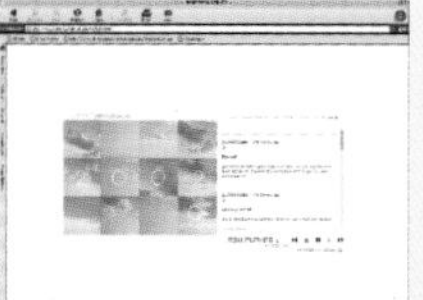

## GRAFIKONSTRUCT
**www.grafikonstruct.com.br**

established: December 1999
location: São Paolo
contact:
Rua Augusta 2445, 6° floor
São Paulo, Brazil
t: +55 (0)11 3088 3179
f: +55 (0)11 3086 2106
e: info@grafikonstruct.com.br

pp. 12–15

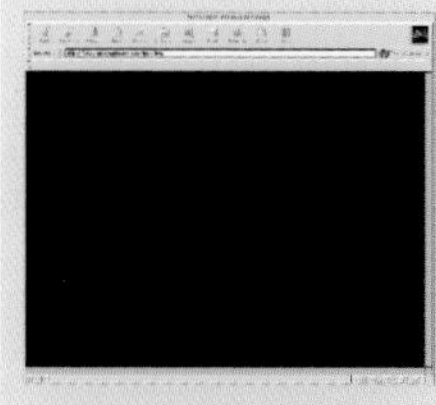

## AMAYA ARZUAGA
**www.amayaarzuaga.com**

established: 2000
location: Spain
languages: Spanish and English
plug-ins: Shockwave
designed by: Quim Nolla
programmed by: Toni Sánchez at Alteraciones
contact England:
Bryan Morel PR
t: +44 (0)20 7437 5654
f: +44 (0)20 7437 5560
e: keith@bryanmorelpr.co.uk
contact Spain:
Mira Bentabol
t: +34 91 308 3783

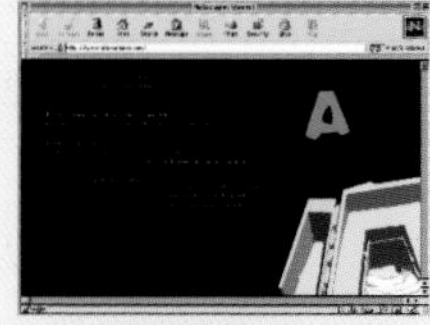

## ALTERACIONES
**www. alteraciones.com**

established: 1999
location: Barcelona
t: +34 93 442 5747
e: toni@alteraciones.com

## QUIM NOLLA

established: 1972
location: Barcelona
contact:
t: +34 93 457 6741
f: +34 93 457 6756
e: quimnolla@eresmas.net

pp. 16-19

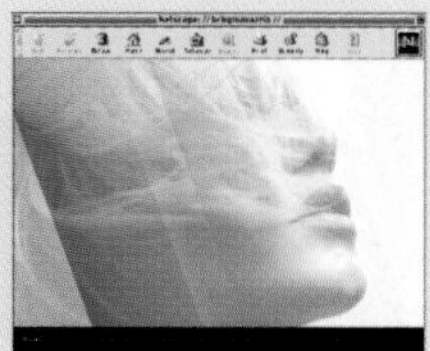

## BCBG MAX AZRIA
**www.bcbg.com**

established: Spring 1997
location: Los Angeles
Language: English
plug-ins: Flash
designed by: Max Azria
programmed by: George Wong, in-house Webmaster
awards: International Web Award, 2000
contact:
BCBG Max Azria
2761 Fruitland Avenue
Vernon, CA 90058, USA
t: +1 213 624 2224
f: +1 323 277 5245
e: www.bcbg.com

pp. 20-5

The site details are in each case above the site designer details, except where sites were designed in-house. In all cases, page references to the discussion of the site in this book are given below the coloured panels.

## CHRISTIAN LACROIX
**www.christian-lacroix.fr**

established: 1998
location: Paris
languages: French and English
plug-ins: Flash, Video Real Player, Video Windows Player
designed by: Anne Lardeur at Aragorn
programmed by: Aragorn
awards: 2000 nomination for the CFDA Best Website Award
contact:
73, rue du Faubourg Saint-Honoré
75008 Paris
t: +33 (0)1 42 68 79 05
f: +33 (0)1 42 68 79 51
e: info@c-lacroix.com

pp. 26–31

## COLETTE
**www.colette.fr**

established: March 1997
location: Paris
languages: French and English
plug-ins: Flash
e-commerce: International
designed by: Nicholas Mir Chaiken, Liz Stirling, James Abramson, Valerie Bellavoine, Phil Wood at SpillNet
programmed by: Nicholas Mir Chaikin, Liz Stirling, James Abramson, Valerie Bellavoine, Phil Wood at SpillNet
contact:
213, rue Saint-Honoré
75001 Paris
t: +33 (0)1 55 35 33 90
f: +33 (0)1 55 35 33 99
e: www.info@colette.tm.fr

pp. 82–5

## COSTUME NATIONAL
**www.costumenational.com**

established: 15 July 1999
location: Milan
language: English
plug-ins: Flash, Shockwave
creative direction: Ennio Capasa
contact: e.capasa@costumenational.com
concept and copywriting: Massimo Torrigiani
contact: massiomo.torrigiani@tiscalinet.it
graphic design: Pino Pipoli and Andrea Zahora at Bigfoot
contact: edmondo@bigfoot.com
music and sound design: Diego Ragini
contact: diego.ragnini@tiscalinet.it
programmed by: Ritram
project coordination: Ilaria Lindholm
contact:
Costume National
Via Mario Fusetti 12
Milan
t: +39 02 838 4420
f: +39 02 838 44252
e: press@costumenational.com

pp. 32–41

## DIOR HOMME
**www.dior.com**

established: January 2001
location: Paris
language: English
plug-ins: Latest Shockwave with a minimal screen resolution of 800x600 in true colour mode
designed by: Hedi Slimane and the Dior Homme Web Team
programmed by: Dior Homme Web Project
contact:
Dior Homme
40, rue François 1er
75008 Paris

pp. 42–5

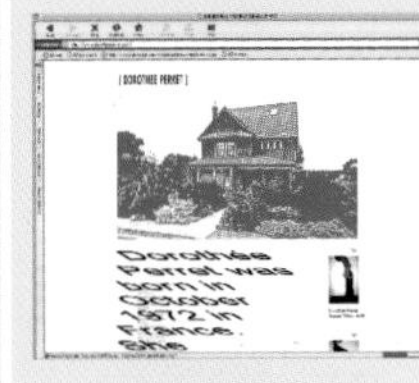

## DOROTHÉE PERRET
**www.dorotheeperret.com**

established: March 2000
location: Paris
language: English
plug-ins: Flash and Real Audio
designed by: The Lonely Line
programmed by: Jean-François Lepage at The Lonely Line
contact:
e: webmaster@dorotheeperret.com
e: dorothee@dorotheeperret.com

pp. 46–9

## DRESSLAB
**www.dresslab.com**

established: February 2000
location: Barcelona
languages: Spanish and English
plug-ins: Flash, Shockwave, Quicktime, Windows Media Player
designed by: Idoia Zubia, Tomas Melinder
programmed by: Toni Rufo, Carles Mezquita, Pedro Mellinas
stylist: Begonia Berges
contact:
Funky Lab, BCN, S.A.
Ramon Turr-100, 6-2
08005 Barcelona
t: +34 93 211 1616
f: +34 93 211 1158
e: talk@dresslab.com

pp. 126–31

## ARAGORN
**www.aragorn.fr**

established: December 1999
location: Paris
contact:
85, Avenue Emile Zola
Paris
t: +33 (0)1 30 88 31 79
f: +33 (0)1 30 86 21 06
e: info@aragorn.fr

## SPILLNET
**www.spillnet.com**

established: 1995
location: Paris and New York
contact:
Spill Europe
34 rue du Sentier
75002 Paris
t: +33 (0)1 44 88 51 33
f: +33 (0)1 44 88 51 32
e: paris@spill.net

Spill USA
391 Broadway
New York, NY 10013
t: +1 212 625 8445
f: +1 212 625 0475
e: nyc@spill.net

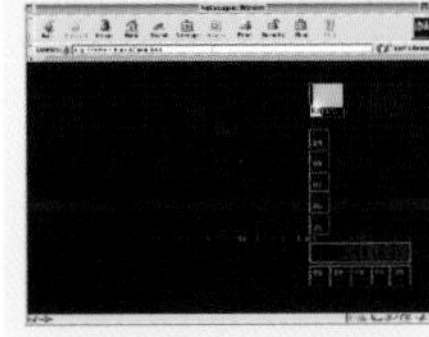

## RITRAM
**www.ritram.it**

contact:
via Marconi 457
40010 Bentivoglio, Bologna
Italy
t: +39 051 664 0932
f: +39 051 664 0938
e: info@ritram.it

## THE LONELY LINE
**www.thelonelyline.com**

established: January 2001
location: Paris
contact:
t: +33 (0)6 77 74 14 57
e: jf@thelonelyline.com

## LAB072
**www.lab072.com**

established: 2000
location: Barcelona
contact:
Ramon Turr-100, 6-2
08005 Barcelona
t: +34 93 211 1616
f: +34 93 211 1158
e: talk@dresslab.com

**ELUXURY**
**www.eluxury.com**

established: June 2000
location: San Francisco
e-commerce: USA only
language: English
plug-ins: Flash, Viewpoint, Zoom
art directed by: Alex Gonzalez of AR Media
awards:
Accessories Council's 2001 Best Accessories Website
Forbes.com Magazine Summer 2001 Best of Web
Webby Awards nominee for Best Fashion Website, 2001
Yahoo January 2002 issue names eluxury.com as the Best Fashion Destination Website

**JOHN GALLIANO**
**www.johngalliano.com**

established: January 2002
location: Paris
language: English
plug-ins: Flash
designed by: Mother
programmed by: Mother
contact:
Mesh Chibber
60 rue d'Avron
75020 Paris
t: +33 (0)1 55 25 11 11
f: +33 (0)1 55 25 11 13

**MOTHER**
**www.mother.fr**

established: June 2000
location: Paris
awards:
Art directors Club Awards, 2001
Webby nomination, 2001
contact:
Helena de Signori, CEO
Nicolas Krenner, Creative Art Director
16 rue de Montmorency
75003 Paris
t: +33 (0)1 44 61 86 06
f: +33 (0)1 44 61 86 07
e: gael@mother.fr

pp. 86–9

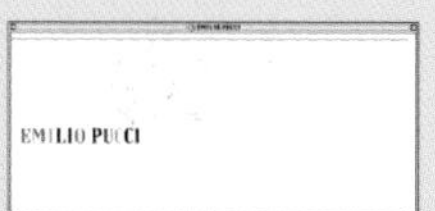

**EMILIO PUCCI**
**www.emiliopucci.com**

established: August 2001
location: Florence
language: English
plug-ins: Flash
e-commerce: through eLUXURY.com (US only)
designed by: DigitalForm
programmed by: DigitalForm
contact:
Palazzo Pucci
Via de Pucci 6
50122 Florence
t: +39 055 261841
f: +39 055 280451

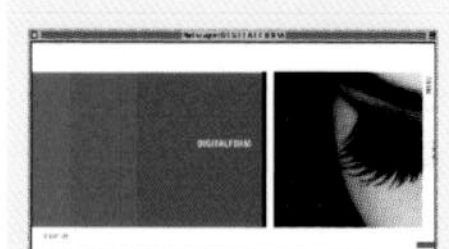

**DIGITALFORM**
**www.digitalform.com**

established: 1997
location: New York
contact:
DigitalForm
584 Broadway, Suite 1201
New York, NY 10012
t: +1 212 677 4321
f: +1 212 677 3334
e: info@digitalform.com

pp. 50–5

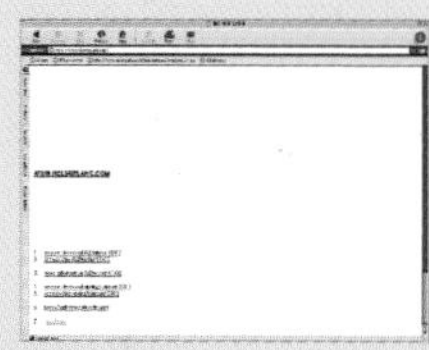

**HELMUT LANG**
**www.helmutlang.com**

established: July 2000
location: New York
language: English
designed by: Corsis
programmed by: Corsis
contact:
80 Greene Street
New York, NY 10012
t: +1 212 334 1014
f: +1 212 334 1950

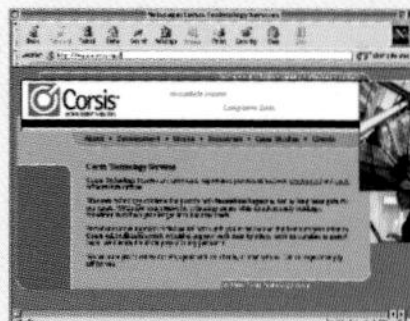

**CORSIS**
**www.corsis.com**

established: 1993
location: New York
contact:
121 West 27th Street, Suite 201
New York, NY 10001
t: +1 917 661 0200
f: +1 917 661 0230
e: info@corsis.com

pp. 56–9

**HINTMAG**
**www.hintmag.com**

established: April 1998
location: New York
language: English
designed by: Lee Carter
programmed by: Lee Carter
awards:
Ellie Award for General Excellence on line, 2001
Winner 5th Annual Webby Awards Best Fashion Website, 2001
contact:
134 Tenth Avenue, #2
New York, NY 10011
t: +1 212 645 0556
f: +1 212 675 6514
e: leecarter@hintmag.com

pp. 132–5

**I LOVE COLETTE**
**www.ilovecolette.com**

established: September 2000
location: Paris
language: English
designed by: Craig Robinson at Flip Flop Flyin'
programmed by: Craig Robinson at Flip Flop Flyin'
contact:
213, rue Saint-Honoré
75001 Paris
t: +33 (0)1 55 35 33 90
f: +33 (0)1 55 35 33 99
e: www.info@colette.tm.fr

**FLIP FLOP FLYIN'**
**www.flipflopflyin.com**

established: May 1999
location: Berlin
contact:
e: craig@flipflopflyin.com

pp. 90–5

**IT FASHION**
**www.itfashion.com**

established: January 1999
location: Barcelona
languages: Spanish and English
plug-ins: Flash
designed by: Estel Vilaseca, Estel Munné, Mireia Sabanés
programmed by: Estel Vilaseca
contact:
C/Códols n°27 pral. 2a
08002 Barcelona
t: +34 (0)6 58 88 1628/(0)6 66 24 6639
e: postmaster@itfashion.com

pp. 136–41

## KIRNA ZÂBETE
**www.kirnazabete.com**

established: Fall 1999
location: New York
language: English
plug-ins: Flash 4
designed by: Tim Miller and Paris Fleezanis at Engine Three
programmed by: Tim Miller and Paris Fleezanis at Engine Three
awards:
Nominee for the 5th Annual Webby Awards Best Fashion Website, 2001
Winner, Print Magazine's Interaction 2001 Interactive Design Annual
contact:
96 Greene Street
New York, NY 10012
t: +1 212 941 9656
f: +1 212 941 5098
e: info@kirnazabete.com

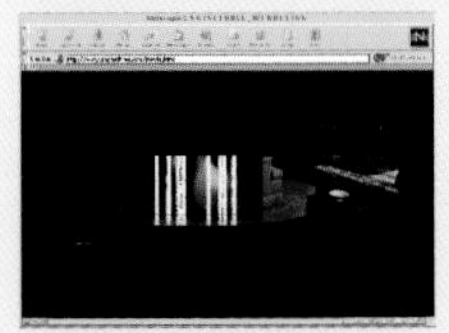

## ENGINE THREE
**www.enginethree.com**

established: 1998
location: New York
contact:
66 West Broadway
New York, NY 10007
t: +1 212 732 9520
e: info@enginethree.com

pp. 96–9

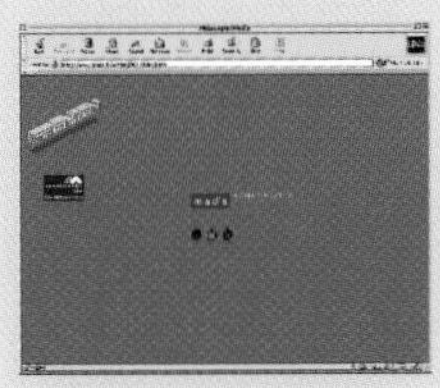

## MAD'S
**www.mads.it**

established: May 2000
location: Verona
languages: Italian and English
plug-ins: Shockwave
designed by: Art directed by Giuliano Garonzi and designed by Alessandro Nicolis at Happycentro+ Sintetik
programmed by: Roberto Comuniello, Stefano Anselmi and Paolo Tezza at Happycentro +Sintetik
awards: Macromedia site of the week, July 2000 and October 2001
contact:
Feeling S.p.A.
Via E. Natta, 40
37026 Z.I. Settimo di Pescatina
Verona, Italy
t: +39 045 676 0676
f: +39 045 676 0678
e: feeling@mads.it

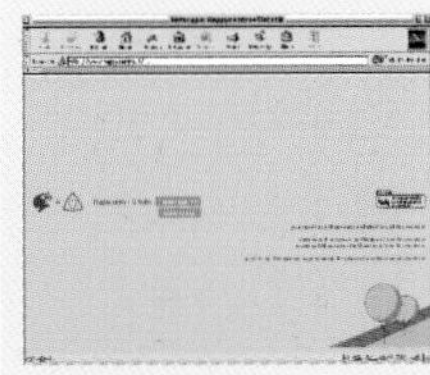

## HAPPYCENTRO +SINTETIK
**www.sintetik.it**

### HAPPYCENTRO
established: February 1998
location: Verona
contact:
t: +39 045 505 993
f: +39 045 823 2552
e: info@happycentro.com

### SINTETIK
established: January 1999
location: Verona
contact:
t: +39 045 820 2272
f: +39 045 823 2552
e: info@sintetik.com

pp. 60–3

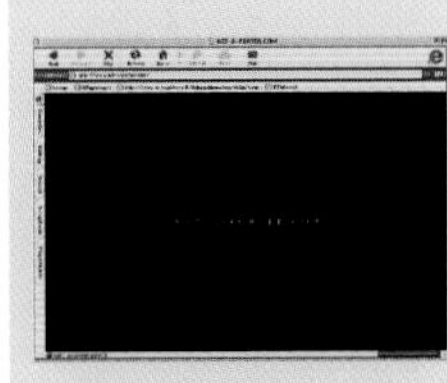

## NET-A-PORTER
**www.net-a-porter.com**

launched: 10 June 2000
established: 5 August 1999
location: London
languages: English and Japanese
e-commerce: Global
designed by: All design over-seen by Megan Quinn-Newall
programmed by: In-house
awards: Glamour's 2002 Award for Service to Glamorous Internet Shopping
contact:
e: editors@net-a-porter.com

pp. 100–5

## NYLON
**www.nylonmag.com**

established: April 2000
location: New York
language: English
creative direction: Marvin Scott Jarrett
designed & programmed by: Flashlight Media
web designer: Midoria Hamada
web designer: Allin Chung
technical lead: Jason Thaxter
techincal consultant: Jude Flannery
producer: Willy Somma
contact:
394 West Broadway, Fl. 2
New York, NY 10012
t: +1 212 226 6454
f: +1 212 226 7738

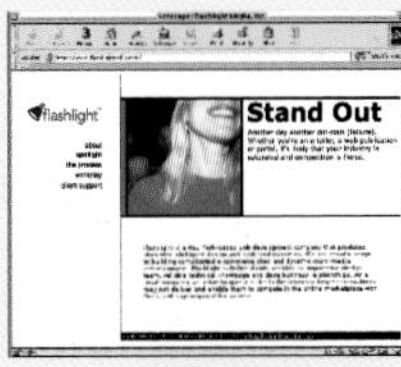
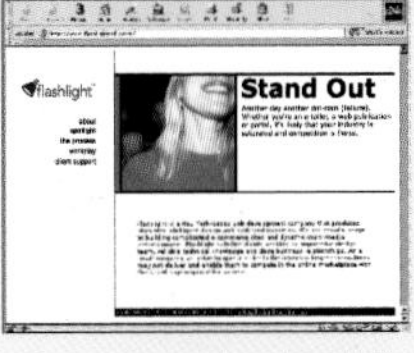


## FLASHLIGHT MEDIA
**www.flashlightmedia.com**

established: April 1999
location: New York
contact:
16 Warren Street
New York, NY 10007
t: +1 917 374 3262
e: wsomma@flashlightmedia.com
e: info@flashlightmedia.com

pp. 142–7

## PLEATS PLEASE
**www.pleatsplease.com**

established: October 1999
location: New York
language: English
plug-ins: Flash 5
designed by: Sayuri Studio, Inc.
flash programmed by: Nelson Wong and Sayuri Shoji
html programmed by: Antonio Cruz
awards:
CFDA Most Stylish.com
Communication Arts Annual
ID Magazine's Interactive Prize
New York Type Director's Club Annual
contact:
Andre Wiesmayr
Issey Miyake USA Corp.
119 Hudson Street
New York, NY 10013
t: +1 212 226 1334
f: +1 212 428 6709
e: info@pleatsplease.com

pp. 64–9

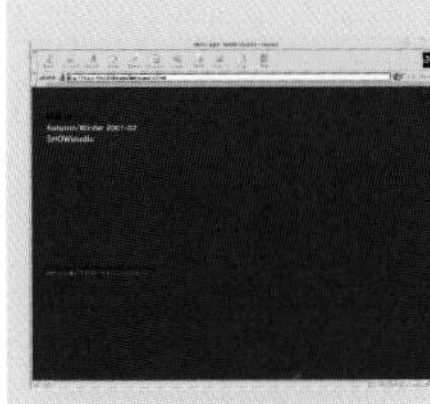

## SHOWSTUDIO
**www.showstudio.com**

established: 27 November 2000, 7:23 pm
location: London
language: English
plug-ins: Flash 5, Shockwave
designed by: Paul Hetherington
contact: paul@showstudio.com
programmed by: Derek Michael
contact: derek@showstudio.com
e-commerce: Yes, International
awards: Dazed and Confused, Top 100 Sites
contact:
SHOWstudio
Export House
25–31 Ironmonger Row
London EC1V 3QN
e: mail@showstudio.com

pp. 148–57

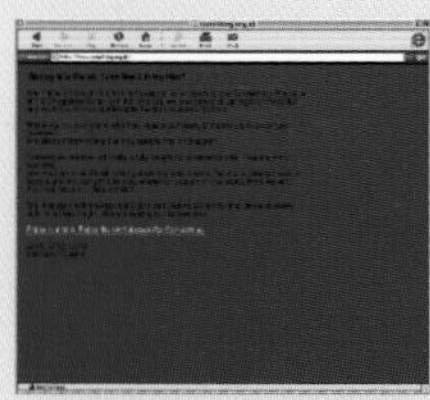

**SOMETHING**
**www.something.org.uk**

established: July 2000
location: London
language: English
plug-ins: Flash
designed by: Marc Hare, Selene Allen, Gareth Parkinson, Paul Bruty and Lee Glasspool
programmed by: Gareth Parkinson at Publicland
contact:
1-3 Chepstow Road
London W2 5BL
t: +44 (0)20 7229 9944
f: +44 (0)20 7229 9696
e: mail@something.org.uk

**PUBLICLAND**
**www.publicland.co.uk**

established: 1 January 2001
location: London
contact:
Public
United House
North Road
London N7 9DP
t: +44 (0)20 7607 5500
f: +44 (0)20 7607 6633
e: hello@publicland.co.uk

pp. 106–11

**SOWEAR**
**www.sowear.com**

established: February 2000
location: New York
e-commerce: USA
language: English
plug-ins: Flash
designed by: Jason Yang
programmed by: Jason Yang
contact:
Jason Yang
635 East 6th Street, 1B
New York, NY 10009
t: +1 212 677 2257
e: jyang@sowear.com

pp. 112–15

**STYLE**
**www.style.com**

established: 18 September 2000
location: New York
language: English
designed: In-house
programmed: In-house
contact:
CondéNet
4 Times Square, Fl. 17
New York, NY 10036
t: +1 212 286 3700
f: +1 212 286 5974
e: feedback@style.com

pp. 116–19

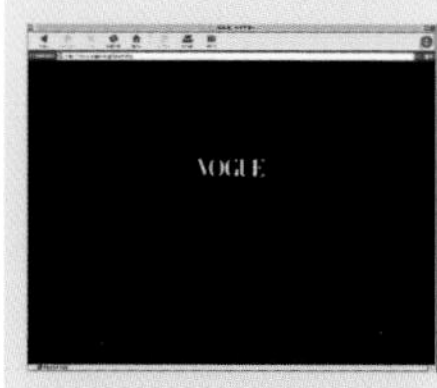


**VOGUE NIPPON**
**www.vogue.co.jp**

established: 28 November 2000
location: Tokyo
language: Japanese
plug-ins: Flash 4, Real Player
designed by: Y.K.CondeNet.jp
senior web editor: Ritsuko Hotta
web coordinator: Yoko Arai
programmed by: DOE Co. Ltd.
contact:
Y.K.CondeNet.jp
Osuga Bldg. 3F, 2-11-8 Shibuya
Shibuya-ku, Tokyo 150-0002
t: +81 (0)3 5485 9150
f: +81 (0)3 5766 3010
e: mail@vogue.co.jp

**DOE CO. LTD.**
**www.doe.co.jp**

contact:
Tosei Bldg., 1-8-8 Kanda Ogawamachi
Chiyoda-ku, Tokyo 101-0052
t: +81 (0)3 3257 0861
f: +81 (0)3 3257 0862
e: info@doe.co.jp

pp. 158–61

**XULY.BËT**
**www.xuly-bet.com**

established: February 1999
location: France
language: French
plug-ins: Flash Player
designed by: Human Technology and the Xuly.Bët team
programmed by: students of the Institute Telecom, Paris
Flash animation, Javascript, html development by Eric Masson (Kaleido28@yahoo.com) and Xavier Zoutou (Xavier.zoutu@xuly-bet.com)
contact:
Xuly.Bët Petite Boutil X-tra Funky
Espace Créateurs du Forum des Halles
1, rue Pierre Lescot
75001 Paris
t: +33 (0)1 42 33 50 40
f: +33 (0)1 48 46 19 65

**HUMAN TECHNOLOGY**
**www.human-technology.com**

established: 1996
location: Paris
contact:
Julien Delafosse
t: +33(0)1 48 87 59 89
m: +33 6 03 00 49 84
f: +33 (0)1 53 69 10 61
e: humantechnology@wanadoo.fr

pp. 70–5

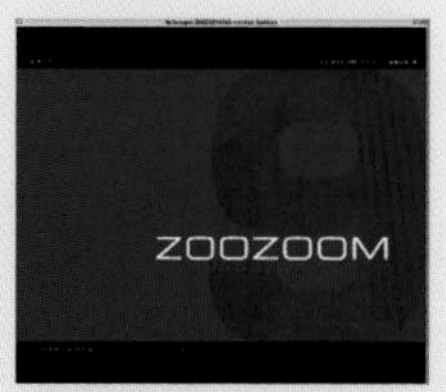


**ZOOZOOM**
**www.zoozoom.com**

established: March 2000
location: New York
language: English
plug-ins: Flash
designed by: Mak
programmed by: Mak
contact:
Kelley Quan
249 West 29th Street
New York, NY 10001
t: +1 212 631 0383
e: kq@zoozoom.com

pp. 162–9

# credits

## INTRODUCTION

p. 1 Photograph from zoozoom.com by Andreas Rhuen/Mint Management, Model: Ruth Spivey at Ford
p. 2 Photograph from net-a-porter.com by Barbara Metz and Eve Racine; Model: Eva at FM
pp. 4–5 Illustrations from dresslab.com
pp. 6–7 Illustration from mads.it
pp. 8–9 Illustration by Christian Lacroix from christian-lacroix.fr

## CHAPTER ONE

pp. 10–11 Images, from left: Photo Dorothée Perret, Costume National, Helmut Lang/Photo: Anthony Ward; Alexandre Herchcovitch; Pleats Please/Photo: © F. Giacobetti
pp. 12–15 All images courtesy of Alexandre Herchcovitch
pp. 16–19 All images courtesy of Amaya Arzuaga; Photo by Manuel Outumuro (16)
pp. 20–5 All designs by BCBG Max Azria; Copyright © 2001 BCBG Max Azria. All rights reserved; Models: Delfine Bafort and Liisa Winkler
pp. 26–31 Copyright © Christian Lacroix; Model: Vivien Solari (29)
pp. 32–41 All images courtesy of Costume National; Models Natasha Vojnovic and Erika Wall (32–3); Photographs by John Akehurst (34–41)
pp. 42–5 All images courtesy of Dior Homme; Photograph by Richard Avedon/ Model XX (42)
pp. 46–9 Copyright © 2000 Dorothée Perret. All rights reserved, Photograph copyright © by Marcus Bayer (49)
pp. 50–5 All images courtesy of Emilio Pucci; Copyright © Alessandro Mossotti/Emilio Pucci Archives/All rights reserved (50–1); Copyright © Photo Marco Severini. All rights reserved; Models: Aurelie N. (International Beatrice Models), Colette Petchecova (Elite), Erin Wasson (Run), Kamila (Women Management), Karolina Kurkova (Why Not) and XXX (52–3); Copyright © Photo Marco Severini. All rights reserved. Model: Karolina Kurkova (54); Copyright © Photo Lumachi. Emilio Pucci Archives. All rights reserved
pp. 56–9 © Copyright 2001 Helmut Lang; Photographs by Anthony Ward
pp. 60–3 Concept and Creativity: Happycento+Sintetik; Photographer: Emilio Casi; Photographer's Assistant: Alberto Peroli; Art direction and graphic design: Giuliano Garonzi (H+S); Creative team: Federico Lorenzo Galvani, Alessandro Nicolis, Roberto Solieri (H+S); Stylist: Daniela Checcini; Fashion designers: Giorgio Albertini, Daniela Checchini, Chiara Fasoli, Paolo Zenatello (Mad's®); Gorgeous George: Patrick Mackenzie; Vinnie: Zoe Havler; Runner: Jon; Tyrone: Doppa; Production: Emilio Casi Management; Organization: Icelandic Models; Spirit of Iceland Guide: Kolla; Hair and makeup artist: Susanna Heidarsdottir; Crew cooker and singer: Botta; Crew bus driver: Thorkell Gudgeirsson (Limousine Buses); Digital Alchemies: O®bit
pp. 64–9 © 2000–1 Issey Miyake Inc. All rights reserved. Photos: F. Giacobetti (64–5, 68–9)
pp. 70–5 Copyright © 1989–99 Xuly.Bët Group Ltd. Copyright reserved

## CHAPTER TWO

pp. 76–7 Images, from left: A.P.C.; Sowear; Colette; eLUXURY; Net-a-Porter, Kirna Zâbete
pp. 78–81 ©A.P.C.; Photo: ©Pierre Bailly (78); Model: Griet Toch; Photos: © Joseph Benita (79–81)
pp. 82–5 © 2001 Colette
pp. 86–9 Copyright © 2000–02 eluxury.com, Inc. All rights reserved
pp. 90–5 All images courtesy of Colette
pp. 96–9 All images courtesy of Kirna Zâbete
pp. 100–5 All images courtesy of Net-a-Porter: Reality Bites (102–3): Photography: Barbara Metz and Eve Racine; Direction: Megan Quinn-Newall; Stylist: Lisa Samoto at A+R; Hair: Lance Lowe at The Mouth that Roars; Makeup: Helen Barnes at Mandy Coakley using Estée Lauder; Prop Styling: Georgia Sion at Smile; Model: Eva at FM; Shot at: Fishtank Studios, London; top tan (104): Photography: Barbara Metz and Eve Racine
pp. 106–11 All images courtesy of something.org.com
pp. 112–15 © 2001 So Collective; Lookbook photography by Sebastian Gollings (115)
pp. 116–19 © 2002 CondéNet Inc. All rights reserved

## CHAPTER THREE

pp. 120–1 From left: Nylonmag/Illustration by Heather Hernon; Dresslab/Photo: Providencia Casanovas; ZooZoom/Photo: Andreas Rhuen/Mint Management; Hintmag/Photo: Mika Nakanishi; SHOWstudio/Photo: Nick Knight; 2fanzine/ Photo: Emilene Galende and Gustavo Menegazzo
pp. 122–5 All images courtesy of 2fanzine; FESTA by Fabia Bercsek (123); Emilene Galende and Gustavo Menegazzo (124–5)
pp. 126–31 All images courtesy of dresslab.com; BNCSM2001 ACCRS: Photography by Cesar, Music: The Avalanches, Since I Left You, DEEPLY by Providencia Casanova; SET 4 by Sonia Soms
pp. 132–5 HIDDEN PLACES (133): Photographer: Mika Nakanishi; Stylist: Christina Naima; Graphic Designer: Lee Carter; Hair: Shalom Sharon at Bradley Curry; Makeup: Clelia Bergonzolia at Bradley Curry; Models: Katie Nauta and Jessica Lindsay at Elite; Photographer's Assistant: Ronnie Kim and Arturo Cubria; Music: Vespertine by Björk; MORROW IS TODAY (134): Interview and design: Lee Carter. PEOPLE USED TO DREAM ABOUT THE FUTURE (135): Text: Lee Carter, Graphics: Lee Carter and Tony King from King & Partners, Models: Erika Wall and Bekah Jenkins; Music: Adult
pp. 136–41 All images courtesy of itfashion.com; Photographs by Jordi Sabanés (137 left middle, 141)
pp. 142–7 NYLON 3 (143): *Model*: Danita Angell, Artist: Kaws; NYLON 5 (143): Model Björk; (144) *Photograph:* Marvin Scott Jarrett; GIDDYUP (145): *Photographer:* Clang; *Stylist:* Anne Marie Creskey; *Hair and makeup:* Bryan Marryshow at Independent; *Model:* Gili Saar at Marilyn; *Photographer's assistants:* Jason Kibbler and Remy Leung; *Stylist's assistant:* Genny Yun; *Location:* Walk House; *Location manager:* Isabelle at site4view.com. DRESS ME UP (146): Illustration by Heather Hernon; LOUD AND PROUD (147): Photographer: Marcelo Krasilcic; *Stylist:* Haidee Findlay-Levin; *Hair:* Rick Gradone for Oribe; *Makeup:* Jun Funahashi for Calvin Klein at L'Atelier; *Model:* Juliana McCarthy
pp. 148–57 All images © showstudio.com; GIVENCHY COUTURE (149): *Photography:* Nick Knight; *Styling:* Katy England at Smile; *Lights Suits:* Alexander McQueen for Givenchy Autumn/Winter 2000 Haute Couture; *Film & Sound Edit:* Adam Mufti; *Models:* Kim Iglinsky at Storm and Eleaonre at IMG Models; *Hair:* Sam McKnight at Premier; *Makeup:* Val Garland at Untitled; *Manicurist:* Natalie Collins for Amalgamated Talent; Shot at Metro Studios, London. SWEET (150–1): *Direction and 3D Photography:* Nick Night; *Costumes:* Jane How at Katy Barker; *Animation Direction:* Dominic Wright at Createc; *Hair:* Sam McKnight at Premier; *Makeup:* Val Garland at Untitled; *Models:* Vivien Solari at Models One; Marleen Berkova at Nathalie; *Text:* Susannah Frankel; *Animation Production:* Peter Martin at Createc; *Music written by:* Adem Inhan; Kiernan Hebden; Samuel Jeffers; Used by kind permission of Universal/MCA Music Ltd. J-WALK (152): *Direction:* Nick Knight; *Walk:* J.

Alexander; *Filmed at:* Audio Motion; *Animation:* Dominic Wright at Createc; *Music:* Jeremy Healey; *Text:* Marion Hume. PLASTICINE (153–5): *Sculptures:* Lone Sigurdsson; *Concept & Direction:* Nick Knight; *Styling:* Jane How; *Art Direction:* Paul Hetherington; *Film edit:* Adam Mufti; *Programming:* Nic Crossaina. SLEEP (156–7): *Direction and concept:* Nick Knight; *Styling:* Sidone Barton; *Models:* Devon Aoki, Zora Star, Natasha Prince and Elise Crombez all at Storm; *Hair:* Sam McKnight at Premier; *Nails:* Marian Newman @ Premier; *Production:* Phillippa Oakley-Hill; *Technical Development:* Chris Raettig; Axis 2100 webcam provided with kind support from Axis Communications Ltd; Pebble lights by Habitat

pp. 158–61 © 2000 Y.K.CondeNet.jp. All rights reserved. Networked by Cable & Wireless. SEXY SPECIAL (159) *Photographer:* Raymond Meier; *Model:* Roos van Bosstraeten. WHAT IS MODERN BEAUTY? (160) *Photographer:* Michael Thompson; *Model:* Guinevere Van Seenus; *Makeup artists:* Scott Andrew, Laura Mercier, Virginia Young, Sharon Dorsett, Dick Page. SHE-VOGUE! (161) *Story and illustration:* Gogh Imaizumi; *Agent 13:* hitomi; *Photographs:* Shuichi Maiyama

pp. 162–9 All images courtesy of zoozoom.com. ISSUE 8 (162) *Photographer:* Anna Palma at Bernstein and Andrulli; *Model:* Agola at Ford; *Hair:* Carmel Bianco at Link; *Makeup:* Kelley Quan at Mark Edward; *Stylist:* Elizabeth McClean. ISSUE 9 (163) *Photographer:* Mak; *Model:* Marianne S. at Ford; *Hair:* George Kyriakos; *Makeup:* Kelley Quan at Mark Edward; *Stylist:* Jamie Kimmelman. BRUCE (163) *Photographer:* Andreas Rhuen/Mint Management; *Text:* Sameer Reddy; *Fashion editor:* Elizabeth McLean; *Makeup:* Janeiro for MAC at Jump; *Hair:* Stacey Ross; *Model:* Ruth Spivey at Ford; *Studio:* Sun Studios, New York City; *Film processing:* DIA Positive; *Digital imaging:* Sox Imaging; *Colour prints:* Bond Street Print Lab. INSPECTED BY... (164–5) *Photographer:* Sabine Liewald/Bradley Curry; *Fashion editor:* Carrena Lukas/Mel Bryant; *Makeup:* Maria Secca/Bradley Curry; *Hair:* Yuki Yamazaki/Bradley Curry; *Manicurist:* Dida Paraschivoiu/Bradley Curry; *Model:* Jennifer Williams at T Model Management; *Studio:* Sun Studios, New York City; *Film processing:* DIA Positive; *Digital imaging:* ADT (Art Digital Technologies); *Retouching:* Felix Fischer/Bradley Curry. TAKE THE HIGH ROAD (166–7) *Photographer:* Karen Detrick; *Fashion editor:* Sarah McGovern; *Makeup:* Andie Markoe-Byrne for Tarte Cosmetics; *Hair:* Miki Mori; *Model:* Kate Davis at Marilyn Models; *Film processing:* DIA Positive; *Colour prints:* Bond Street Print Lab; *Thanks:* Dorothy Cowfield and Charles Reidy. UNITED BAMBOO (168–9) *Photographer:* Karen Pearson; *Fashion editor:* Elizabeth McClean; *Makeup:* Andie Marcoe-Byrne for Defile Cosmetics; *Hair:* Benoit Moeyart at Susan Price for Kim Lepine Salon; *Model:* Breanna Goebel at Q Models; *Film processing:* DIA Positive; *Digital imaging:* ADT (Art Digital Technologies); *Colour prints:* Bond Street Print Lab



# acknowledgments

2FANZINE: Lucia Dossin; Dudu Bertholini, Kleber Matheus
A.P.C: Emmanuel Berard, Jessica Allen, Rik Bas Backer
ALEXANDRE HERCHCOVITCH: Alexandre Herchcovitch, Fanny Oster
AMAYA ARZUAGA: Keith Wallace, Quim Nolla
ARAGORN: Anne Lardeur
BCBG MAX AZRIA: Kristin Dykstra, Kristine Westerby, Max Azria
CHRISTIAN LACROIX: Bérangère Broman, Laure du Pavillon, Tessa and Vivien Solari at Models 1
COLETTE/I LOVE COLETTE: Sarah
COSTUME NATIONAL: Ana Milisic/The News, Ennio Capasa, Massimo Torrigiani
DIGITAL FORM: Asa Mader, Ayshe Farman-Farmaian, Farhad Farman-Farmaian
DIOR HOMME: Cyril Bréjon, Hedi Slimane, Sabisha Freiberg
DOROTHÉE PERRET: Anne-Claude Scherer, Dorothée Perret
DRESSLAB/FUNKY LAB BCN: Alex Segura, Jordi Belda, Eduardo Nofuentes, Begonia Berges
ELUXURY: Jennifer Schram Maxwell, Al Lacago and Michael Manhas/Look Models, Amanda Moore/Next Models, Anne Helper, Don Flood, Hope Sidman, Jen Palmer, Jessica Barist, Ronni Heyman, Sarah Seyfried, Stewart Shining
EMILIO PUCCI: Laudomia Pucci, Ilaria Sartori, Marco Severini, Paola Giannini/Karla Otto, Aurelie N./Paola at International Beatrice Models, Candela/Alfonso at Major Models, Colette Petchecova/Lele at Elite Models, Erin Wasson at Run Models, Kamila at Women Management, Karolina Kurkova/Tiziana Dagali at Why Not Models
ENGINE THREE: Tim Miller, Paris Fleezanis
FLASHLIGHT MEDIA: Allin Chung, Willy Somma
FLIP FLOP FLYIN': Craig Robinson
GRAFIKONSTRUCT: Rodrigo Teco, Fernando Kreigne, Joao Paulo Martins
HAPPYCENTRO+SINTETIK: Roberto Comuniello
HELMUT LANG: Anthony Ward, Kim Stringer
HINTMAG: Lee Carter
HUMAN TECHNOLOGY: Jeremie Dumont, Julien Delafosse
IT FASHION: Estel Vilaseca, Estel Munné, Mireia Sabanés
JOHN GALLIANO & TEAM
KIRNA ZÂBETE: Beth Buccini, Sarah Hailes
THE LONELY LINE: Jean-François Lepage
MAD'S: Laura, Mariano Buglioni
MAGGIE MORRIS
MOTHER: Elisabeth Lazaroo, Helena de Signori
NET-A-PORTER: Hayley Mitchell, Megan Quinn-Newall, Natalie Massanet
NYLON: Crystal Meers, Marvin Scott Jarrett
PETER BRAUNSTEIN
PLEATS PLEASE: Andre Wiesmayr, Nancy Knox, Sayuri Shoji, Stephanie Phair
PUBLICLAND: Gareth Parkinson
SHOWSTUDIO: Charlotte Wheeler, Nick Knight, Phillippa Oakley-Hill
SOMETHING: Marc Hare, Selene Allen
SOWEAR: Jason Yang
SPILL NET: Nicholas Mir Chaikin
STYLE: All of my wonderful colleagues
VOGUE NIPPON: Gene Krell, Ritsuko Hotta, Yoko Arai
XULY.BËT: Aurore, Lamine Badian Kouyaté
ZOO ZOOM: Kelley Quan

AND ANNE BUFORD, whose idea it was, MY PARENTS for their love, M.T., HELEN FARR, NIKI MEDLIK, who is responsible for the wonderful design, and JAMIE CAMPLIN for believing in me.